A History of Religion in America

A History of Religion in America: From the First Settlements through the Civil War provides comprehensive coverage of the history of religion in America from the precolonial era through the aftermath of the Civil War. It explores major religious groups in the United States and the following topics:

- Native American religion before and after the Columbian encounter
- Religion and the Founding Fathers
- Was America founded as a Christian nation?
- Religion and reform in the nineteenth century
- The first religious outsiders
- A nation and its churches divided

Chronologically arranged and integrating various religious developments into a coherent historical narrative, this book also contains useful chapter summaries and review questions. Designed for undergraduate religious studies and history students, *A History of Religion in America* provides a substantive and comprehensive introduction to the complexity of religion in American history.

Bryan F. Le Beau is retired from the University of Saint Mary in Leavenworth, KS, where he served as Professor of History, Provost, and Vice President for Academic Affairs. He is the author of several books on American cultural and religious history.

For student and instructor resources to accompany *A History of Religion in America*, visit the dedicated companion website at: www.routledge.com/cw/lebeau

Perfect for use in the classroom or as an aid to independent study, the website includes:

- Recommended Further Reading
- Supplementary Chapter Information
- Audio Chapter Introductions

The companion website includes material which covers both volume one: *A History of America, from the First Settlements through the Civil War* and volume two: *A History of America, From the End of the Civil War to the Twenty-First Century.*

A History of Religion in America

From the First Settlements through the Civil War

Bryan F. Le Beau

Routledge
Taylor & Francis Group

LONDON AND NEW YORK

First published 2018
by Routledge
2 Park Square, Milton Park, Abingdon, Oxon OX14 4RN

and by Routledge
711 Third Avenue, New York, NY 10017

Routledge is an imprint of the Taylor & Francis Group, an informa business

British Library Cataloguing-in-Publication Data
A catalogue record for this book is available from the British Library

Library of Congress Cataloging-in-Publication Data
A catalog record for this book has been requested

ISBN: 978-0-415-81924-4 (hbk)
ISBN: 978-0-415-81925-1 (pbk)
ISBN: 978-0-203-57628-1 (ebk)
ISBN: 978-1-138-05991-7 (2 volume set, pbk)

Typeset in Times New Roman
by Apex CoVantage, LLC

Visit the companion website: www.routledge.com/cw/lebeau

Contents

Figures

Acknowledgments

Books such as this may take only a few years to write, but they rely on a professional lifetime of research. And even then, the author is heavily dependent on the scholarship of others to fill in the gaps in the story that even a lifetime of research cannot fill. I am deeply grateful for all those who contributed – albeit unknowingly in most cases – to the story I have told. I hope that I have fairly represented their work.

As with all of my past publications, this book would not have been possible without the professional research assistance, willing and encouraging ear, and good counsel of my wife and outstanding reference librarian, Chris Le Beau. I owe so much of my career to her.

I want to acknowledge the very capable assistance of my editors at Routledge, Taylor and Francis Group. Their editorial assistance from the very start has been invaluable. And finally, I want to thank the several readers who took the time to review this book while it was still at the manuscript stage and to offer much wise advice. My book is far better for all of their insights.

Introduction

The principal themes of this history of religion in America are growth, diversity, adaptation, and accommodation, which are actually major themes in American history as a whole, religious or secular. These themes help to explain the unique persistence of religion in America, when it appears to be in decline throughout most of the Western world. They also allow us to address the perennial question of whether the United States is, or ever was, a Christian nation. This study focuses on religion in the context of American history. But it also addresses questions concerning that history, namely the challenges posed to religious bodies living outside the boundaries of traditional beliefs or even belief itself, as well as the resistance to new religions – at least new to the United States – which has waxed and waned but nevertheless persisted, over the centuries. Studying such resistance helps us not only to better understand the history of religion in America but also our cultural underpinnings and our understanding of ourselves.

Although each chapter is organized around a particular theme, this story of religion in America is told more or less chronologically. The themes provide the central points around which this history has been written. The chronological approach affords the opportunity to make connections between religious and secular history, thereby presenting a more coherent story. It also shows how secular events – revolution and civil war, for example – influenced, and in many cases were influenced by, religious developments. The two were inextricably linked and cannot be understood properly in isolation.

And finally, two things quickly occur to anyone who has tried to write such an expansive histories. First, given the limits of space, it is impossible to include everything and still provide enough depth to provide a satisfactory level of understanding. As a result, this history is somewhat subjective, and readers will find that some religious groups and topics have been excluded. Second, the author must rely on the work of hundreds of scholars, past and present, who have devoted their professional lives to the study of various topics of religion in American history. This author hopes that this single volume has done justice to their very fine scholarship, much of which has been cited in the numerous endnotes and recommendations for further reading following each chapter.

In the way of a brief overview, Chapter 1 explores both the diversity and common elements among the many Native American religions. It addresses the impact of European contact, settlement, and religious missions – Spanish, French, British, and American. As a result of that contact, Native Americans would be decimated and their religions nearly disappear. But both would survive, at the same time that both, while struggling and ultimately successful in maintaining their integrity, would be forced to adapt to their ever-changing environment and adopt significantly new beliefs.

Chapter 2 focuses on British colonization and the origins of what would become the dominant religious force for centuries in the United States – the Protestant establishment. It shows how in religious, and in political and economic, terms, British colonization was an extension of the English Reformation, both in its extension of that reformation and in the dissent it caused among colonists. It points to the diversity of religions, by the standards of the day, that came to exist in the colonies by the end of the colonial period and the seemingly inescapable acceptance of religious tolerance that resulted. Finally, it addresses the First Great Awakening, the nation's first great revival, and how it helped shape the nature of religion in America.

Chapter 3 explores the Great Awakening's impact on the generation of the American Revolution, relating New Light theology, millennial thought, and evangelical rhetoric to the growing disenchantment with what an increasing number of Americans saw as British immorality and corruption. God's visible power in the Great Awakening convinced many religious leaders and those born again that the pace of history was accelerating; that the Second Coming, or God's millennium on Earth, was close at hand; and that the millennium might well begin in America, a land settled by God's chosen people, with independence from the country God had abandoned. As such, American religion was as much shaped by, and helped shape, the American Revolution. It ushered in a period of significant change in the lineup of religious bodies. Some denominations went into rapid decline, while others grew exponentially. And finally, this chapter will discuss how under the influence of the Enlightenment – conceived in Europe but realized in America, as one historian put it – a public civil religion developed for the new nation, while the centuries-old traditions of church establishment and restraints on the freedom of diverse religious expressions were gradually discarded.

Chapter 4 examines the historical process by which disestablishment and the free exercise of religion were gradually realized at the state and national levels. As it is a question that persists even today, it will treat at some length what constitutional scholars label original intent: What did the Founding Fathers intend by their revolutionary constitutional provisions for the separation of church and state and free exercise of religion included in the First Amendment? It addresses the subject of deism, which for the first time challenged in a significant manner mainstream, revealed religion. And it addresses the Second Great Awakening, which helped drive home the dramatic populist or democratic emphasis on religion in America.

Chapter 5 picks up on the ideas of perfectionism, postmillennialism, and pursuit of the Kingdom of God on Earth to explore the important role religion played in the great era of reform in America. It discusses American Transcendentalism as a movement that reflected many of the main currents of religion and reform in the nineteenth century, and it provides an overview of the unprecedented proliferation of reform movements with religious roots. The final section of this chapter takes up the significantly greater role women came to play in American religion during this period, sometimes referred to as the feminization of American culture. The home became the American woman's nearly exclusive sphere, it has been argued, and she became the moral guardian of the nation. This led to her extending her sphere of influence beyond the church to various social and cultural reform efforts.

To this point, with the exception of Native American religion, this has been a story of religious insiders, those religious groups that dominated, or came to dominate, American religion, defined the mainstream, and commanded the adherence of most Americans at the nation's founding. Chapter 6 looks at the increased importance of two religious groups that lay outside America's mainstream at that point – African Americans and Roman Catholics – as well as the appearance of the young nation's first major native born religion, the Church of Jesus Christ of Latter-day Saints, all of which faced similar challenges.

The discussion of African Americans will include religious life in the slave community and among free blacks, including the ongoing debate over the extent to which the character of African American religion retained ties to the group's African past. The small number of Roman Catholics in the early nineteenth century may not have lessened suspicion toward them, but it did protect them from the more hostile treatment which they faced with the arrival in large numbers of Irish and German Catholics at mid-century. And finally, the Church of Jesus Christ of Latter-day Saints in many ways was distinctly American. Nevertheless, seen as religious outsiders, Mormons were subjected to levels of hostility matching, and even exceeding at times, that experienced by Roman Catholics, forcing them to move west, seeking their Zion in the Utah Territory.

The American Civil War was not only the crucial, even seminal, event in American secular history, it also served to reshape and redirect American religious history. Both the nation and its churches were torn asunder, and although both would survive and even grow stronger, they would be significantly changed by the experience. Chapter 7 will begin by discussing the role of religion in the Antislavery Movement and the response of Southern religious leaders to criticism by Northern evangelicals to their "peculiar institution." It will examine the divisive influence of slavery on the nation's churches, leading in some cases to the creation of separate institutions. It will discuss the role of the churches in the Civil War and the reformulation of religious thought in the war's aftermath. And it will conclude with a section on the religious beliefs and expressions of President Abraham Lincoln, especially as they appeared in his public pronouncements, which remain some of the most oft-quoted "founding documents" in American history.

This history of religion in America ends amidst the aftermath of the Civil War. It is the most common line of demarcation for surveys of American history, religious or secular, as the specter of the nation divided provides an appropriate point at which to conclude a coherent story of the nation from its first settlements to its near destruction. But it also sets the stage for anyone wishing to further explore the role of religion in American history from that point to the present, which will be the subject of a subsequent volume. The themes remain the same, even if the historical events and the major characters change.

Chapter 1

Native American religion and its European encounter

The importance and challenges of studying Native American religion

For most Americans, their history begins with the English settlement of North America. Barely a thought is given to Spanish and French efforts, and not much more attention is paid to those who occupied the land before any Europeans arrived. This foreshortened history has largely been abandoned, for good reason. For one thing, not to tell the full story is to perpetuate a short-sightedness induced by a preoccupation with America's European cultural heritage. Second, it limits our understanding of the complex character of religion that is not as readily apparent in the exclusive study of the West.[1]

"Savages we call them," wrote Benjamin Franklin of Native Americans, "because their manners differ from ours, which we think the perfection of civility."[2] Much the same can be said of many Americans' attitudes toward Indian religion. Religion, however, has always been central to the Native American experience, to its identity, and to its vitality. Some continue to describe it as primitive, but in that the word primitive implies a belief system devoid of deep feelings and subtle thought it is inappropriate. Historically, Native American religion has been marked by rich symbolism and profound thought concerning the most basic concerns of man: the creation of the world, the origin of human life, and the nature of the supernatural and of the afterlife.[3]

The study of Native American religion poses three problems. First, there is the problem of sources. Whereas most of the major world religions have literary traditions, Native American religion has been handed down as oral tradition. Such oral accounts have little sense of linear time. And though quite lovely in their telling, metaphorical and symbolic language abounds and past and present are collapsed into a single continuum. Similarly dangerous is the use of the records of the first European and American observers of Indian culture. Explorers, traders, and missionaries witnessed firsthand many aspects of Indian life, but their accounts are framed by their cultural biases.[4]

Second, the title "Native American religion" is actually a misnomer and perhaps might better have been put: "Native American religions." Native American religion was, and still is, as diverse as the Euro American religions with which it came into contact. In brief, there were as many Indian religions as there were Indian tribes.[5] The phrase Native American religion, then, is a fiction, but it is a convenient fiction, which will be employed, at least in part. What follows is a discussion of both the diversity that separates and the commonalities that unite Native American religions.

Third, there is the challenge of describing a phenomenon that is ever changing. Like subsequent inhabitants of North America, Indians were immigrants, and like those who followed, they were forced to adapt – to adjust their life patterns – to their new environment, the other tribes they encountered, and in time, and most challenging, to European culture and Christianity. What is often described as traditional behavior is really the product of extensive alteration over many centuries in response to all of those encounters. This was true for Native Americans in the Pre-Contact Period, between the migration of their northeast Asiatic ancestors beginning perhaps 30,000 years ago to 1492, during which hundreds of distinct Native American cultures emerged. And it was true in the period after 1492, when Indian tribes were forced into foreign environments to which they had to adapt, encountered hitherto unknown tribes with different religious beliefs that influenced their own, and faced the oftentimes forced acculturation that followed confrontations with European and American agents of culture and religion[6]

Common characteristics of Native American religion(s)

As Peter Williams has argued, among Native Americas, as with many traditional societies,

> the religious life of a people is coextensive with the people itself, and seldom extends beyond a coherent social group. . . . Society, culture, religion, and cosmos are coincident, and together constitute the sum of reality for a particular people as long as they manage to cohere as a self-sufficient group.[7]

Thus, it is not surprising that anthropologists have identified at least 500 different Native American cultures in the area that would become the United States on the eve of European contact. Euro Americans may have insisted that the truths of their religion were universal, that Christianity transcended culture, but Native Americans believed that each society or group of people had its own sacred stories and rituals.[8] Nevertheless, it is possible to identify many common characteristics among Native American religions.

Four prominent features linked the diverse expressions of North American Indian religion: a similar world-view, a shared notion of cosmic harmony, emphasis on directly experiencing powers and visions, and a common view of the cycle of life and death. Native Americans generally believed that human existence was designed by the creator divinities – in some cases holding a single, particularly powerful, creator god primarily responsible – at the time of the "first beginnings." They agreed that, in those days, all beings were more or less human but that a change took place that turned many primeval beings into animals and birds. Thus the close affinity that remains between people and animals, as well as the animistic concept of spirits as animals and animals as spiritual.[9]

Although clearly not monotheistic, as were principal Western religions, the Native American notion of cosmic harmony emphasized the unitary system of the universe made up of humans, animals, trees, and plants – nature as a whole – and the supernatural. The roots of this idea may be traced to Indian hunting origins, thereby explaining its continued prominence in later hunter-gatherer tribes, but it was equally at home among agricultural Indians. Simply put, all living beings had their supernatural guardians. Each animal had its guardian, usually a mysterious spirit larger than ordinary members of the species. In the case of humans, a Supreme Being played a superior but not exclusive role.[10]

Native Americans emphasized the direct experience of powers and visions. Among the Great Plains Indians, this was commonly represented in the vision quest, one of the most powerful rituals in Native American religions. The vision quest may have originated as a puberty rite, where young men were required to seek the assistance of a guardian spirit to withstand the trials of existence and luck in hunting, warfare, and love. Parents or elders sent young men into the forest or wilderness to fast, suffer from the cold, and be subject to the attacks of wild animals, from which might result a vision of the spirit that henceforth would become a guardian spirit. The vision quest was transformed, however, on the Plains into a ritual for grown men, wherein hunters or warriors repeatedly withdrew into the wilderness to seek guardian spirits, each serving a different purpose.[11]

Native Americans, in contrast to those living in Western culture, conceived of time as cyclical, rather than linear. Rather than seeing time as a straight line, from an origin through the present into the future, implicit in which is the notion of progress, American Indians understood time to be an eternally recurring cycle of years and events. So too each person made a cycle of time from birth to death, death marking both the end of the old and the beginning of a new life, either on this earth, reincarnated into another human or some animal form, or in a transcendent hereafter.[12]

Native Americans possessed a strong sense of continuity between the self and outside realities and between themselves and the things they held sacred. They saw reality as more mysterious and symbolistic and what they saw as more holy and mysterious as closely related to, if not inseparable from, their daily existence. Whereas Euro Americans conceived of a three-level universe of God, human beings, and nature, each inhabiting different realms, Native Americans envisioned a world to which all were bound by ties of kinship. There were grandfathers who were Thunder Beings, there was Grandmother Spider, and there was the Corn Mother. Animals took on human form, like Coyote the Trickster, and shamans – holy people – who were said to fly like birds and talk to animals.[13]

In the Western world-view, the natural world was a resource for man; as noted in Genesis 1:28, man was "to have dominion over . . . every living thing that moves on earth." The secular and the sacred were distinct, and the human relationship to the natural environment fell into the secular sphere. Native Americans made no such distinction. For them, land belonged, for lack of a better word, to the tribe only insofar as they were inhabiting it and making use of it. While occupying that land, however, they made certain aspects of that space symbolically important. Mountains, for example, could be associated with a particular god or gods or with a unique story of creation. But Indians also conceived of animal and plant guardians as sacred beings, who, at some point in the distant past, had pledged the bodies of their species as food for man. This led Native Americans to create elaborate rituals for hunting and planting, offering gifts to the spirits of the life they took and being careful not to waste any portion of that which they killed or harvested.[14]

For the agricultural-based tribes of the Southwest, harmony with nature was paramount, and that was expressed in their rituals that marked the changing of the seasons and that honored the Father Sun, Mother Earth, and the gods that brought precious rain. Prime among the last group were the kachinas, who visited villages during the first half of the year, bringing rain from their homes in the nearby mountains. Kachinas (see Figure 1.1) were not so much worshipped, as they were considered friends. They were represented by male dancers, who danced themselves into a state in which their spirits were joined with the kachinas they impersonated. As part of the rituals, the dancers gave carved dolls to the children, which were not intended as toys but rather as sacred objects for the home.[15]

Native Americans held sacred the inner world as well. Dreams revealed holy, hidden things that often could not be known in other ways. Tribes had rituals wherein individuals brought their dreams to tribal councils or holy men so that their meaning could be discerned. Especially on the Plains, leaders of the hunt were chosen from among those who had dreams

Figure 1.1 Kachina dancers

Source: Granger Historical Picture Archive/Alamy Stock Photo

deemed relevant to the hunt, while many tribes believed that, in dreams, the soul was free to travel to distant places to learn and to return with information, or visions, from guardian spirits.[16]

The inner world that dreams disclosed was intimately related to the outer world, and in order to bridge the gap between the two, people were given a name that indicated their kinship with nature and that told something of their inner essence. Those names could, and often were, changed as significant deeds or events occurred. Black Hawk, for example, might become Afraid of Horses, White Rabbit, or Moves from Your Sight Little Red Star. And the colors were significant, in that each of the four directions had its color, and each color its quality: the red of the north might signify wisdom; the white of the south, innocence; the black of the west, deep thought or introspection; and the yellow of the east, inner light.[17]

Belief in shape-shifting was common. Trickster figures such as the Coyote could assume any form they chose, even in the very midst of their adventures. Thus, they were seen as beings of creative power, who had helped put the present world in order, as well as disorder, and who often disturbed the regular working of society. Shape-shifting tricksters could shift from sly cunning creatures, who could outwit their opponents, to the fool, who, according to one tale, fought himself because his right arm and left arm did not know that they belonged to each other. They were without boundaries, able to become whatever inspiration and circumstance decreed, and belief in such transformations reminded Native Americans that the world was, after all, one substance.[18]

Native Americans lived their lives in accordance not only with the four directions, as noted above, but also with sacred numbers – four, for the directions of the compass, for example, and seven, which added a vertical dimension to the four, namely the zenith, nadir, and center – and with shapes, most notably the circle. Circles were sacred for Native Americans because they reflected shapes they saw in nature both in space and time. To be in harmony with nature meant to live as part of the circle, or the medicine wheel of the world. It meant living securely in what they saw as the middle of that circular world from which they did not venture toward the edges, or frontier.[19]

Also similar were Native American accounts of their origins as humans on earth. Most tribes pictured their primordial ancestors as having ascended from the darkness under the earth. A hero, often accompanied by a god, liberated them, freeing them to emerge from the darkness into the light. Those who came to Earth ascended a tree (alternately a vine or mountain) in the order to which they would assume their place in society, chiefs and shamans first. That tree, with its roots in the underworld and crown in the upper, was represented by such ritual structures as the sun dance post or sacred pole.[20]

Native Americans generally ascribed the origin and existence of good and evil to dual creation, or to the product of two creative spirits – often twins – almost always related but in conflict. They commonly credited the good spirit with having fashioned a positive and beneficent world for human beings. They saw the evil one as having introduced into the world elements that would thereafter frustrate them and make their lives more difficult, like disease and pestilence. Similar accounts told of the heroes or gods, who gave men such indispensable gifts as fire, the ability to hunt, and skill in planning.[21] Central to Native American religion was the quest to align themselves with good, or benevolent, spirits and to distance themselves from the bad, harmful, or evil spirits.

Illness was seen as the result of a lack of harmony between the afflicted and the spiritual world. Disharmony might be the result of natural causes, in which case herbal medicine might be applied. Illness might also result from contact with ghosts, witchcraft (in this case meaning the intentional use of spiritual powers by an individual to harm others), or "soul loss," in which case a supernatural remedy was required to reestablish harmony. Such remedies were the province of medicine men, especially shamans. Shamans – who, depending on the tribe could be male or female – were recognized by their communities as intermediaries between humans and the supernatural. They accessed the supernatural through dreams or visions, and they applied that knowledge to healing the sick.[22]

Similarities existed in Native American attitudes toward death and the afterlife. To begin with, there was no sharp difference between the existence led by the living and the dead, the two realms of which were more in continuity than disjunction. Some tribes espoused theories of reincarnation, wherein the deceased person might return to earth in a different form, commonly an animal. At the same time, their three-level view of the universe led Native Americans to believe that the deceased departed for either the level above, where they might enjoy a happy life of plenty and contentment, or the level below the earth, of darkness, which did not necessarily involve torture but that was deprived of warmth and satisfaction. Good people would be rewarded in the afterlife, and the bad not, thereby providing a sense of the world as a moral place which favored good and opposed evil.[23]

Most Native Americans believed in ghosts, or the spirits of the recently departed existing for an interim period between earth and their final dwelling places. They commonly performed ceremonies to appease such spirits, especially for the first year following a person's death. Visits from the deceased in their survivor's dreams were common, thereby relaying important messages about decisions that needed to be made and warning of problems that lay ahead. And finally, the retelling of myths – meaning stories that explained the ways of the cosmos – assured harmony between humans and the spirits, or powers, of the universe. Myths varied from tribe to tribe, but what they had in common was their assuring a sense of order out of chaos – to maintaining, or restoring, harmony between humans and the divine.[24]

European contact and the impact of Christian missions

Native American religion was never static, even in the pre-Columbian period. Change was never so swift, however, as it was when Indians came into contact with Europeans and Euro Americans, especially Christian missionaries. One of the great motivating forces underlying Christian European expansion into the New World was the missionary spirit of Christianity. A central agent in its colonization was the Christian church, leading some to describe the process of colonization as "colonialism in the name of Christ." The belief that the heathen should be converted as a Christian duty was not limited to priests and ministers. Financial supporters of the earliest expeditions, ministers of state and colonial officials, sought to carry out what they regarded as a moral duty. Colonization was closely equated with the spread of civilization, the carrying of an alleged superior European and later American culture to the so-called primitive areas of the world.[25]

Missionaries were constantly frustrated by the reluctance of most Indians to be converted, the very idea of a native Christian identity being culturally problematic. Indians recognized no line of distinction between religious and cultural life; once an Indian became a Christian, he was seen as having rejected more than the religious component of his former life. He called into question the cultural values by which he had been nurtured, resulting in the mind of many in deracination. Because, at the same time, the convert was seldom fully accepted into white society, conversion could result in isolation from both the white and Native American worlds.[26]

Frustration among the Indians led to many revitalization movements. To a large extent, these were primitivist movements or attempts to return to their cultural and religious origins. But as Anthony F. C. Wallace argued in his seminal essay on revitalization movements, and as we will see, they were more complicated than that. These movements commonly blended elements of the old and new, often proving to be "both restorationists and revolutionaries."[27]

Wilcomb Washburn has argued that, despite the number of converts and the apparent strength of the Christian movement among Native Americans, the effects of conversion were too often either "peripheral, divisive, or narcotic." Christianity "helped the Indian accept the poor place the white world offered him and helped him overcome the rage and despair he might otherwise have felt because of his inability to prosper in that world." But Richard White may have put it best when he summarized the results of Christian missions in one story with two endings. The story: "Indians are the rock, European peoples are the sea, and history seems a constant storm." The two outcomes: "The sea wears down and dissolves the rock; or the sea erodes the rock but cannot finally absorb its battered remnant, which endures."[28]

Spanish missions

Spanish and French missions in North America preceded, and differed in significant ways from, English and American missions, largely as the result of the number of settlers and the type of society they tried to create. Francis Parkman recognized the difference a century ago when he wrote that, in North America, "Spanish civilization crushed the Indian; English civilization scorned and neglected him; French civilization embraced and cherished him." By some estimates, as many as 15,000 European clergy arrived in areas of the Americas controlled by Spain and Portugal between 1500 and 1800. They were a mixed lot of diocesan priests, Dominicans, and Jesuits, but Franciscans dominated at over 8,000 strong.[29]

The Spanish moved quickly in colonizing and christianizing most of what we now call Latin America following Columbus's arrival in the Western Hemisphere in 1492. At least at first, Columbus found those inhabitants he encountered likely prospects for conversion. So, in 1493 and 1494, by a series of papal bulls and the Treaty of Tordesillas, Spain was granted control of most of the hemisphere – save only Portuguese Brazil. It was the Pope's wish that this assignment of responsibilities would facilitate bringing the natives into the Catholic faith. Further to that end, in 1510, Spain issued the *Requerimiento*, a proclamation to the native inhabitants on the necessity of their conversion to "the one true church." And in 1527, the church appointed a bishop – the first official Western religious leader in the hemisphere – in Mexico.

The first missionary efforts on what would become United States soil occurred in the Southeast and Southwest under Spanish auspices. The Florida governor's first choice to establish Indian missions was the Jesuits, newly established in 1534 to lead the Catholic Counter Reformation. Their efforts began in earnest after the first permanent Spanish settlement was established at Saint Augustine in 1563. But after several failed attempts the Jesuits withdrew, leaving the field to the Franciscans. In 1595, the Franciscans launched a major effort in what is today Florida and Georgia, cut short by a revolt of the Guale Indians two years later in Georgia, which resulted in the deaths of several clergy. Thereafter, they made some progress, but by 1708, their efforts, not supported by any significant Spanish migration to the area and subject to constant harassment from their British neighbors to the north, the Franciscan mission system was all but destroyed.[30] In 1763, Florida became a British territory.

Roman Catholic missionary activity in the Southwest progressed under the cover of Spanish military power, which through 1541 was marked by scandalous scenes of plunder and slaughter. When, in 1541, Francisco Coronado's expedition failed to find wealth to match that of Mexico and Peru, the Spanish military withdrew from the area, leaving the field open to those who would propagate the Word of God through less violent means.[31]

As an important aside, it should be noted that the violence perpetrated on the Native Americans by the Spanish military – or conquistadors – did lead to imperial reforms, at least on paper. In 1537, Pope Paul III, in *Sublimus Deus* (From God on High), proclaimed that Native Americans were fully human, and Christians were not only obligated to convert them to Christianity but also to treat them as humans. The Pope's stance led the Spanish Crown to proclaim the New Laws in 1542, which forbade Indian enslavement and demanded their humanitarian treatment. But perhaps most dramatically, in 1550 in Valladolid, Spain, scholar Juan Ginés de Sepúlveda and Bartolomé de las Casas debated the nature of Native Americans and whether their continued enslavement could be justified. Sepúlveda argued that the Native Americans were somewhat less than fully human and therefore appropriately subject to slavery. Las Casas, who became known as the "Apostle of the Indies," argued to the contrary – that they should be treated as fully human. Las Casas – perhaps whose greatest legacy is his *History of the Indies*, among the earliest accounts of Indian life following European contact – is commonly credited with persuading the Spanish Crown to forbid further enslavement of Native Americans and to end their continued mistreatment, but, once again, neither practice ended anytime soon. One particular setback came in 1585, when the bishops of New Spain forbade the ordination of Native Americans, whom they had worked so diligently to convert.

The most significant Spanish missionary efforts in what would become the United States began in the 1590s and early 1600s. In 1598, Juan de Oñate moved into the heart of the Pueblo region, in what is now New Mexico, near what is today Santa Fe, with about 400 colonists, some soldiers, and a number of Franciscan missionaries. His purpose was to colonize the area, which was inhabited by between 40,000 and 50,000 Indians – Zuni, Hopi, and Acoma – living in four or five dozen villages. He authorized grants of land (*encomiendas*) in the most populous eastern and northern pueblos of the upper Rio Grande to Spanish settlers with the right to utilize the services of Indians living on those grants (*repartimentos*). Missionaries built churches on the edges of Indian villages, baptized Indians, and introduced new agricultural methods.[32]

In 1680, a general Pueblo revolt against the Spanish, led by the shaman Popé and resulting in the death of an estimated 30 missionaries and 400 Spaniards and the destruction of many churches, caused a major setback for Spanish rule and Franciscan missions in the area. His initial success notwithstanding, Popé found himself facing the opposition of Indians who were unwilling to abandon all of the modern ways brought with the Spanish and who were unpersuaded by his preaching of the purity of the ancient ways. The insurrection did not lead to a revival of Pueblo culture, which continued to decline. The Spanish and the Franciscans re-established control by 1740.[33]

In the meantime, beginning in the early 1700s, the Franciscans established a chain of missions along the San Antonio River in what is now the State of Texas. The first, actually resulting from the transfer of an earlier failed mission on the Rio Grande in 1718, was named Mission San Antonio de Valero, later to be known as the Alamo. Despite repeated attacks by Apaches and Comanches, the Texas missions did well until about 1775, when the effects of European diseases, acculturation, and intermarriage took too great a toll on the Indian population and distinct identity.

Jesuits moved into Spanish holdings in Baja (lower) California in 1683, led by the Italian Eusebio Francisco Kino. But when his efforts failed, he moved north into Alta (upper) California, in what is now the state of California. He obtained an exemption for the Indians they encountered from the forced labor or demands for tribute employed in colonization efforts and brought cattle with him to create a food supply for his missions. He achieved some measure of success but was forced to leave when the Jesuits were expelled from the Spanish Empire in 1767 leaving the field to the Franciscans.[34]

The prevailing pattern of Spanish missionary activity Serra created over the next fifteen years was the establishment of largely self-contained missions, centered around the physical church, to which the Indians of the area were attracted for food and medicine, as well as to learn about the missionaries' God and to practice the arts of "civilized" men. Serra considered it his mission to bring the Indians to Christ quickly in anticipation of Jesus's imminent return – to be baptized as soon as possible, pursuing more extensive instruction thereafter. Thus, he and his fellow Franciscans actively, and some would argue harshly, sought to prohibit the continued practice of native rites, destroying kachina figures and raiding kivas. Although initially the missionaries tried to learn the many different Indian tongues they encountered, they soon gave up and forced Indians to receive instruction in Spanish.[35]

Serra, like most of his fellow missionaries, initially saw the Indians as prelapsarian innocents, lacking both civilization and Christianity, comparing them to Adam in paradise before the Fall. He believed the "harvest of souls" among such innocents would be easy and considerable. But when in time the Indians proved to be unreceptive to the missionaries' teachings, Serra and others began to see then as "a pitiful, childlike people of slow intelligence, who were overcome by . . . rude ignorance," or worse, "a savage people of 'brutal appetites' prone to all kinds of vices." Innocents or savages, the Indians' behavior and even culture had to be eliminated, the Franciscans concluded, before Christianity could take root.[36]

Although the records are incomplete, the evidence suggests that Serra was successful in baptizing a comparatively large number of Indians. In one 5-year period, he and his fellow priests baptized 2,500, or more than 1 a day. By another estimate, by the time Serra died, he baptized more than 4,600 Indians. But baptism, especially as most occurred among children, did not necessary mean conversion. What they experienced and even learned, they did not necessarily understand or believe. But as Serra and his fellow missionaries commonly reported, even an unexamined participation in rites and rituals could be a hopeful sign of things to come, and clearly many Indians did embrace Christianity and internalize it in their own way, commonly mixing elements of Christianity and their native religion in a way meaningful to them.[37]

As Steven Hackel summarized it: Indians entering the Franciscan mission of California,

> entered a distant world, where, regardless of age, they were treated as juveniles in the eyes of the Catholic Church, they were 'spiritual children'; before the Spanish state and its laws, they were minors. And with that status came both limited protection and extensive discrimination. In the realm of introduced religion, Indians learned a catechism pitched to a child's level of comprehension, yet, when they approached the Catholic sacraments, they found themselves subject to adult standards of comprehension and conduct.[38]

Legally, the Indians associated with the missions had the status of wards. Missionaries had complete control over "their" Indians except in criminal matters. But such parental control extended beyond that. "The management, control, punishment, and education of baptized Indians pertain exclusively to the missionary Fathers," the *reglamento* read. But more directly, the priests controlled every aspect of a neophyte's religious and social life.[39]

Serra was met with considerable resistance, especially at first. In August 1769, soon after their arrival at San Diego, local Indians attacked the missionaries and their lay protectors, killing one and wounding three. In 1775, also at the San Diego mission, following the rape of several Indian girls by Spanish troops, local Indians attacked and burned the mission, murdered and mutilated a priest, and killed several Indian workers. But Serra persisted. He even went so far as to absolve from full blame the Indians who attacked the San Diego mission. In part, he blamed the soldiers for the crimes they perpetrated on the Indians. But he also exonerated the Indians because of the theological concept of "inculpable ignorance." In brief, they could not be held responsible for their transgression of Christian and/or even natural law, because they did not know or understand either law, given their primitive state. Instead, they had been led to such acts by Satan. Thus, Serra resolved to redouble his efforts.[40]

Serra insisted that the Franciscans have control over the Indians and their punishments, once again, except in criminal matters. In part, this was an attempt to stop, or at least control, the abuse of the Indians by Spanish military and other lay inhabitants. In 1773, Serra petitioned Spanish Viceroy Antonio Bucareli in Mexico City and was granted a "Bill of Rights" for the Native Americans. But to be sure, the Franciscans and Serra himself considered corporal punishment integral to their missionary efforts to "correct" their "spiritual children." Serra himself was one of a small group of ascetics known as "fervents," who practiced self-flagellation in an attempt to mortify the flesh, often doing this in full sight of his Indian wards. But although not totally abandoned, the missionaries' use of physical punishment – usually whippings, often administered by Indian assistants – grew less over time, due both to its ineffectiveness as a corrective measure and because of hostile reactions.[41]

Similarly, the Franciscans sought to control the use by force of Indian labor by Spanish lay officials. But they insisted that those Indians associated with their missions provide them with labor. The Franciscan missions of California were self-sustaining, cultivating a variety of crops and raising cattle, a way of life in which local inhabitants were at first welcome and later pressured to join while learning the ways of Christianity. The Franciscan mission system incorporated the Spanish *encomienda*, whereby labor was required of those Indians who chose to live near, and participate in, the missions, estimated at perhaps 20,000 by 1800. The result was an institution that shaped all aspects of the lives of resident Indians – a "benevolent paternalism," basically Spanish but representing, as well, a cultural fusion. It was successful, compared to other missionary efforts, but in time, it too lost ground to the secularization and eventually dismantling of the missions throughout the Southwest under Mexican and later American control beginning in the 1820s. Serra's missionary approach, rooted in scholastic and medieval practice, gave way to the more "enlightened" process of integration of California Indians into society, the results of which were hardly more satisfactory.[42] The intense controversy with which it was met for many years notwithstanding, in 2015, the Roman Catholic Church proclaimed Serra a saint.

The number of recorded conversions among the Indians of the Southwest was high, and many remained Catholic even after the power of Spanish Catholic missions was broken. They regularly attended mass, observed feast days, and participated in the sacraments, if with less understanding of the dogma and theology involved to fully satisfy the missionaries. But by the early years of the nineteenth century, Indians of the Southwest had modified Roman Catholic rituals in ways commensurate with their traditional ways, to better serve their spiritual needs. The result was a syncretic religion marked by ceremonial calendars that were based on traditional Native American beliefs and practices, but to which were added an amalgam of Catholic elements.[43]

For a brief period, 1821–1846, the Southwest came under the control of the newly independent Mexico, which secularized missions throughout the Southwest. In 1846, the United States moved in, initiating a new period of Indian-white relations, this time Protestant as well as Catholic, and reservations were established for the various tribes. Once again, in what was termed syncretism, or hybridization, many Indians continued to at least formally accept Catholic ritualism, but they did so while preserving much of their traditional religious culture. They learned to live in two worlds simultaneously through mental and physical compartmentalization.[44]

French missions

French missionary efforts were located in the vast expanses of North America called New France, today largely Canada but also in the area around the Great Lakes and along the Mississippi River Valley as far south as present-day Louisiana. Their efforts were built on the fur trade, and in that the fur trade required little more than the trading of goods desired by Native Americans for furs, the relationship between the French and the Native Americans was different from that of the Spanish and the English. Military conquest was unnecessary and large settlements were not required. By 1660, only 2,000 Frenchmen lived in New France, compared to 20 times that number of Englishmen in New England alone.[45]

The French took a page from the Spanish missionaries of California and relied on persuasion. But they also differed from the Spanish in that, whereas the Franciscans lived in their missions and brought the Indians to them, the French Jesuits lived among the Native Americans. They moved into Native American villages, learned their languages, allowed those Christianized to retain their traditional dress, and even incorporated some of their rituals into their own. For the French, it was a policy born of weakness, but out of it came the most lastingly amicable relations between Europeans and Native Americans on the continent. Fur traders paved the way for this approach by freely mixing with the Indians, in many cases taking Native American mistresses and wives. In Nova Scotia by 1676, one authority has noted, virtually all French families had Native American blood in their veins, and in the 1660s, Colbert, Louis XIV's architect of imperial reorganization, called for full-fledged integration in order to "civilize" them.[46]

The Jesuits arrived on the coast of New France in 1609 but saw no significant success for another fifteen years. In 1625, led by Fathers Jean de Brébeuf and Gabriel Lalemont, the Jesuits moved inland to Quebec and in 1634 established a mission among the Hurons of the Great Lakes area – called Huronia – where they worked for "the greater glory of God" with considerable success. Other French missionaries, most notably the Jesuit Jacques Marquette, found success among the tribes of the Mississippi River Valley, eventually extending their efforts to the Gulf of Mexico. Catholicism had some advantages over reformed Protestantism, which was to follow, in the quest for converts.

Whereas their Puritan neighbors denied that people could do anything to achieve salvation, but nevertheless insisted they have faith, Catholics encouraged prospective converts to seek salvation through good work, right living, and faithful worship. Catholicism was much more liturgical, thereby appealing to all the senses, as well as reason. And in New France, as in New Spain, the Jesuits – the "black Robes" as they were called – were more willing than the Puritans to accept that Native American beliefs in a supreme being, in the immortality of the soul, and in supernatural forces could be revised sufficiently to find acceptance from the Christian God. Whereas the Puritans insisted that Native Americans discard their values, renounce their way of life, and abandon their religious beliefs as a starting point in accepting Christianity, the Jesuits studied the Native American structure of belief and attempted to change it slowly rather than replace it. As one student of Brébeuf has put it: "He strove not to wrench the Hurons away from their old beliefs but to translate the gospel into their language and into their world [often using "native exhorters"] so that they might see through their own eyes a new face of God." The Jesuits detailed their work among the Hurons in the *Jesuit Relations*. Originally published in the 1630s and 1640s, it is among the most important sources of information on Indian culture.[47]

Nevertheless, the Jesuits also fell short in their missionary efforts, but for reasons quite different from their Spanish and English counterparts. A major attraction for the Jesuits among the Hurons was the protection offered them by French soldiers and traders, with whom the Jesuits maintained amicable relations, as all did with the Hurons. By the mid-seventeenth century, however, European diseases having wreaked havoc among the Hurons, and the French combined presence remaining insufficient to protect them from their enemies, the

Hurons fell victim to the Iroquois, who resisted the European incursion and Jesuit mission-ary efforts. In 1649, Iroquois attacks overwhelmed the Hurons, killing hundreds of them and torturing and killing several Jesuit missionaries in the process, including Brébeuf and Lalemont. Both, as well as six other missionaries who died in the attack, were canonized in 1930. Brébeuf was recognized as patron saint of Canada in 1940.[48]

And there is the story of Kateri Tekakwitha, known as Lily of the Mohawks or the Iro-quois Virgin. Born in 1656 in northern New York to an Algonquin Catholic mother and Mohawk warrior father, Kateri lost both of her parents and a younger brother to smallpox at age 4. The epidemic also left Kateri badly scared and with impaired eyesight; Tekakwitha means "she who bumps into things." At age 10 her village was destroyed by an inter-tribal war, and she moved to her uncle's longhouse nearby. While still a teenager, she embraced Catholicism and at age 20 was baptized by Jesuit missionaries. Shunned by her uncle and other members of her tribe for her decision, as well as for rejecting an arranged marriage, Kateri fled to Canada. She joined the Jesuit mission at St. Francis Xavier du Sault in Quebec, near Montreal, where she led a model devotional life, took an oath of perpetual virginity and charity, and practiced self-mortification. She died in 1680 at age 24 and was proclaimed a saint in 2012, making her the first Native American saint.

As previously noted, French missionaries moved down the Mississippi River in the 1680s and 1690s but did not reach the lower Mississippi River valley until after 1700. Led largely by a sporadic number of Carmelites and Capuchins, their success along the Gulf Coast was hindered by the limited number of French settlers, lack of support, resistance from mer-chants and political figures, and threats of attack by the British from the east and Spanish from the west. Nevertheless, Catholicism established a foothold among the native popula-tion that occupied the area, which passed into Spanish hands in 1763 and into American possession in 1803.[49]

British missions

As historian Jon Butler has written, "The story of Native American religion during the Brit-ish colonial period is simultaneously a tale of disappearance, change, and resilience." In this regard, the Native American experience in British North America was similar to that of Spanish and French America. The English did not successfully plant colonies in the Western Hemisphere until 1607, 115 years after Christopher Columbus's arrival. They arrived with a split image of Native Americans. On the one hand, reflecting Columbus's earliest observa-tions, some Englishmen expected Indians to be a gentle people, receptive to Christian "civi-lizing" efforts. Some even conjectured that the Indians were one of the lost tribes of Israel, perhaps corrupted by the devil, but still capable of final salvation through Christ. But that impression was replaced over time by an image of Native Americans as savage and hostile, a people cursed by God by their having been denied the presence and teaching of Christ. A flood of pamphlets described the natives as brutal, loathsome, and even cannibalistic, leav-ing little room for optimism concerning their reception of European civilization.[50]

Concern for the conversion of Native Americans was pursued in at least a modest manner early on in the British colonies. As per the king's charter to the Virginia Company of London for the settlement of Virginia, the company was to concern itself with bringing the Christian religion to such people "as live in darkness and miserable ignorance of the true knowledge and worship of God." Similar provisions would be included in later charters, but from the start, such goals were always a distinct second to that of making a profit. Historian Reginald Horseman would state the problem more directly: "From the time the first English settlers arrived . . . the fundamental struggle with the aboriginal inhabitants was over the possession of land."[51]

British Protestant efforts at Christianizing Native Americans along the East Coast of North America were undertaken by a relatively few clergy, "whose faith did not easily lend itself to intercultural understanding." One early missionary gave up in disgust after three years, despairing: "Heathen they are, heathen they will remain." This did not discourage the English from pursuing a policy of intimidation, but they were largely rebuffed by a resilient native culture, including religious traditions. One company plan to appropriate money to educate young Native Americans in Virginia homes and special schools, separating the children from their families by force if necessary, failed by 1622. In a pattern that occurred all along the East Coast, as more Virginians pushed inland to carve out tobacco plantations, what had been an abrasive and sometimes violent relationship became disastrous. Disease (e.g. smallpox, diphtheria, and scarlet fever) proved a devastating, if unintended, weapon, but war played a significant part in the destruction of the Native Americans as well. When a Native American attack in 1622 wiped out almost one-third of the white population, Virginians resorted to a ruthless policy in which colonists would no longer be obliged to "civilize" the Native Americans. They would simply be kept apart. In 1676, the Virginians went to war with the Native Americans, reducing the colony's native population to fewer than 1,000.[52]

The policy of separation was quickly adopted elsewhere in the British colonies. As a social and political movement, Puritanism, largely concentrated in New England, intended to reverse the march of disorder and wickedness in English society by creating a model regenerated social order, a "city on a hill," as John Winthrop put it. In order to reform their society, they assumed responsibility, moral stewardship, over those around them. They, the elect, were not only to save themselves, but they were also to assume the burden of reforming their native neighbors. If they were not receptive to Puritan efforts, they might have to be coerced and controlled, directed, and dominated.[53]

Among the first New England settlers somewhat sympathetic to the Native Americans was Roger Williams, himself an outcast from the Puritan Massachusetts Bay colony. Williams criticized Massachusetts leaders for taking Indian lands without either compensation or treaty. But he also urged them not to force Native Americans to abandon their religious beliefs. When he moved to Rhode Island, Williams insisted on having the land upon which he planted a new colony deeded to him by the Narragansett. He studied their language and religion, and for a time, he spoke favorably of the ethical, religion-based traditions of their daily life. But ultimately, as relations between them and British New Englanders grew worse and broke out into war, he succumbed to the dominant Puritan understanding of the Indians' "wicked, devilish origins."[54]

The charter of the Massachusetts Bay Company called for the conversion of the Native Americans to Christianity. The "principal end of this plantation," it read, was to "win and incite the natives of [the] country to the knowledge and obedience of the only true God and savior of mankind and the Christian faith." The colony's seal depicted a Native American pleading: "Come over and help us." Such references in these and other official expressions of purpose, however, reflected a secondary motive, if that, rather than the central priority. Massachusetts missions, rather than being an end in themselves, were in reality intended to enhance the colony's political power at the natives' expense. So it is not surprising that no missionary activity was to be initiated for the first thirteen years of the colony's existence. By then, the rapidly increasing number of settlers and their thirst for land only hastened the Puritan impulse to follow the Virginia model of removing Indians to the interior.[55]

The Native Americans stood as a vivid reminder of what the English knew they must not become. Their nature was the counterimage of civilized man, and Puritans could achieve control of themselves only if they could control and civilize that counterimage. Toward that end, the Puritans attempted to bring them under civil government, making them strictly accountable to the ordinances that governed white behavior. The earliest missionary effort was undertaken by Thomas Mayhew, Jr., in 1642 among the Wampanoag Algonquians (also referred to as Algonkians) on Martha's Vineyard. Mayhew was committed to drawing the Wampanoags away from devil worship, as he saw it, and false gods. But he also respected their cultural traditions and instructed them in their native tongue. By 1652, the number of Mayhew's converts reached 300 adults, and the work was continued following his untimely death by drowning in 1657 by his father, his widow, and his sons. By the high point in their work, 1675, two churches had been built on the island and their work expanded to nearby Nantucket Island.[56]

The most successful English missionary was John Eliot, who, with aid from the Society for the Propagation of the Gospel in New England, built the Indian College at Harvard, Massachusetts in 1655. Like Mayhew, Eliot also sought to employ the natives' language, and he established a printing press that published an Algonquian translation of the Bible. Titled "Apostle to the Indians" by the Puritan divine Cotton Mather, Eliot, like most New England missionaries, concentrated his efforts on tribes whose numbers had been deeply diminished by epidemics and the Pequot War and who had already lost much of their land and become economically dependent on the colonists. Eliot sought to instruct the Native Americans in "civility" and religion, hoping that some would experience conversion and be brought to church membership. Eliot's effort won the approval of Parliament, which passed a bill encouraging the propagation of the Bible among the Indians. This in turn led to financial contributions from some wealthy British supporters, which paved the way for the creation of "praying Indian" towns, which prior to King Philip's War in 1675 numbered 14 and contained over 4,000 inhabitants.[57]

"Praying Indians" were required to reject their native lifestyle and adopt that of the British. They learned English in books of agriculture; adopted English hairstyles, dress, and customs; and were nurtured on the Bible and other devotional works, translated by Eliot into their language. There was an estimated 2,300 to 4,000 conversions, although by some accounts fewer than 20 percent were baptized. The end of Eliot's Indian communities was signaled by the outbreak of King Philip's War, which led to the decimation of the remaining native population of New England. Massachusetts officials ordered all Native American men, women, and children residing in the colony – including those living in the Praying Towns – interned on Deer Island in Boston Harbor, a move Eliot protested to no avail. Nearly half of New England's settlements were laid waste by Philip's (Metacom's) warriors, but the losses for the natives were even greater. The Praying Towns were allowed to reopen following the war, but their populations rapidly declined and, in short order, closed.[58]

Attempts to convert Native Americans continued in the eighteenth century, but expectations shifted from bringing entire tribes into the fold to small group and even individual conversions. The Great Awakening of the 1730s and 1740s provided examples of pious converts and zealous missionaries, one of the most famous being Samson Occom, a Mohegan. Born in 1723 near New London, Connecticut, of a convert Christian mother, Occom found "salvation through Jesus Christ" at age 17 at the hands of New Light minister James Davenport. After studying with Eleazar Wheelock, who established a school for Native Americans at Lebanon, Connecticut, he was ordained by the Presbyterians a minister to the natives of

Long Island. Wheelock's plan for Occom and other talented young Native Americans was to train them as missionaries to other tribes. Finding his greatest success in Occom, Wheelock sent the charismatic young convert to England where he successfully raised funds for the Indian Charity School. But Occom broke with Wheelock when Wheelock insisted on divorcing students from their native culture. The school failed in its original mission, but it relocated to New Hampshire, where it was transformed into a school to train white New England clergy and renamed Dartmouth College. Striking out on his own, Occom took his mission west to the Oneida and Mohawk.[59]

The First Great Awakening spawned increased interest in missions to the Native Americans. Among the most renowned missionaries of the period was David Brainerd, whose activities were made widely known by his friend, the New Light minister, Jonathan Edwards. When, in the early stages of the Awakening, Edwards announced that the "great work of redemption" had begun in New England, he included the Native Americans among those affected. As evidence, he wrote about Brainerd's conversions among the Delaware of Pennsylvania, only one of several sites Brainerd would establish at times attracting over a hundred participants to his outdoor gatherings. By the spring of 1747, tuberculosis ridden, Brainerd retreated to the Edwards's Northampton home, where he soon died. But thanks to Edwards's account of Brainerd's activities, he became the missionary prototype of his day, no doubt influencing Edwards's own efforts among the Housatonic of Stockbridge.[60]

Space precludes our discussing British missions in all thirteen colonies, but in general, few were much more successful than those in Massachusetts and Virginia, and all fell victim to the same process of Native American decline, decimation, and dispossession. The colony of Pennsylvania bears mention for its brief but genuine attempt to deal fairly with the Native Americans. So too does the colony of Georgia, because of its proprietor's comparatively better relations with the natives. The United Brethren, or Moravians, were among the most active and successful missionaries of eighteenth-century British America, if on a small scale. But British missions were met with increasing resistance as they moved inland. Interior tribes, such as the Iroquois, Creeks and Cherokees, were not impressed with most institutions of British life, including religion, and they saw no reason to replace what they had with them.[61]

Representative of the resistance among northern tribes was the preaching of Neolin, "The Enlightened One," a charismatic Delaware prophet. As would several subsequent prophets, Neolin preached that Native Americans should return to the state they were in before the whites arrived, or face extinction. In Neolin's vision, the Master of Life told him that salvation for his people lay in returning to their ancient customs; foreswearing rum, clothing, and other elements of white culture; and in population control through abstinence. His disciples carried Neolin's message throughout the western territories, attracting large numbers of Native Americans, including the Ottawa leader, Pontiac. Pontiac made Neolin's doctrine the spiritual underpinning of the failed uprising he led against the English in the Ohio River Valley in 1763. Neolin was among the Shawnee and Delaware that surrendered at Fort Pitt in 1765. In his speech on that occasion, he said that the Great Spirit had commanded the Native Americans to lay down their arms and smoke the peace pipe, after which Neolin and his visions disappeared from the pages of history.[62]

In time, most Native Americans in British America took a page from those of New Spain and New France and engaged in their own syncretism, or hybridization, joining their native beliefs and rituals with those of the new dominant Christian culture. As Linford D. Fisher has found, this syncretism, the appropriation of Christian forms that began as early as the seventeenth century, although a practical response, occurred in surprising and nominal ways that can be seen among Native American churches today (e.g. steeples and pulpits) and rituals that can be easily identified as Christian but subtly indigenized with Natives American elements. As Linford has concluded, in many ways, contemporary Native American Christians "seem to profess Christianity despite the long history of evangelization and education, not because of it."[63]

Native Americans and the new American nation

Attitudes toward Native Americans had not changed on the eve of independence. The Declaration of Independence charged George III with trying to loose on the frontier "the merciless Indian savages, whose known rule of warfare is an undistinguished destruction of all ages, sexes, and conditions." During the American Revolution, most tribes remained loyal to the British, who they hoped (no doubt encouraged by British agents) would defend them and their land from the onrush of settlers. The result did not bode well for the Native American inhabitants of the new nation, and clashes between tribes on the frontier and citizens of the new nation continued unabated until they were forced to sign the Treaty of Greenville in 1795.[64]

Soon after his inauguration in 1789, George Washington established the new nation's Native American policy – one of assimilation. Washington expected all natives living east of the Mississippi to be acculturated within fifty years. They would be taught English and farming, and their land would be divided among them in severalty. Once that happened, the Indians would be admitted to the republic as full and equal citizens, their tribes denationalized, and their remaining lands ceded to the federal or state governments.[65] Missionaries were an integral part of this policy.

Federal plans for "civilizing" the Indians centered on the Civilization Fund, an annual sum first appropriated by Congress in 1819 but supplemented over the years by various missionary groups. Missionaries, among whom Protestants were almost exclusively represented and for a time organized under the interdenominational American Board of Commissioners of Foreign Missions, established schools, including boarding schools, which grew to include model farms and training in mechanical skills as well as religious instruction. The first head of the Bureau of Indian Affairs was so impressed that he predicted that, through such efforts, within one generation, the Indians would be "civilized," but attendance records were poor and parental disinterest marked. Native American students found it impossible to cope with their old world, from which they felt estranged, after having been educated for the new world, entrance into which they were denied.[66]

Throughout the first half of the nineteenth century, missionaries – Presbyterians, Congregationalists, Baptists, Methodists, and Moravians – at first welcomed the task assigned them by the War Department, the government office which was in charge of Indian policy. But as their attitudes toward the Native Americans changed from one of "paternalistic pity" for a people beholden to "primitive concepts of the infancy of the human race" to increasing respect, missionaries struggled to maintain a political neutrality. When their missionary boards instructed them to refrain from any defense of Cherokee rights, for example, and to acquiesce in President Jackson's removal policy, some openly resisted. Nevertheless, the Cherokees' resistance to the missionaries grew.[67]

Protestant missionary activity burgeoned in the 1790s prompted by the defeat of the Ohio Indians in the Battle of Fallen Timbers and the Treaties of Fort Stanwix (1784) and Greenville (1795). Stimulated by the Second Great Awakening, several religious organizations were created committed to the idea that civilization must go hand in hand with Christianization if either was to succeed. "In the school and in the field, as well as in the kitchen," one missionary wrote, "our aim was to teach the Indians to live like white people." But missionary efforts at "civilizing" the Indians had to work within the context of the equally new American nation's policy of Indian removal. Although justified on humanitarian grounds, as well as on the need for American territorial expansion – to protect Native Americans as well as provide land for a rapidly increasing population – the Indian removal policy provoked resentment, resistance, and armed conflict.[68]

Resistance occasionally took the form of new revitalization movements. It was hoped that they would provide Native Americans with a renewed strength, whereby they could regain their spiritual and physical well-being and even expel whites from their lands. In about 1800, Handsome Lake led such a movement among the Seneca in northern New York. Quaker missionaries were already working among the Seneca, something Handsome Lake not only resisted but confronted by bouts of drunkenness, terror, and destructiveness. Following one such episode, Handsome Lake "suffered the agonies or hangover and guilt," as one historian put it, received visions and underwent a profound spiritual change. Following on one of those visions, Handsome Lake called for a return to the Indians' ancient religion and for reforms that included the banning of alcohol, witchcraft, and intermarriage with whites. In what came to be known as the Religion of the Longhouse, Handsome Lake focused on four rites: the Thanksgiving Ceremony; the *adowe*, or individual prayers and thanksgivings; the communal Bowl Game; and the Dance of Worship, all of which actually constituted a syncretic mix of elements of traditional religion and Christianity.[69]

Tenskwatawa and his brother Tecumtha (Tecumseh) led a similar and more widespread movement among the Shawnee, largely as a negative response to Handsome Lake. In 1805, Tenskwatawa too had a visionary experience, also in the wake of drunkenness and depression, which brought him into the presence of the Master of Life. He also spoke of heaven and hell and what was necessary for a person to enter paradise, most importantly avoiding the contamination that follows associating with whites, as well as shunning alcohol, polygamy, and witchcraft. Few believed him at first, however, until he warned that continued disbelief would lead to "darkness come over the sun," which in fact occurred as if in fulfillment his prophecy in the 1806 solar eclipse. Tenskwatawa's brother, Tecumseh, used the appeal of Tenskwatawa's vision to pursue a pan-Indian alliance to force whites from the territory. The Shawnees' Prophetstown, which became the center of Tenskwatawa's activities, attracted the concern of white observers, especially the army. That concern ultimately escalated into war and Tecumseh's defeat, despite Tenskwatawa's pronouncement that their faith would make them invincible, even immune from the white man's bullets. Tenskwatawa fled in disgrace. Both revitalization movements, that led by Handsome Lake and the other by Tenskwatawa, were short-lived, but they were not the last.[70]

The Cherokees were among the groups that resisted removal. Their intent was to prevent encroachment on their native lands and maintain their right to self-government, while at the same time obtaining economic assistance from the federal government. Culturally, they sought to adopt select aspects of the white man's culture and Christian beliefs and practices, while retaining those traditional beliefs, customs, and ceremonies to which they tied their identity as a people. They sought a delicate balance, which, through the inculturation they welcomed, led them to be proclaimed "the most civilized tribe in America."[71]

In 1808, having acquired the benefits of "civilization" and expressing a preference for severalty and citizenship, they formally requested exclusion from the new Indian removals policy. Jefferson rejected their appeal. Between 1808 and 1823, scores of treaties were negotiated providing for the relocation of nearly all remaining tribes located east of the Mississippi, but still the Cherokee resisted, peaceably. In 1811–1813, a movement arose among the Cherokee to assert their identity as a people and their cultural identity. Although no single leader rose to the fore, many Cherokees were visited by the spirits of their ancestors in dreams and visions, urging them to oppose the white man's intrusion and to return to traditional ways. When a series of earthquakes struck, many were convinced that they were signs of the necessity of following the will of their ancestors. In 1824, a similar movement grew out of the dreams of an elderly Cherokee prophet, whose visions told him to proclaim white doctrines false and to be resisted, thereby earning their passage to an afterlife in a land of beauty and abundance.[72]

In 1827, a messiah, incongruously named Whitepath, appeared, appealing to the Cherokee to reverse their direction and to return to their more traditional ways, but the movement was squelched by those who chose to continue their course. It was the culmination of years of growing antimission sentiment and Cherokee nationalism, but once again, it was not entirely a reactionary movement seeking a return to a lost past. The rebels were not opposed to all acculturation, but they resisted the constant missionary assault upon their customs and beliefs. It was a movement that pitted Whitepath, an elderly respected chief, against largely younger Cherokee leaders, who saw acculturation as the only way to survive. The movement failed and Whitepath was martyred.[73]

And then came President Andrew Jackson. Jackson's policy was not to seek treaties with the Indians, but rather to force them to relocate, regardless of the terms of any existing treaties. He presented his plan – the Indian Removal Bill of 1829 (passed in 1830) – as a benevolent one, intended to protect the Indians from their rapacious white neighbors by moving them to a safe area west of the Mississippi on lands they would hold in perpetuity. The missionaries did not know how to respond; some sought to remain neutral, at least openly, while others sought to prevent removal, even aggressively opposing the policies and actions of the federal government and of the States of Georgia, Alabama, and Mississippi.[74]

When the Cherokees failed to gain presidential and congressional protection from the State of Georgia, they turned to the United States Supreme Court, where they also failed in cases heard in 1831 and 1832. In 1832, the Cherokee case actually was successfully argued before the United States Supreme Court in *Worcester v. Georgia*, but Chief Justice John Marshall's majority opinion that federal, not state, law prevailed and that Georgia had acted in haste and contrary to previous federal treaties, was ignored. President Jackson's remark, "John Marshall has made his decision, now let him enforce it," may be apocryphal, but it accurately reflects Jackson's refusal to use executive power to implement the Court's defense of the Cherokees. Cherokee removal across the Mississippi to Indian Territory, later to become the state of Oklahoma (Choctaw for "red people"), known as "the trail of tears," resulted in the deaths of more than 4,000 Cherokees.[75]

Cherokee religion did not disappear along the Trail of Tears, and as a concluding note, it might be helpful to offer a brief note on John Ross, who has been credited with providing the leadership that helped hold advocates of the old and new religion together during the just described period of stress.[76] Ross, only one-eighth Cherokee (on his mother's side), was born in Tennessee in 1790 and raised and educated in the white man's world in Kentucky. He fought with Jackson against the Creeks in the War of 1812. A member of the Methodist Church, he engaged in several business ventures, including the ownership of slaves, before becoming active in Cherokee political affairs. In 1817, he became a member of the Cherokee

National Council, serving as Council President from 1819 to 1826, and he threw his support behind those who opposed Indian removal. He led the Cherokees in creating a democratic government, adopting a constitution much like that of the United States, and he pushed for, and succeeded in, building roads and irrigation ditches, schools and churches and providing artisan training on tribal lands. Ross worked closely with the missionaries in these various endeavors with the overall goal of modernizing the Cherokees, while retaining those elements of their traditional culture that provided the tribe's sense of identity. Joining Ross in these efforts, and better known for his efforts, was Sequoyah – also of mixed ancestry – whose white name was George Guess. Sequoyah is credited with developing a Cherokee alphabet, which led to publication in 1828 of the *Cherokee Phoenix* newspaper.[77]

In 1828, Ross was elected Principal Chief of the Cherokees, from which post he fought both President Jackson and the State of Georgia, to retain tribal lands. When that failed, he led approximately 17,000 Cherokees on the "trail of tears." In 1839, Ross was elected Tribal Chief of the United Cherokee Nation. He took on the challenge of a battered and badly divided people, divided between those who favored and those who opposed any further accommodation with the dominant white culture and Christian religion. Ross's approach was to combine select Christian beliefs, ritual, and symbols with those of the Cherokee to form a syncretic adaptation that best met the needs of the Cherokee. For his efforts, after 1832, the Cherokee accepted Ross as prophet as well as their chief. Ross died in 1866.[78]

Not all of the tribes of the Southeast left their lands peacefully. Among the more fierce resisters were the Seminoles, who instead of accepting land dispossession, rallied behind a warrior named Osceola, yet another leader of mixed ancestry, who merged his military skills with spiritual visions for his people. Gathering in Florida, Osceola's resistance precipitated the Second Seminole War of 1836–1838, which ended in his death.[79]

In 1831, the Nez Perce sent delegations to St. Louis seeking religious instruction. Missionaries of various denominations responded by relocating to the Northwest, the best known of which were the Methodists Jason Lee, Marcus and Narcissa Whitman, and Henry Spalding and the Jesuit Catholic Pierre Jean de Smet. These early missionaries had some success in persuading various tribes to combine the ways of their ancestors with Christian teachings, but they struggled in vain to protect them from the onrush of white settlers. Indian wars began, precipitated by the murder of the Whitmans by a group of Cayuses in 1847, and by 1860, nearly all tribes of the Northwest were confined to reservations.[80]

In 1865, Congress created a joint committee to inquire into the condition of the Native American tribes and "especially into the manner in which they are treated by civil and military authorities of the United States." Taking its unlikely name from the senator who chaired the Committee, James Doolittle, the Committee reported that, except for the tribes in the Indian Territory, the native population was rapidly declining as the result of disease, intemperance, war, and the pressure of white settlement. Although the Committee recommended a reorganization of the Indian service and provided the impetus for the creation of a reservation system, the importance of the Committee lay not in immediate legislation but in its effort as the Christian conscience of reform-minded humanitarians in the East.[81]

Congress established the Board of Indian Commissioners in response to demands for a non-partisan organization to oversee the administration of Indian affairs. Staffed by distinguished reformers, the board was frequently at odds with the Interior Department and thus largely ineffective in becoming a voice for Native Americans. They prompted several attempts at reform, but until 1887, federal policy remained focused on concentrating Indians on reservations and providing them with Christianized civilization.[82]

Summary

As Catherine Albanese has written:

The story of American Indian religion is a microcosm of the religious encounters that would confront each of the immigrant peoples to America. All would come with the ways of their ancestors; all would intend to preserve them. Yet each people was among many . . . and the presence of other ways led to changes in traditional religions.

Change was particularly marked in the period after 1492, during which time Indian culture encountered, and was nearly overwhelmed by, European and Euro American culture. The European conquest of America was nearly total, but battered remnants of Indian culture, including Native American religion, endured and in the twentieth century witnessed a revival.[83]

Review questions

1   Why is it important to study Native American religion?
2   What challenges do we encounter when studying the history of Native American religions?
3   What are some of the characteristics common to Native American religions?
4   What are some of the differences and what might account for those differences?
5   How would you compare Spanish, French, British, and Euro American missions to the Native Americans, as to their approaches and results?

Notes

1 Although Native American is now preferred, the word Indian is still commonly used historically. Both will be used herein, the latter to be consistent with historical references and to avoid confusion with those more popularly labeled American. Peter W. Williams, *America's Religions from Their Origins to the Twenty-First Century*, 3rd edn. (Urbana: University of Illinois Press, 2008), 14.
2 Gary B. Nash, *Red, White, and Black: The Peoples of Early North America*, 3rd edn. (Englewood Cliffs, NJ: Prentice Hall, 1992), 3.
3 Ake Hultkrantz, *Native Religions of North America* (San Francisco, CA: Harper and Row, 1987), 10; Harold E. Driver, *Indians of North America*, 2nd edn. (Chicago: University of Chicago Press, 1969), 396.
4 Howard L. Harrod, *Becoming and Remaining a People: Native Americans on the Northern Plains* (Tucson: University of Arizona Press, 1995), xvi, 15; Gregory H. Nobles, *American Frontiers: Cultural Encounters and Continental Conquest* (New York: Hill and Wang, 1997), 29; Tracy Neal Leavelle, "American Indians," in *The Blackwell Companion to Religion in America*, ed. Philip Goff (Hoboken, NJ: Wiley-Blackwell, 2010), 400.
5 Hultkrantz, *Native Religions of North America*, 16; Robert F. Berkhofer, *The White Man's Indian: Images of the American Indian from Columbus to the Present* (New York: Alfred A. Knopf, 1978), 3.
6 Alvin M. Josephy, ed., *America in 1492: The World of the Indian Peoples before the Arrival of Columbus* (New York: Alfred A. Knopf, 1992), 280; Nash, *Red, White, and Black*, 9; Alvin M. Josephy, *The Indian Heritage of America* (New York: Alfred A. Knopf, 1970), 23–4.
7 Williams, *America's Religions*, 17.
8 John Butler, Grant Wacker, and Randall Balmer, *Religion in American Life: A Short History*, 2nd edn. (New York: Oxford University Press, 2011), 17; Catherine Albanese, *America: Religions and Religion* (Belmont, CA: Wadsworth Publishing Company, 1992), 25–6.

9 Hultkrantz, *Native Religions of North America*, 21–2.

10 Hultkrantz, *Native Religions of North America*, 27–8.

11 Hultkrantz, *Native Religions of North America*, 31; Sam D. Gill, *Native American Religions: An Introduction* (Belmont, CA: Wadsworth Publishing Company, 1982), 97–101.

12 Hultkrantz, *Native Religions of North America*, 33.

13 Denise Lardner Carmody and John Tully Carmody, *Native American Religions: An Introduction* (New York: Paulist Press, 1998), 8; Albanese, *America*, 26–7.

14 Nash, *Red, White, and Black*, 25–6; Carmody and Carmody, *Native American Religions*, 235–7.

15 Hultkrantz, *Native Religions of North America*, 96–7, 102; Albanese, *America*, 39–40.

16 Albanese, *America*, 28.

17 Albanese, *America*, 28.

18 Albanese, *America*, 28–9; Gill, *Native American Religions*, 27–9.

19 Albanese, *America*, 30.

20 Carmody and Carmody, *Native American Religions*, 219–20; Hultkrantz, *Native Religions of North America*, 25.

21 Carmody and Carmody, *Native American Religions*, 221.

22 Williams, *America's Religions*, 23–4; Butler et al., *Religion in American Life*, 19.

23 Carmody and Carmody, *Native American Religions*, 239, 244, 250; Ake Hultkrantz, *Belief and Worship in Native North America* (Syracuse, NY: Syracuse University Press, 1981), ch. 11.

24 Hultkrantz, *Native Religions of North America*, 33.

25 Nash, *Red, White, and Black*, 28; James Axtel, *The Invasion Within: The Contest of Cultures in Colonial North America* (New York: Oxford University Press, 1985), 329; Francis Jennings, *The Invasion of America: Indians, Colonialism, and the Cant of Conquest* (Chapel Hill: University of North Carolina Press, 1975), 4, 6, 43–4.

26 Wilcomb E. Washburn, *The Indian in America* (New York: Harper and Row, 1975), 111–2, 115; Axtell, *Invasion Within*, 330.

27 Anthony F. C. Wallace, "Revitalization Movements," *American Anthropologist*, 58 (1956): 246–81; Leavelle, "American Indians," 404.

28 Washburn, *The Indian in America*, 116; Richard White, *The Middle Ground: Indians, Empires, and Republics in the Great Lakes Region, 1650–1815* (New York: Cambridge University Press, 1991), ix.

29 Butler et al., *Religion in American Life*, 24; Nash, *Red, White, and Black*, 88. Due to space limitations, Dutch missionary efforts, which were comparatively few, are not included. See, Nash, *Red, White, and Black*, 92–3.

30 Butler et al., *Religion in American Life*, 29; James Hennessey, *American Catholics: A History of the Roman Catholic Community in the United States* (New York: Oxford University Press, 1981), 11–13.

31 Washburn, *The Indian in America*, 117; Nash, *Red, White, and Black*, 112.

32 Edward H. Spicer, *Cycles of Conquest: The Impact of Spain, Mexico, and the United States on the Indians of the Southwest, 1533–1960* (Tucson: University of Arizona Press, 1962), 156–9; Henry Warner Bowden, *American Indians and Christian Missions: Studies in Cultural Conflict* (Chicago: University of Chicago Press, 1981), 9–10.

33 Russell Bourne, *Gods of War, Gods of Peace: How the Meeting of Native and Colonial Religions Shaped Early America* (New York: Harcourt, Inc., 2002), 9.

34 Washburn, *The Indian in America*, 117–19; Spicer, *Cycles of Conquest*, 120–6, 315; Ramon A. Gutierrez, *When Jesus Came, the Corm Mother Went Away: Marriage, Sexuality, and Power in New Mexico, 1500–1846* (Stanford, CA: Stanford University Press, 1991), 46–94.

35 Washburn, *The Indian in America*, 117; Butler et al., *Religion in American Life*, 136.

36 Steven W. Hackel, *Children of Coyote, Missionaries of Saint Francis: Indian-Spanish Relations in Colonial California, 1769–1850* (Chapel Hill: University of North Caroline Press, 2005), 132; James A. Sandos, *Converting California: Indians and Franciscans in the Missions* (New Haven, CT: Yale University Press, 2004), xv.

37 Sandos, *Converting California*, xvi, 33; Hackel, *Children of Coyote*, 162–5.

38 Hackel, *Children of Coyote*, 3.

39 Sandos, *Converting California*, 53.

40 Sandos, *Converting California*, 42, 49, 61, 64; Williams, *America's Religions*, 168.

41 Sandos, *Converting California*, 36, 39, 49; Hackel, *Children of Coyote*, 324, 330–1.
42 Butler et al., *Religion in American Life*, 37; Williams, *America's Religions*, 169, 260; Sandos, *Converting California*, 69.
43 Albanese, *America*, 43–4.
44 Peter Nabokov, *Native American Testimony: A Chronicle of Indian-White Relations from Prophecy to the Present, 1492–1992* (New York: Viking, 1991), 54–6; Richard White, *"It's Your Misfortune and None of My Own": A History of the American West* (Norman: University of Oklahoma Press, 1991), 11–2; Spicer, *Cycles of Conquest*, 326–7.
45 Nash, *Red, White, and Black*, 104–5.
46 Nash, *Red, White, and Black*, 106–9.
47 Axtell, *Invasion Within*, 272–3, 277–9; Nash, *Red, White, and Black*, 107–8; Bowden, *American Indians and Christian Missions*, 75–95; Peter A. Dorsey, "Going to School with Savages: Authorship and Authority among the Jesuits of New France," *William and Mary Quarterly*, 3rd sers, 55 (1998): 399–401; Bourne, *Gods of War*, 101. The Jesuits detailed their work among the Hurons in the *Jesuit Relations*, originally published in the 1630s and 1640s, is among the most important sources of information on Indian culture
48 Williams, *America's Religions*, 170; Butler et al., *Religion in American Life*, 41–2; Bourne, *Gods of War*, 112–13.
49 Butler et al., *Religion in American Life*, 44–6.
50 Butler et al., *Religion in American Life*, 94; Bourne, *Gods of War*, 3–4; Berkhofer, *White Man's Indian*, 13–14; Nash, *Red, White, and Black*, 37–9, 43.
51 Nash, *Red, White, and Black*, 45; Reginald Horsman, *Expansion and American Indian Policy, 1783–1812* (East Lansing: Michigan State University Press, 1967), 1.
52 William T. Hagan, *American Indians* (Chicago: University of Chicago Press, 1961), 9; Nash, *Red, White, and Black*, 60–5; Williams, *America's Religions*, 171.
53 Nash, *Red, White, and Black*, 68–9.
54 Bourne, *Gods of War*, 44–5, 49–50.
55 Richard W. Cogley, *John Eliot's Mission to the Indians before King Philip's War* (Cambridge, MA: Harvard University Press, 1999), 2–3; Theodore Dwight Bozeman, *To Live Ancient Lives: The Primitivist Dimension in Puritanism* (Chapel Hill: University of North Carolina Press, 1988), 97; Francis Jennings, *The Invasion of America: Colonialism and the Cant of Conquest* (New York: Norton, 1976), 53, 238.
56 Bourne, *Gods of War*, 144–5.
57 Roy Harvey Pearce, *The Savages of America: A Study of the Indian and the Idea of Civilization* (Baltimore: Johns Hopkins University Press, 1965), 3–24; Jennings, *Invasion Within*, 233; Alden T. Vaughan, *New England Frontier: Puritans and Indians, 1620–1675*, 3rd edn. (Norman: University of Oklahoma Press, 1995), 44–52.
58 Neal Salisbury, "Religious Encounters in Colonial Context: New England and New France in the Seventeenth Century," *American Indian Quarterly*, 16 (1992): 503; John F. Freeman, "The Indian Convert: Theme and Variation," *Ethnohistory*, 12 (1965): 113–28; Williams, *America's Religions*, 171; Butler et al., *Religion in American Life*, 96–7; Cogley, *John Eliot's Mission*, 4–5, 139–71; Bourne, *Gods of War*, 124–30, 134–8.
59 Bourne, *Gods of War*, 224–40, 259–60; Williams, *America's Religions*, 172.
60 Bourne, *Gods of War*, 194–213.
61 Hagan, *American Indians*, 11–2, 16; Paul A. Wallace, ed., *Thirty Thousand Miles with John Heckewelder* (Pittsburgh, PA: University of Pittsburgh Press, 1958), 3, 31, 189–200; Axtell, *Invasion Within*, 225.
62 Nash, *Red, White, and Black*, 266; Anthony F. C. Wallace, *The Death and Rebirth of the Seneca* (New York: Alfred A. Knopf, 1970), 118; Bourne, *Gods of War*, 242–53.
63 Linwood D. Fisher, *The Indian Great Awakening: Religion and the Shaping of Native Cultures in Early America* (New York: Oxford University Press, 2014), 214–23.
64 Hagan, *American Indians*, 31, 36, 49–50; Josephy, *Indian Heritage of America*, 314–16.
65 William G. McLoughlin, *Cherokees and Missionaries, 1789–1839* (New Haven, CT: Yale University Press, 1984), 2.
66 Hagan, *American Indians*, 87–8, 90–1, 134–6; Ronald H. Satz, *American Indian Policy in the Jacksonian Era* (Lincoln: University of Nebraska Press, 1975), 253, 263, 288; Francis Paul Prucha, *The*

Great Father: The United States Government and the American Indians (Lincoln: University of Nebraska Press, 1984), 1: 283–92.

67 McLoughlin, *Cherokees and Missionaries*, 4–5, 180.

68 Prucha, *The Great Father*, 1: 145; Robert F. Berkhofer, *Salvation and the Savage: An Analysis of Protestant Missions and American Indian Response, 1787–1862* (Lexington: University of Kentucky Press, 1965), 1, 10; Bowden, *American Indians and Christian Missions*, 167–9; Satz, *American Indian Policy*, 2; Reginald Horsman, *The Origins of Indian Removal, 1815–1824* (East Lansing: Michigan State University Press, 1970), 15.

69 Bourne, *Gods of War*, 321–3. Although not included in this story, readers may enjoy taking a few minutes to explore the legendary Hiawatha. A follower of the Great Peacemaker, the sixteenth-century leader of the Onondaga, or the Mohawks, is credited with founding the Iroquois Confederacy.

70 Bourne, *Gods of War*, 324; Adam Jortner, *The Gods of Prophetstown: The Battle of Tippecanoe and the Holy War for the American Frontier* (New York: Oxford University Press, 2011).

71 McLoughlin, *Cherokees and Missionaries*, 2; Berkhofer, *Salvation and the Savage*, 159.

72 McLoughlin, *Cherokees and Missionaries*, 82–3, 95–6, 190–1.

73 Hagan, *American Indians*, 55, 66–7, 74; Horsman, *Origins of Indian Removal*, 5–13; McLoughlin, *Cherokees and Missionaries*, 213.

74 McLoughlin, *Cherokees and Missionaries*, 240–65.

75 Satz, *American Indian Policy*, 11; Hagan, *American Indians*, 11; Bourne, *Gods of War*, 366.

76 See, for example, McLoughlin, *Cherokees and Missionaries*, 348.

77 Bourne, *Gods of War*, 374–5.

78 McLoughlin, *Cherokees and Missionaries*, 348–50.

79 Bourne, *Gods of War*, 374–5.

80 Josephy, *Indian Heritage of America*, 326–7; Washburn, *The Indian in America*, 123–4; Robert Ignatius Bums, *The Jesuits and the Indian Wars of the Northwest* (New Haven, CT: Yale University Press, 1966), 31–116.

81 Prucha, *The Great Father*, 1: 485–500.

82 Hagan, *American Indians*, 111–2, 121.

83 Albanese, *America*, 48; James Axtell, *After Columbus: Essays in the Ethnohistory of Colonial North America* (New York: Oxford University Press, 1988), 101, 108.

Recommended for further reading

Berkhofer, Robert F. *The White Man's Indian: Images of the American Indian from Columbus to the Present.* New York: Alfred A. Knopf, 1978.

Deloria, Vine, Jr. *God Is Red: A Native View of Religion.* Golden, CO: Fulcrum, 1994.

Ehle, John. *Trail of Tears: The Rise and Fall of the Cherokee Nation.* New York: Anchor Books, 1988.

Fisher, Linwood D. *The Indian Great Awakening: Religion and the Shaping of Native Cultures in Early America.* New York: Oxford University Press, 2014.

Gutierrez, Ramon A. *When Jesus Came, the Corn Mother Went Away: Marriage, Sexuality, and Power in New Mexico, 1500–1846.* Stanford, CA: Stanford University Press, 1991.

Horsman, Reginald. *Race and Manifest Destiny: The Origins of American Racial Anglo-Saxonism.* Cambridge, MA: Harvard University Press, 1981.

Jennings, Francis. *The Invasion of America: Indians, Colonialism, and the Cant of Conquest.* Chapel Hill: University of North Carolina Press, 1976. Rpt. New York: W. W. Norton, 1975.

Martin, Joel W. *The Land Looks after Us: A History of Native American Religion.* New York: Oxford University Press, 2001.

Sandos, James A. *Converting California: Indians and Franciscans in the Missions.* New Haven, CT: Yale University Press, 2004.

White, Richard. *"It's Your Misfortune and None of My Own": A History of the American West.* Norman: University of Oklahoma Press, 1991.

Chapter 2

British colonization and the origins of American religion

England prepares for colonization

"God is English," an English clergyman told his parishioners in 1558,[1] but England did little to convince the world of that or at least to establish the Church of England in the New World until over a hundred years after Columbus arrived in the Caribbean. A British clergyman, Richard Hakluyt, deserves considerable credit for finally bringing that about.

In *A Discourse on Western Planting* (1584), Hakluyt argued the allied causes of Protestantism and England. In speaking of spreading the word of God through colonization, he wrote: "It remains to be thoroughly weighed and considered by what means and by whom this most godly and Christian work may be performed of enlarging the glorious gospel of Christ." But, he continued, it should be done by those "who have taken upon them the protection and defense of the Christian faith," namely the Kings and Queens of England. Having been named Defenders of the Faith, they "are not only charged to maintain and patronize the faith of Christ, but also to enlarge and advance it."[2] That charge grew out of the English Reformation, which first delayed and then made more urgent English colonization of America.

During the reign of King Henry VIII, England severed its ecclesiastical ties with Rome, but this marked only the beginning of the turbulence that rocked England for generations. When Henry died, the kingdom veered sharply toward Protestantism under Edward VI, then toward Catholicism under Mary I, before arriving at a "settlement" under Queen Elizabeth. A measure of stability returned as the Church of England steered a middle course between Roman Catholicism and the Protestantism of either Calvin or Luther, but such a course did not please everyone. The most quarrelsome of the dissidents became known as the Puritans, who, despairing of the degree of reform effected, withdrew into their own churches and then, when they came under increasing attack by the Stuart kings, from England altogether.[3]

The Virginia colony

On April 10, 1606, King James I chartered the London Company, and almost exactly one year later, the company cast anchor off the coast of Virginia, establishing a colony named for its monarch, Jamestown. Tragedy marked the first years of the settlement. Of little more than a hundred settlers in May, half were dead by September, and so the pattern continued for several years in the face of Indian attacks, disease, and starvation. It would be at least a dozen years before reasonable men could believe that Virginia might survive.

There was no question from the start that the Church of England would be the Established Church in Virginia. At its initial meeting in 1619, the House of Burgesses confirmed what had been stipulated in its founding charter. The Church in Virginia, however, found itself incapable of duplicating the Church left behind. First, parishes were not neat parcels of land centered on the village green. They were measured in miles, not blocks, and they were sparsely settled mostly with single young men. Virginia offered little to a potential pastor but personal hardship and hostile country. Although provided a set salary from taxes levied on the colonists, he was paid in a fixed amount of tobacco or corn, the value of which fluctuated undermining a stable income. In 1662, Roger Green bitterly complained of a clerical shortage so severe that settlers "see their families disordered, their children untaught, the public worship and service of the great God they own neglected."[4]

Further adding to the difficulties of the Church of England in Virginia was the absence of theological training for prospective ministers, the poor quality of those ministers attracted to the colony from England, and troubles between the clergy and the laity, the last being complicated by uncertain and uneven church discipline. Virginia had no bishop and no ecclesiastical court to examine orthodoxy or enforce discipline. That left such matters to individual congregations and the men elected to the church vestry. Under such circumstances, the rector was sometimes at the mercy of an unsympathetic vestry, while the vestry was sometimes under the spell of an unworthy minister.[5]

Despite these handicaps, as the colony grew so too did the Church. There were twenty parishes in Virginia by 1650 and twice that number by the end of the century. In 1693, the College of William and Mary was chartered "to the end that the Church of Virginia may be furnished with a seminary of ministers to the gospel." Nevertheless, Anglicanism lost favor and following to the rapidly growing forces of dissent. After England adopted its Act of Toleration in 1689, the Church's restrictive walls crumbled, and Presbyterians, Baptists, and Methodists made deep inroads. Part of the growth of the dissenting or non-conforming churches resulted from new immigration; the rest migrated from New England and the Middle Colonies. The pattern had begun that would be repeated throughout the colonies, regardless of which particular group was responsible for that colony's settlement: "Where once there was one, there soon appeared many."[6]

New England

In 1620, the Pilgrims sailed for the New World. Like other Puritans, the Pilgrims contended that England's established church had not completed its reformation. Unlike other Puritans, they had given up trying to reform it from within. Having become Separatists, they fled England to escape the heavy penalties of the law – first to Amsterdam, in 1607, then to Leyden, where though they had more freedom they did not feel at home, and finally to America. With "great hope and inward zeal," William Bradford, soon to be governor of Plymouth Colony, wrote, they set out to lay "some good foundation for propagating and advancing the gospel of the Kingdom of Christ in those remote parts of the world; yea, though they should be but even as stepping-stones unto others for the performing of so great a work."[7]

Authorized to settle in Virginia, the Pilgrims made landfall off the coast of New England, where, with supplies short and winter near, they decided to remain. The site of Plymouth (Plimoth) was chosen, a compact agreed to for social order, and a community begun. Bradford recorded his observations upon arrival: "The season, it was winter," he wrote, and they were "subject to cruel and fierce storms." They had arrived in "a hideous and desolate wilderness, full of wild beasts and wild men," and "what could now sustain them but the Spirit of God and His grace?"[8]

By the following spring, half of the settlers had died, but the colony itself did not perish. By fall, the Pilgrims and Indians, who had done much to insure the Pilgrims' survival, shared a thanksgiving feast, and soon the colony was on more firm footing. Growth in Plymouth, however, was never great, as second and third generations left to settle new towns and were not replaced. It was soon eclipsed by the far larger migration of their Puritan cousins to Massachusetts Bay. By the middle of the seventeenth century Plymouth still numbered fewer than 1,000 inhabitants; Massachusetts Bay was nearly twenty times as large.

Unlike the Pilgrims, the Puritans of Massachusetts Bay had not separated from the Church of England. For them, the Church, though having lost its way, remained their church, and they bore the responsibility of reforming it. To do so, however, in 1630, they would emigrate to a new land 3,000 miles from England's ecclesiastical courts, where they would be free to create a true Church of England, a church purified. Soon to be Governor, John Winthrop, explained their mission on board the flagship *Arbella* before they disembarked, in a lay sermon titled "A Model of Christian Charity." They were "to do more service to the Lord" by increasing "the body of Christ where of [they were] members" and to preserve themselves and their posterity "from the common corruptions of this evil world." They would "work out [their] salvation under the power and purity of [God's] holy ordinances" and become "a city on a hill," which would serve as a model for those they left behind. But if they failed? Winthrop was quite clear:

> The eyes of all people are upon us. So that if we shall deal falsely with our God in this work we have undertaken, and so cause Him to withdraw His present help from us, we shall be made a story and a by-word through the world . . . [and] we shall surely perish out of the good land whither we pass over this vast sea to possess.[9]

In Puritan Congregationalism, the "New England way," each local church ruled itself, joining with other churches only for counsel, admonition, and fellowship. In contrast to the Church of England's hierarchical structure, the local congregation was the highest earthly ecclesiastical authority. Only those who gave evidence of conversion were eligible for church membership, and the church was formed by means of a voluntary covenant among the converted.[10]

The Puritans, standing firmly in the tradition of John Calvin, indulged in no sentimental illusions about the nature of man. Man was a sinner, and his salvation was by God's grace and predestination, the belief that God had already determined who was to be saved, or not. As a result, New England Puritans acknowledged the need for law, discipline, and control. In addition to a church covenant and a covenant of grace, a civil compact was provided. Because Massachusetts was a commonwealth, all were equally subject to the active dominion of God. Because it was a Puritan commonwealth, the saints were in charge, and the entire experiment rested on the premise that church and state would be one, not in their organization – Massachusetts was not a theocracy in which ministers wielded secular authority – but in their common recognition of the sovereignty and omniscience of God. As Edwin Gaustad put it: "New England was not 'priest-ridden' in the sense that clergymen forced reluctant magistrates to do their bidding. The colony was 'piety-driven' . . . in the sense that basic religious motives propelled the state no less than the church."[11]

Decades ago, Perry Miller exposed what he referred to as the New England Puritans' Augustinian strain of piety.[12] More recent scholarship, however, has shown that, beyond being intellectual, Puritanism was as well an upwelling of religious emotion bounded and articulated by Reformed Protestantism. This piety was established in conversion, spiritually the soul's rebirth, wherein fear of God and self-humiliation over one's unworthiness and incapacity to achieve salvation gives way to peace, joy, and love for God and fellow saints from recognition that God's grace is freely given. Such love then provides a measure of spiritual potency to obey God's laws and reform society, which in turn was seen as a necessary step in the restoration of the church order buried under more than a millennium of Catholic corruption and human Innovation.[13] To ensure religious orthodoxy and uniformity, especially among the clergy, the colonies of Massachusetts and Connecticut established Harvard College in 1636 and Yale in 1701.

Church covenants and civil compacts ensured that dissenters would be excommunicated, disenfranchised and even banished. Nevertheless, some chose to dissent from the Massachusetts dissenters' establishment. Roger Williams, who took Holy Orders in the Church of England but became a Puritan, arrived in Boston in 1631, whereupon Governor Winthrop received him as one of the "godly ministers." Boston offered Williams its pulpit, but he declined because, as he later wrote, "I durst not officiate to an unseparated people." The people of New England must separate "holy from unholy, penitent from impenitent, godly from ungodly." Williams accepted an offer from Plymouth, where the Pilgrims, themselves separatists, found nothing objectionable in Williams's separatism. Not finding the Plymouth congregation sufficiently separated, however, in 1633, he moved to Salem.[14]

In his ministry, Williams not only took separatism to the extreme, wherein he could find no visible church, but also he became one of the earliest proponents of religious freedom and separation of church and state. He attacked not only church government but also civil government, arguing that magistrates should not punish Sabbath-breakers or violators of any other religious requirement. Massachusetts authorities saw Williams's religious zeal as misdirected and threatening to the peace and covenanted harmony upon which their "errand into the wilderness" depended, but Williams responded by arguing that civil magistrates had no power to punish him or anyone else for their religious opinions. (He also questioned Massachusetts' right to the land it occupied without first having purchased it from the Indians.) In 1635, Massachusetts authorities brought Williams to trial, found him guilty of having "broached and divulged new and dangerous opinions against the authority of the magistrates and churches," and ordered him to depart Massachusetts's jurisdiction. Williams moved to Narraganset Bay and what would become Providence, Rhode Island.[15]

Promising freedom of religion to all comers, Williams's colony became a haven for dissenters and the persecuted. Williams remained as zealous in his faith as ever, but he believed that state compulsion was not conducive to that end. He is credited with being the first to use the phrase "wall of separation" in matters of church and state. Rather than arguing that the state had to be protected from ambitious religionists, however, as his words might be interpreted today, he argued that Christianity had to be protected from the state, the "garden of Christ" from the "wilderness of the world." As he explained in *The Bloody Tennent of Persecution* (1644), "persecution for cause of conscience [was] against the Doctrine of Jesus Christ."[16] Religion must be voluntary, not forced; church and state must be separate. In 1663, when Rhode Island received a colonial charter, religious liberty remained a guarantee, not only for Christians but also for Jews. Ten years later, Jews dedicated what is now the oldest surviving synagogue in British America, the Touro Synagogue in Newport, Rhode Island.

Anne Hutchinson, too, came as an insider, having followed her clerical hero, John Cotton, from England. She heard Cotton preach that, prior to the Fall, God gave Adam and his heirs a covenant of works. That having failed, God promised man a new covenant of grace, which Jesus Christ sealed when he gave himself to death on the cross. Cotton favored the second covenant, Hutchinson accepted it exclusively. She opposed those who suggested that salvation could be achieved through obedience to moral law, arguing even, it was charged, that once people were under the covenant of grace or had received God's saving grace, they were absolved from the necessity of obeying moral law. Massachusetts Puritans rejected the covenant of works as well, but they had tacitly allowed, if not encouraged, a preparationist understanding of obedience to moral law and taught that people under the covenant of grace would necessarily lead a holy life. Her enemies called Hutchinson's heresy Antinomianism; they feared it would lead to lawlessness and anarchy.[17]

Instead of keeping her religious views to herself, Hutchinson expounded on them to increasingly large crowds of men and women in her home. She also attacked Cotton's fellow-minister, John Wilson, for having lapsed back to the covenant of works. To colonial authorities of church and state, she had gone too far. Anne Hutchinson had preached falsely, they charged, and she had violated good practice and church order.

When tried before the Massachusetts General Court, in 1637 and 1638, Hutchinson asked what law she had broken. Officials cited the Fifth Commandment because, while it only demanded respect for father and mother, they interpreted it to include all other authority in church and state as well. Hutchinson asked whether true children of God were obliged to obey parents, if those parents asked them to do wrong. But Winthrop chose not to debate the matter, responding: "We do not mean to discourse with those of your sex.[18]

Hutchinson made it clear that she followed a higher law than that laid down by religious authorities. Moreover, she insisted that individuals could communicate with the spirit of Christ and interpret biblical teachings on their own. This, Winthrop convinced the Court, was the root of all Hutchinson's mischief. Church and state could never survive such capricious assertions. They could not tolerate claims that God spoke new words apart from Scripture to Hutchinson or anyone else. Hutchinson and her followers were either banished or silenced.[19] The Reverend John Wheelwright, Hutchinson's brother-in-law, moved to New Hampshire, where he joined others in planting that colony. Hutchinson, her family, and others moved to Rhode Island. Still the eye of the storm even among Rhode Islanders, following the death of her husband, she moved to the Pelham Bay area of Long Island Sound where she was killed in an Indian attack in 1643.

A less inflammatory form of discontent led the Reverend Thomas Hooker, in 1634, to petition the Massachusetts General Court for permission to leave. Finding Massachusetts too contentious, Hooker moved to what is now northern Connecticut. Three years later, the Reverend John Davenport, finding Massachusetts too compromising, led a group to the port of New Haven. Their contrasting ideological origins notwithstanding, the two colonies were joined under one colonial charter in 1665.

Other individuals and groups – including Baptists and Quakers – continued to challenge Puritan rule. Authorities attempted to close their doors to such radicals, but in a pattern that would be repeated throughout American history, they ultimately failed and had to adjust. By 1660, Philip Gura has found, an ideological system evolved that, while it could not fully satisfy the longings of all radicals, harnessed enough of the potential energies of their ideas to garner the support of the majority of settlers. The dissenters became members of the congregational order from which Winthrop and others had worked to exclude them.[20]

Adding to the challenges posed by dissenters was the loss of religious fervor among second- and third-generation New Englanders and increased immigration from England, Scotland, and France, who though Protestant, did not share in the "Puritan way," preferring instead to be Baptists, Huguenots, Quakers, and Anglicans. As Jon Butler has found, Congregational (Puritan) church membership, which had been as high as 70 percent to 80 percent in the 1630s and 1640s, fell by half by the 1670s. In Salem, only 30 percent of taxpayers belonged to the town's Puritan church. All of this declension manifested itself in other ways in New England as well, including underscoring the witch trials of 1692. Although not the direct cause, the unraveling of Puritan New England's religious experiment at the end of the century made fertile soil for witch-hunting. What David Hall has described in his analysis of popular religion as a long-standing tension between orthodox ministerial expectations and deeply embedded, centuries-old magical and occult beliefs broke down.[21]

As Hall and Richard Godbeer have found, the people of seventeenth-century New England lived in "an enchanted universe" – "a world of wonders" – and the practice of magic was widespread, as it had been for centuries in Europe. Horoscopes, astrology, the use of charms, and recognition of those who claimed to be learned in fortune-telling or to be able to employ magical practices to cure diseases or do harm, were widespread. Moreover, the use of folk magic in early New England was commonplace even among Puritan church members, who switched from one to the other without any sense of wrongdoing much to the consternation of the Puritan ministry. By way of example, in 1692, one Rebecca Johnson of Salem in an attempt to determine if her son was dead or alive, had her daughter perform "the turning of the sieve." If the sieve turned, she believed, he was dead. To properly execute this bit of folk magic, however, she repeated the phrase: "By Saint Peter and Saint Paul, if [her son] be dead let this sieve turn around," which indeed it did. If that was harmless enough, however, in the same year and town, in the face of various untoward circumstances, all went terribly awry, as it had numerous times over the course of the last 250 years in Western Europe. White magic became black magic, associated with evil spirits and pacts with the Devil. Political conflicts with Great Britain, Indian wars, community tensions, land disputes, and socio-economic cleavages were charged to those accused of doing the Devil's bidding.[22]

It all began in Salem Village (now Danvers), a community well known for its family disputes, commonly involving a series of failed ministers, in the home of one of which, Samuel Parris, the first signs appeared. Parris's daughter and niece, ages 9 and 11, were the first afflicted and accusers, only to have one of those they accused, Parris's Caribbean servant Tituba, confess and be the first to name others. That set off a conflagration of newly afflicted accusers, including other young women in the village, and accused, mostly older women and men associated with them (e.g. husbands). The trials that followed and the near certain condemnation that resulted in its early stages often based on the use of "spectral" evidence available only to the afflicted, soon spread to other communities in eastern Massachusetts before burning out due to its own overheated excesses, at one point threatening to implicate the Governor's wife.[23]

Before the Salem witch trials ended, nineteen people were hanged and one pressed to death for refusing to enter a plea and stand trial. Over 150 people from 24 towns and villages were jailed, where several died and many remained for months. Compared to other witch-hunts in the Western world, it was but "a small incident in the history of a great superstition," but it was the largest of its kind in the British colonies of North America. It has left its mark on the historical conscience of Americans and, some would argue, marked the turning point from the more medieval reformation religious world of the seventeenth century to the modern period that followed. Puritan hegemony had been broken, forever.[24]

The Middle Colonies

No other section of the American colonies is less visible in the literature than that called the Middle Colonies. It may be the case, however, that it was those colonies, in their great diversity of faiths, more so than the more homogenous Puritan New England and Anglican South, that demonstrated that voluntarism, or denominationalism; the free exercise of religion; and disestablishment were not necessarily destructive to belief in God and that out of diversity can come unity: *e pluribus unum*. New York, New Jersey, and Pennsylvania present the most striking pictures of religious diversity in British America.[25]

New York began as the colony of New Netherlands, established by the Dutch West India Company in 1623 at the mouth of the Hudson River. Although established with the express purpose of bringing to Holland "a share of the rumored riches of the New World," largely through the fur trade and with no reference to religion in the company's charter, colonial promoters proposed that ministers be sent to instruct both the settlers and the Indians "in religion and learning."[26] In 1629, the Dutch Reformed Church was officially established, but the directors of the company followed a liberal policy encouraging colonists of many faiths to settle there, including Jews.

The first Jews in the American colonies, mostly Sephardic (observing Spanish and Portuguese Judaic traditions) arrived in New Amsterdam in 1654 from Brazil, after the Portuguese captured the Dutch colony there. Most left within a few years, however, and were replaced by a second wave of Jewish settlers in the 1680s, who established the first permanent synagogue in New York City in 1695. Their numbers, however, never exceeded 2 percent of the city's total population in the colonial period. Other than those who settled in Newport, Rhode Island, the only other significant, yet small, groups of Jews settled in Philadelphia, Charleston, and Savannah.[27]

In 1664, the Dutch colony came under British rule. The Dutch Reformed Church was permitted to remain, and New York's comparatively liberal policy attracted Congregationalists from New England, Presbyterians from Scotland and Ireland, Quakers from a number of locations, and Lutherans from the Palatinate. Anglican leaders were not pleased by such promiscuous mixing, but once the English Toleration Act was passed, exclusion ceased to be an option. Instead, the colony of New York adopted new laws to encourage the building of Anglican churches and the growth of an Anglican ministry. By the mid-eighteenth century, largely the result of the efforts of the Society for the Propagation of the Gospel, about sixty Anglican churches existed in the Middle Colonies. In 1754, Anglicans succeeded in establishing in New York City King's College, later to be renamed Columbia, but actual establishment of the Church of England was limited to the four counties around New York City.[28]

New Jersey's even more liberal policy toward dissenters attracted diverse religious groups as well. Among the largest groups added to the founding Dutch Reformed Church were Presbyterians out of Scotland and Ireland, New England Congregationalists, who would become Presbyterians, and Quakers from England. By 1746, Presbyterians had gained sufficient strength of numbers to establish synods in Philadelphia and New York and to secure a charter for the College of New Jersey, later known as Princeton.[29] English Quakers settled in West New Jersey – for a time separated from East New Jersey – from which, the Quaker William Penn later wrote, they laid "a foundation for other ages to understand their liberty as men and Christians that they may not be brought in bondage but by their own consent."[30] Penn would soon, however, set his sights elsewhere, creating his own colony of Pennsylvania.

William Penn was no stranger to intolerance. During the reign of Charles II, 15,000 Quakers had been confined to British jails, where more than 400 died. In 1670, he wrote a passionate defense of religious liberty, *The Great Case of Liberty of Conscience*, wherein he argued that force had no place in matters of the spirit. Much as had Roger Williams, Penn insisted that when force is used in religion – a direct reference to an established church using its position to silence dissenters – God is dishonored, the Christian religion overthrown, reason violated, and government undone.[31]

Penn launched his "Holy Experiment" in 1681, when King Charles II, in payment for a debt, granted Penn the area that was to become the colonies of Pennsylvania and Delaware (separated from Pennsylvania in 1701). Penn intended his colony to be a model of what men of good will could be, when guided by the inner light of God's spirit the Quaker way. Penn's generous land policy and offer of religious freedom attracted other religious groups as well. Tens of thousands of Reformed, but mostly Lutheran, Germans began arriving as early as 1683 led by Francis Daniel Pastorius, and by 1740, they equaled nearly one-third of the entire Pennsylvania population. Scotch-Irish Presbyterians, equaling another third, began to arrive in large numbers during the second and third decades of the eighteenth century, moving to the frontier where they became one of the most formidable groups of frontiersmen in American history. There were also smaller but significant numbers of Mennonites, Catholics, Amish, German Baptist Brethren (or Dunkers), Jews, and Anglicans.[32]

In that "Penn's Woods" attracted and accommodated such diversity, Penn's Holy Experiment was a success. While Penn worked for "a blessed government, and a virtuous, ingenious and industrious society,"[33] however, the Quakers' leadership was soon rent with disputes. Civil authority grew tangled and corrupt, and Quaker pacifism was compromised by the colony's frontier conditions. In sum, Penn's much-exalted Quaker belief in the "holy law within," upon which the colony was to be built, disappeared.

The Southern Colonies

In contrast to the Middle Colonies, the Southern Colonies followed Virginia's example in attempting to maintain its Anglican establishment. Maryland was the single exception. In 1632, King Charles I granted to Cecil Calvert, Lord Baltimore, a charter for lands around Chesapeake Bay north of Virginia. Lord Baltimore was the only Roman Catholic proprietor among American colonists. Although intended as a haven for Catholics, Maryland – honoring both England's last Catholic monarch and the Virgin Mother – also welcomed Protestants, but the latter arrived in such large numbers that the founders' original intent was repeatedly and ultimately successfully challenged. In 1649, in response to one such challenge, Calvert sought to protect the Catholic minority by framing a toleration act, whereby "no persons professing to believe in Jesus Christ should be molested in respect of their religion, or in the free exercise thereof, or be compelled to the belief or exercise of any other religion, against their consent."[34]

Opposition from resident Protestants continued until, in April 1689, they persuaded King William to make Maryland a royal colony. In 1692, the Maryland colonial assembly adopted an act "for the service of Almighty God and the establishment of the Protestant religion," and the new governor administered English test oaths and oaths of office to all office-holders, with which Catholics could not comply. In 1718, the Maryland legislature disfranchised Catholics altogether.[35]

The first permanent settlement in the Carolinas was established in 1670 at Charleston. The colony attracted settlers from Barbados, Jamaica, and other Caribbean islands, as well as immigrants from England, Ireland, and France and migrants from New England. Nearly all were Protestant, but a major center of colonial Judaism arose in Charleston. As in Virginia, the arrival of such dissenting groups in what was to be officially a Church of England preserve caused some alarm. Anglican leaders viewed dissenters as interlopers, not only forgetful of colonial prerogatives and royal wishes, but also a threat to the peace and security they believed establishment and uniformity of belief guaranteed.

Quaker John Archdale made matters worse, when he urged all in authority to give up their quarrelling over "poor trifles and barren opinions." In 1707, Archdale wrote: "It is stupendous to consider how passionate and preposterous zeal not only veils but stupefies oftentimes, the rational powers." Reasonable men should consider the qualifications of prospective settlers as settlers, not on their religious beliefs. If Carolina were to take away freedom of conscience or deprive men of their liberty and property because of their religious beliefs, Archdale continued, settlers would leave or not be attracted to the colony in the first place. It was a telling argument, heard again and again all along the Atlantic coast, not only against the Anglican Establishment but also against the Puritans of Massachusetts and Connecticut. The result, in the Carolinas as elsewhere was an increase in religious toleration, eventually leading, as we shall see, to religious freedom.[36]

The area that was to become North Carolina had no settlements until about 1653, when colonists began to migrate from Virginia into the region around Albemarle Sound. Many were Quakers, their affiliation encouraged by George Fox's visit in 1672. By the early years of the eighteenth century, over 4,000 inhabited the area, but the region developed a reputation for its rough ways. Anglican missionaries were appalled at the lack of "decency and order." Although the colonial assembly made legal provision for Anglicanism as early as 1715, successful implementation of the law depended, as always, on the sentiment and sympathy of the people, and the people of North Carolina were unwilling or unable to establish effectively the Church of England in their midst.[37]

In 1731, Thomas Bray, founder of the Anglican Society for the Propagation of the Gospel and Society for the Promotion of Christian Knowledge, commissioned an organization "for instructing the Negroes in the Christian religion and establishing a charitable colony for the better maintenance of the poor of this kingdom, and for other good purposes." He attracted James Oglethorpe to his cause, and soon thereafter Oglethorpe petitioned King George III for a land grant south of South Carolina for imprisoned debtors and impoverished unemployed. In 1733, the King granted him a charter and about a hundred men, women and children embarked for King George's colony.[38]

Oglethorpe made clear his intent to instruct and convert blacks in the charter's prohibition against slavery. He was forced to remove the restriction, however, in 1749. The poor were nevertheless conspicuous among the colony's first settlers, and the "charitable colony" welcomed Lutherans fleeing persecution in Salzburg, Moravians leaving the protection of Saxony, and Scottish Presbyterians escaping political and economic distress. Even Jews, although officially forbidden to come, arrived in 1733, whereupon Oglethorpe not only permitted them to stay but also granted them land. In 1740, George Whitefield started an orphanage in Bethesda, near Savannah.[39]

In 1758, the Georgia Assembly formally recognized the Church of England as the colony's official denomination, created eight parishes, and stipulated a salary for eight nonexistent clergymen. Like the 1715 law in North Carolina, however, this act had little force for lack of actual church buildings and ministers. Failing, as did Anglicans in the other British colonies, to have a bishop appointed, Georgia Anglicans met little more than frustration in their efforts to solidify their hold on a colony that became an attractive destination for dissenters.[40]

The First Great Awakening

The transplanting of European religion to the New World was made more difficult by the environment into which it entered. Given the unsettled, frontier-like world into which immigrants plunged – the absence of church, ministry, or even community – it was easy for many to simply fall into non-practice. Given the presence of so many religious groups among those who might wish to practice, rather than one established church as had been the case in Europe, no one church could permanently claim any turf as its own. They would have to compete both with the wilderness and one another to win believers. The First Great Awakening constituted one such competition.

Initial impulses for the First Great Awakening arrived from Europe – from pietistic movements that tried to fire up casual believers, like the revivals that shook Britain during the 1730s and 1740s. But something new arose in America in the 1730s, an awakening that took many shapes, forms, and expressions. It is hard to prove that religious participation was low before the stirrings and greatly increased thereafter, supporting those who claim it was a Christian revitalization movement. Moreover, the Awakening was really a series of loosely connected outbreaks, each of which took on the color of its local milieu. No central person or religious organization planned or coordinated it; "no single plot unfolded."[41] Nevertheless, something of significance did happen during the fourth and fifth decades of the eighteenth century.

The Great Awakening can be seen as a move toward the development of modern religion in the West, in general, and American religion, in particular. At its heart was the notion of choice: Colonists were obliged to choose Jesus Christ, to decide to let the Spirit of God work in their hearts, and to select one version of Christianity over another. In this regard, the Great Awakening changed the landscape of the American religious community. As Martin Marty has put it: "Where once a single steeple towered above the town, there soon would be a steeple and a chapel, old First Church and competitive Separatist Second Church or Third Baptist Chapel – all vying for souls."[42] Most of the mainline Protestant churches of the modern period exist because they set out to convert people during the First and Second Great Awakenings. Those, like the Anglicans/Episcopalians, who shunned them, were left behind. One figure, Jonathan Edwards, looms especially large in the history of the movement.

Jonathan Edwards, a religious thinker and evangelical preacher, towered above all others of his time. No one both participated in and studied the Awakening more thoroughly. No one interpreted the psychology of conversion or the meaning of the revival for community life better than he did. Finally, Edwards salvaged the central points of Puritan authority by modernizing its outmoded metaphysics with the enlightened harmonies of Isaac Newton and John Locke, thereby paving the way for the New England mind becoming the American mind.[43] Edwards's story, however, like that of most evangelicals of the Great Awakening, makes best sense when set against the background of the immediate world in which he lived, that is the early eighteenth-century Connecticut River Valley, that had been presided over by his grandfather Solomon Stoddard. Stoddard ministered to the region for over fifty-seven years, earning the title "pope" from his detractors due to his pervasive influence.

Stoddard and Edwards inherited a problem that each would address, but in different ways, the declining number of "visible saints" who were to govern church and state in Puritan New

Whitefield, it may be said, was responsible for whipping the flames of the local revivals into the general conflagration known as the Great Awakening. He also came to represent the most controversial aspect of the Awakening, itinerancy.

Whitefield started coming to America from England to advance the cause of Georgia's Bethesda orphanage. Arriving in the late 1730s, however, he became one of the Great Awakening's most ardent proponents. Whitefield whipped people into enthusiasm for God with a voice and style that led actor David Garrick to assert enviously that Whitefield could melt an audience merely by pronouncing "Mesopotamia." He also adopted up-to-date marketing techniques to merchandize his product: religion. Advertising his feats in print, hawking his journals, and staging confrontations to attract publicity, he gained unparalleled notice. When Benjamin Franklin heard Whitefield address crowds in Philadelphia, despite his initial skepticism, he offered to be Whitefield's publisher and made a donation for the erection of a meeting-house and the Georgia orphanage.[50]

Whitefield drew praise for his work among the unconverted, condemning lying, cursing, Sabbath-breaking, and other forms of irreverence. He helped form and was president of England's first Methodist conference. But he relinquished that position to John Wesley to pursue his evangelical work. His evangelical style and itinerancy, however, provoked opposition. In England and America, he was barred from some churches as an enthusiast, so he took his crowds into the streets and open fields. By Franklin's estimate, Whitefield preached to up to 30,000 people upon one occasion in Philadelphia. In doing so, he further undercut the Establishment, both within his own Church of England that generally opposed the Awakening and in other churches that were divided on the issue. He joined with those who attacked Old Light/Old Side, or even neutral, ministers as preaching an unknown and unfelt Christ, for allowing laxity and for not promoting the preaching of grace.[51]

Although the Great Awakening influenced nearly every colonial denomination to some extent, New England Congregationalists and their Calvinist Presbyterian cousins of the Middle Colonies were most affected. Some have found the first stirrings of the Awakening in the Middle Colonies among German radical Pietists in the 1720s. Others have pointed to the work of the German-born Dutch Reformed minister Theodorus Frelinghuysen, who in the mid-1720s created a storm in New Jersey's Raritan Valley by seeking to awaken the spiritually dead and contented. But the Awakening reached its greatest heights among Presbyterians, beginning in the 1730s and peaking during the 1740s.[52]

The Presbyterian awakeners were led by the Tennent family. William Tennent, a Scotch-Irish immigrant, operated what was popularly known as the Log College near Philadelphia, which trained much-needed ministers for the church. Its graduates were listed among the most fervent evangelicals. William's son Gilbert became the leader of the Awakening in Presbyterian circles, as well as one of its most divisive forces. As supporters rallied to his call in large numbers, critics faulted him for claiming that he could look at people's faces and see whether they would be saved or damned; for his causing those who listened to his preaching to cry out "under the impression of terror and love"; and when in Nottingham, Pennsylvania, for offering one of the most heated sermons of the entire Awakening, wherein he spoke of "the dangers of an unconverted ministry." In 1741, one year after the Nottingham sermon, the Presbyterian Synod of Philadelphia split into two parties – Old Side and New Side, or more formally, the Synod of Philadelphia and the Synod of New York – which were not reunited until 1785.[53]

The Great Awakening only temporarily altered patterns of church adherence, which soon settled back into a pattern of more gradual but sustained growth.[54] However, the Great Awakening did leave its mark on American religious, as well as secular, history. In the short term, it politicized religious tensions. Longer term, disputing the propriety of letting an unregenerate pastor keep his pulpit sanctioned similar arguments against corrupt imperial officials. Organizing churches to advance denominational goals modeled the mechanisms ultimately used to prompt patriot dreams. Protestations against local infringements of religious liberty habituated colonists to advance similar defenses against Imperial threats. And finally, the Great Awakening challenged traditional notions of social stratification, insisting instead that the true value of a man lies in his moral behavior not his social class, or, as it would soon be written, that "all men are created equal."[55] Not all historians agree with this assessment, however, but more on that in the next chapter. In other respects, the effects of the Great Awakening were long term. If the First Great Awakening ended, revivals did not; they became permanent features of the American religious landscape. In this respect, the Great Awakening was not an interpretative fiction. It may well have been a turning point in the Christianization of the colonies, or the churching of America.

Summary

By the end of the colonial period, the American religious landscape was dramatically different from what it was only a century earlier. More than 85 percent of the approximately 1,200 religious congregations in the colonies on the eve of the American Revolution were founded after 1680. Moreover, America stood poised to become one of the most religiously diverse countries in the world. Before 1690, 90 percent of all congregations in Colonial America were either Congregationalist (concentrated in New England) or Anglican (largely in the South). By 1770, only 20 percent of all congregations were Congregationalist and 15 percent Anglican. Presbyterians accounted for 18 percent; Baptists, 15 percent; and Quakers, Lutherans, and Reformed, 5 percent to 10 percent each. Non-English congregations accounted for 25 percent of the total, including a number of comparatively small German sects such as the Mennonites, Amish, and Moravians. Within that diversity, however – excluding the much smaller populations of Catholics and Jews – there was considerable unity. Nearly all believers were Protestant and most were Reformed, or Calvinist.[56]

There was, therefore, widespread agreement on certain principles. First, Protestantism was a religion of the Word, the Word of the Bible, and colonists rebuked the Catholic Church for having drifted from that mandate toward sacramentalism. Second, most colonists believed that, without God's help through the grace of Jesus Christ, humans were powerless to effect their own salvation. They were sinners, who on their own could not do anything to win the grace of God. Nevertheless, just as God must perform a decisive act to save them, so they must live out their loyalty to him by decisive action in the world.

Third, colonial Protestant ministers, much like their European Calvinist counterparts, preached justification through faith. Justification was a legal term used to connote salvation, and faith meant the trust that human beings felt for God in Jesus. Faith was not, as in the Catholic Church, a collection of doctrinal truths to be accepted. Instead, it was a response to a divine and trustworthy person. Such faith put the emotional experience of an individual at the center of religion, an emphasis that Protestantism renewed in the First Great Awakening.

Fourth, colonists continued the Protestant insistence on the priesthood of all believers, once again departing from the medieval church with its sacramental understanding of the role of the priest as a ritual leader who represented the community before God. Among Roman Catholics, the community offered a common act of worship. Protestants brought individualism into the communal consciousness of the church. If each person was a priest, then each as an individual was offering worship to God.

These basic principles did not significantly distance colonial Protestants from their European counterparts. They did not remain static, however, but rather in their New World environment evolved into beliefs that were more distinctly American. The emphasis on individualism, for example, would become increasingly important in the new nation. It spoke to the new middle class that would quickly come to dominate the population, underscoring individualism in the social and economic sectors, as well. Further, these Reformation principles came to complement what British Americans saw as a call for moral action in the world. Reformers did not call humans to be idle but instead to witness their beliefs by their deeds. As Catherine Albanese has put it: "Protestantism led out of the churches and into the world."[57]

Review questions

1 What delayed England's entrance into the competition for empire in North America, and what difference did that delay make in its goals?
2 How did the role of religion in the colonization of New England, the Middle Colonies, and the South Colonies differ? In what ways was it similar?
3 What contributions did dissenters such as Roger Williams and Anne Hutchinson make to the development of religious freedom in America?
4 What were the initial impulses for the First Great Awakening? Who were its major proponents, and what was its legacy?
5 How was the religious landscape different on the eve of the American Revolution from what it was upon the planting of the thirteen British colonies in North America?

Notes

1 Carl Bridenbaugh, *Vexed and Troubled Englishmen, 1590–1642* (New York: Oxford University Press, 1968), 13.
2 Edwin Scott Gaustad, *A Religious History of America* (New York: Harper and Row, 1966), 28.
3 Wallace Notestein, *The English People on the Eve a/Colonization, 1603–1630* (New York: Harper Torchbooks, 1962), 146–71.
4 Gaustad, *Religious History of America*, 40–1.
5 Gaustad, *Religious History of America*, 41.
6 Gaustad, *Religious History of America*, 41–2, 45.
7 William Bradford, *Of Plymouth Plantation, 1620–1647* (New York: Modern Library, 1981), 26.
8 Bradford, *Of Plymouth Plantation*, 70–1.
9 Perry Miller and Thomas H. Johnson, eds., *The Puritans: A Sourcebook of Their Writings*, 2 vols. (New York: Harper Torchbooks, 1963), 1: 197, 199.
10 Gaustad, *Religious History of America*, 50.
11 Gaustad, *Religious History of America*, 54.
12 Perry Miller, *The New England Mind: The Seventeenth Century* (New York: Macmillan Company, 1939), ch. 1.
13 See: Charles Cohen, *God's Caress: The Psychology of Puritan Religious Experience* (New York: Oxford University Press, 1986); Theodore Dwight Bozeman, *To Live Ancient Lives: The Primitivist Dimension in Puritanism* (Chapel Hill: University of North Carolina Press, 1988).
14 Gaustad, *Religious History of America*, 64. Mary Dyer's punishment was exceptional for Massachusetts. She was hanged in 1660 for repeatedly defying a law banning Quakers from the colony.

15 Miller and Johnson, *Puritans*, 1: 214–15; Gaustad, *Religious History of America*, 65. See also: John M. Barry, *Roger Williams and the Creation of the American Soul: Church, State, and the Birth of Liberty* (New York: Penguin Books, 2012).
16 Miller and Johnson, *Puritans*, 1: 217.
17 Edmund Morgan, "The Case against Anne Hutchinson," *The New England Quarterly*, 10 (1937): 635–49; Fairfax Withington and Jack Schwartz, "The Political Trial of Anne Hutchinson," *The New England Quarterly*, 51 (1978): 226–40.
18 Glenda Riley, *Inventing the American Woman: A Perspective on Women's History* (Arlington Heights, IL: Harlan Davidson, 1987), 21; Lyle Koehler, "The Case of the American Jezebels: Anne Hutchinson and Female Agitation during the Years of Antinomian Turmoil, 1636–1640," *The William and Mary Quarterly*, 3rd sers, 31 (1974): 55–78; Lad Tobin, "A Radically Different Voice: Gender and Language in the Trials of Anne Hutchinson," *Early American Literature*, 25 (1990): 253–70.
19 Amanda Porterfield, *Female Piety in Puritan New England: The Emergence of Religious Humanism* (New York: Oxford University Press, 1992), 99; Riley, *Inventing the American Woman*, 20. For a documentary history of Hutchinson's ordeal, see: David D. Hall, *The Antinomian Controversy, 1636–1638: A Documentary History*, 2nd edn. (Durham, NC: Duke University Press, 1990). See also: Michael P. Winship, *The Times and Trials of Anne Hutchinson* (Lawrence: University Press of Kansas, 2005).
20 Philip F. Gura, *A Glimpse of Sion's Glory: Puritan Radicalism in New England* (Middletown, CT: Wesleyan University Press, 1984), 6, 14. See also: Janice Knight, *Orthodoxy in Massachusetts: Rereading American Puritanism* (Cambridge, MA: Harvard University Press, 1994), 5.
21 Jon Butler, Grant Wacker, and Randall Balmer, *Religion in American Life: A Short History*, 2nd edn. (New York: Oxford University Press, 2011), 58–9; See: David D. Hall, *Worlds of Wonder, Days of Judgment: Popular Religious Belief in Early New England* (New York: Alfred A. Knopf, 1989).
22 Hall, *Worlds of Wonder*, 71–116, Rebecca Johnson is noted on pages 99–100; Richard Godbeer, *The Devil's Dominion: Magic and Religion in Early New England* (New York; Cambridge University Press, 1992), x.
23 Paul Boyer and Stephen Nissenbaum, *Salem Possessed: The Social Origins of Witchcraft* (Cambridge, MA: Harvard University Press, 1974), 1–21; Bryan F. Le Beau, *The Story of the Salem Witch Trials*, 2nd edn. (Upper Saddle River, NJ: Prentice Hall, 2010), 51–64; Carol F. Karlsen, *The Devil in the Shape of a Woman: Witchcraft in Colonial New England* (New York: W. W. Norton, 1987), 46–76.
24 John Demos, "Underlying Themes in the Witchcraft of Seventeenth Century New England," *American Historical Review*, 75 (1970): 1311; See: John Demos, *Entertaining Satan: Witchcraft and the Culture of Early New England* (New York: Oxford University Press, 1982); Le Beau, *The Story of the Salem Witch Trials*.
25 Patricia U. Bonomi, *Under the Cope of Heaven: Religion, Society, and Politics in Colonial America* (New York: Oxford University Press, 1986), 72–3. See also: Douglas Jacobsen, *An Unprov'd Experiment: Religious Pluralism in Colonial New Jersey* (Brooklyn: Carlson, 1991).
26 Gaustad, *Religious History of America*, 80.
27 Butler et al., *Religion in American Life*, 78–80.
28 Arthur Lyon Cross, *The Anglican Episcopate and the American Colonies* (Hamden, CT: Archon Books, 1964), 1–2, 36–53, 88–113.
29 See: Leonard J. Trinterud, *The Forming of an American Tradition: A Reexamination of Colonial Presbyterianism* (Freeport, NY: Books for Libraries Press, 1949); Bryan F. Le Beau, *Jonathan Dickinson and the Formative Years of American Presbyterianism* (Lexington: The University Press of Kentucky, 1997), chs. 2, 9.
30 Gaustad, *Religious History of America*, 91.
31 Gaustad, *Religious History of America*, 92–3.
32 Gaustad, *Religious History of America*, 92–9.
33 Catherine Albanese, *America: Religions and Religion* (Belmont, CA: Wadsworth Publishing Company, 1992), 94·
34 Gaustad, *Religious History of America*, 73; John D. Krugler, "Lord Baltimore, Roman Catholics and Toleration: Religious Policy in Maryland during the Early Catholic Years, 1634–1649,"

Catholic Historical Review, 65 (1979): 49–75; Kenneth Lasson, "Free Exercise in the Free State: Maryland's Role in Religious Liberty and the First Amendment," *Journal of Church and State*, 31 (1989): 423–32.

35 John D. Krugler, "With Promises of Liberty in Religion: The Catholic Lords Baltimore and Toleration in Seventeenth Century Maryland, 1634–1692," *Maryland Historical Magazine*, 79 (1984): 36–8; Lasson, "Free Exercise in the Free State," 432–8.

36 Gaustad, *Religious History of America*, 100–1.

37 Gaustad, *Religious History of America*, 103.

38 Gaustad, *Religious History of America*, 104.

39 Gaustad, *Religious History of America*, 104–6.

40 Gaustad, *Religious History of America*, 104–6.

41 See: William Reginald Ward, *The Protestant Evangelical Awakening* (Cambridge: Cambridge University Press, 1991); Jon Butler, *Awash in a Sea of Faith: Christianizing the American People* (Cambridge, MA: Harvard University Press, 1990); Frank: Lambert, *Inventing the "Great Awakening"* (Princeton, NJ: Princeton University Press, 1999); Bonomi, *Under the Cope of Heaven*, 37; William G. Mcloughlin, *Revivals, Awakenings, and Reform: An Essay on Religion and Social Change in America, 1607–1977* (Chicago: University of Chicago Press, 1978), 51–3.

42 Martin E. Marty, *Pilgrims in Their Own Land: 500 Years of Religion in America* (New York: Penguin Books, 1986), 109.

43 See: Bozeman, *To Live Ancient Lives*; Perry Miller, *Nature's Nation* (Cambridge, MA: Harvard University Press, 1967). For a more recent corrective on Edwards, see: Stephen J. Stein, "The Spirit and the Word: Jonathan Edwards and Scriptural Exegesis," in *Jonathan Edwards and the American Experience*, ed. Nathan O. Hatch and Harry Stout (New York: Oxford University Press, 1988), 118–30.

44 McLoughlin, *Revivals, Awakenings, and Reform*, 51.

45 Marty, *Pilgrims in Their Own Land*, 113; Sydney E. Ahlstrom, *Religious History of the American People* (New Haven, CT: Yale University Press, 1971), 282.

46 Marty, *Pilgrims in Their Own Land*, 114; Ahlstrom, *Religious History of the American People*, 282; George M. Marsden, *Jonathan Edwards: A Life* (New Haven, CT: Yale University Press, 2003), 161–9.

47 Marty, *Pilgrims in Their Own Land*, 115.

48 Ahlstrom, *Religious History of the American People*, 301.

49 Marty, *Pilgrims in Their Own Land*, 116; Ahlstrom, *Religious History of the American People*, 302–3.

50 Marty, *Pilgrims in Their Own Land*, 118; David T. Morgan, "A Most Unlikely Friendship: Benjamin Franklin and George Whitefield," *The Historian*, 47 (1985): 208–18; See: Frank Lambert, *Pedlar in Divinity: George Whitefield and the Transatlantic Revivals, 1737–1770* (Princeton, NJ: Princeton University Press, 1994); Harry S. Stout, *The Divine Dramatist: George Whitefield and the Rise of Modern Evangelicalism* (Grand Rapids, MI: William B. Eerdmans Publishing Company, 1991).

51 Trinterud, *Forming of an American Tradition*, 87–8.

52 See: Charles H. Maxson, *The Great Awakening in the Middle Colonies* (Gloucester, MA: Peter Smith, 1958); Martin E. Lodge, "The Great Awakening in the Middle Colonies," Ph.D. dissertation (Berkeley: University of California, 1964).

53 Trinterud, *Forming of an American Tradition*, 58–64; Marty, *Pilgrims in Their Own Land*, 125. See also: Milton J. Coalter, *Gilbert Tennent, Son of Thunder: A Case Study of Continental Pietism's Impact on the First Great Awakening in the Middle Colonies* (Westport, CT: Greenwood Press, 1986).

54 Butler, *Awash in a Sea of Faith*, 293.

55 Bernard Bailyn, *The Ideological Origins of the American Revolution* (Cambridge, MA: Harvard University Press, 1967), 249, 273–4, 299–300. See also: Thomas S. Kidd, *God of Liberty: A Religious History of the American Revolution* (New York: Basic Books, 2010).

56 Roger Finke and Rodney Stark, *The Churching of America, 1776–1990: Winners and Losers in Our Religious Economy* (New Brunswick, NJ: Rutgers University Press, 1994), 55.

57 Albanese, *America*, 105.

Recommended for further reading

Bonomi, Patricia U. *Under the Cope of Heaven: Religion, Society, and Politics in Colonial America.* New York: Oxford University Press, 1986.

Butler, Jon. *Awash in a Sea of Faith: Christianizing the American People.* Cambridge, MA: Harvard University Press, 1990.

Demos, John, *Entertaining Satan: Witchcraft and the Culture of Early New England.* New York: Oxford University Press, 1982.

Godbeer, Richard. *The Devil's Dominion: Magic and Religion in Early New England.* New York: Cambridge University Press, 1992.

Hall, Timothy L. *Separating Church and State: Roger Williams and Religious Liberty.* Champaign: University of Illinois Press, 1998.

Hatch, Nathan O. *The Democratization of American Christianity.* New Haven, CT: Yale University Press, 1989.

Kidd, Thomas S. *The Great Awakening: The Roots of Evangelical Christianity in Colonial America.* New Haven, CT: Yale University Press, 2007.

Lambert, Frank. *Inventing the "Great Awakening."* Princeton, NJ: Princeton University Press, 1999.

Miller, Perry. *Errand into the Wilderness.* Cambridge, MA: Harvard University Press, 1956.

Stout, Harry S. *The Divine Dramatist: George Whitefield and the Rise of Modern Evangelicalism.* Grand Rapids, MI: Eerdmans, 1991.

Chapter 3

Religion and the American Revolution

Questions concerning religion and the American Revolution

"No subject in American religious history is as ideologically freighted as the role of religion in the American founding era." So wrote Thomas Kidd in his recent historiographical essay on religion and the American Revolution. Did religion give the movement for American independence ideological energy, or was it a secular event? Whichever historical perspective one takes, Kidd continued, "holds implications in today's debates about religion's place in America's public sphere."[1]

The period from 1763 to 1789 brought momentous changes to Americans. They confronted, then overthrew, the only government they had known, and they established new governments and what they hoped would be a new society. But the era of the American Revolution held immense consequences for religion in America as well, much of which was stimulated by fears of low-level church adherence on the eve of independence, of the potential for religious instability during the Revolution, and of the fate of the republic if republican virtues, necessary to its survival, were not underscored by organized religion. These fears proved to be unfounded. Organized religion not only survived but also prospered. In the process, however, the new nation underwent two more revolutions. In the first, church and state, which had been united for ages, were separated. In the second, in the minds of at least some leaders of church and state, religion became a matter of reason more than the heart.[2]

Religious support for the Revolution

The role of religion in the American Revolution failed to receive any great attention until Carl Bridenbaugh published his *Mitre and Sceptre* in 1962. He drew attention to the "bishop question," wherein Dissenters denounced alleged Anglican plots to install a colonial bishop while colonial assemblies were fighting off taxes and the escalation of imperial authority. Other historians soon followed, stressing the importance of the evangelical style and moral message in shaping both the Great Awakening and the American Revolution by providing a unifying force for the masses.

The bishop question

The bishop question was significant because it undermined trust in British politicians and their motives. It began at nearly the inception of colonization, but it grew much worse in the mid-eighteenth century when Dissenters came to constitute a majority of Americans. They feared an Anglican bishop, because they knew how they had fared under Anglican establishment in England. As Dissenters in New England showed, given the chance, they were not necessarily opposed to an establishment of their own faith, but by the mid-eighteenth century, none would have such a chance.

The Anglican-Dissenter contest over a bishop for America surfaced regularly until the 1760s, when it was joined to colonial protests against taxes and other English efforts at imperial centralization. It climaxed in protests against the Quebec Act of 1774, through which the English government recognized the Roman Catholic Church in the conquered territories of Canada. Beyond its stated purpose of offering freedom of religion to Catholics, the Quebec Act helped perpetuate colonists' belief in Catholicism's secret association with every attempt at tyranny in England since the 1640s, and especially with the reign of the Stuart kings.[3] It also resonated with colonial anti-Catholicism, which had been a staple of British life for two centuries.

Protestant Christianity and Whig political convictions

Protestant Christianity reinforced the Whig political convictions that lay behind early revolutionary rhetoric. In brief, growing out of seventeenth-century England's civil war and "Glorious Revolution," Whigs identified two threats to political freedom: a moral decay among the populace and its representatives that would give rise to despotic rulers and the tendency for encroachment of the crown on parliament if left unchecked. Whig sentiment extended throughout the colonies generally rather than from the more narrow sources of revivalism. As a result, religious support for the Whigs was not limited to evangelical Dissenters. The basic Whig texts – John Locke's *Second Treatise of Government* (1689), for example – were disseminated throughout the colonies, and reached more than evangelicals. Whiggism did not guarantee homogeneity, however. More than minor subtleties separated the Whiggism of Anglicans, Congregationalists, and Baptists, and on the eve of the Revolution, the religious implications of their Whiggism were not entirely clear.[4]

Systematic public discussion of virtue and morality came more frequently from ordained Christian clergymen than from any other single source. Clerics' emphasis on virtue, responsibility, and morality helped make sense of revolutionary rhetoric about corruption and evil among English politicians and society. And as protest escalated, some ministers discussed revolutionary politics specifically. This could occur in Sabbath sermons, but in New England, it more often happened during mid-week fast days and thanksgiving sermons, as best fitted the state church tradition. As they had done before, the ministers excoriated the unchurched, criticized the British, and promoted the quest for salvation, but now they also brought Christianity directly to bear on the revolutionary crisis.[5]

John Adams singled out the Reverend Jonathan Mayhew of Boston as one of the first to promote the cause of liberty. After some participation in the Great Awakening as a youth, Mayhew parted company with its proponents and followed the path of "reasonable Christianity" to being accused of Arminianism. Adams and his peers, however, remembered him for setting forth ideas of revolution a generation before the wave of independence.[6]

In *A Discourse Concerning Unlimited Submission and Non-Resistance to the Higher Powers* (1750), Mayhew took on the biblical text of Paul, in Romans 13, which stated that, since God established all authorities, whoever resisted authority resisted God and must be condemned. Since Paul presumably wrote these lines while Nero was persecuting Christians, his words would have meant that believers should obey evil rulers. Mayhew, however, argued that rulers had no authority from God to do mischief. Bad rulers were ministers of Satan, not God, and Christians were obliged to disobey any laws they might promulgate that ran contrary to the word of God.[7]

In 1762, Mayhew led a ministerial attack on the rumored appointment of an American Anglican bishop, and three years later, he preached his most inflammatory sermon in opposition to the passage of the Stamp Act. Once again, he used a text from Paul: "Ye have been called unto liberty."[8] The date was August 25, 1765, five months after the passage of the Stamp Act, and Mayhew's sermon helped ignite it by hinting that some local people were conniving with the British. The mob had already burned in effigy Andrew Oliver, stamp collector. The day after Mayhew preached, they burned Lieutenant Governor Thomas Hutchinson's house, and Governor Bernard accused Mayhew of fomenting the disorder.[9]

Ministerial support for the Revolution extended beyond New England. Despite some probable exaggeration in his report on the "thunder and lightning" that marked the Philadelphia ministers' weekly anti-British sermons, John Adams was not alone in remarking on the local clergies' political involvement. Thomas Jefferson commented that, in Anglican Virginia, "pulpit oratory ran like a shock of electricity through the whole colony." One minister, he continued, "did very pathetically exhort the people in his sermons to support their liberties . . . and, in the room of God save the king, he cried out: God preserve all the just rights and liberties of America."[10]

Nevertheless, ironically, the most common denominator among pro-revolutionary ministers was a state church pulpit, whether it be in New England among Congregationalists or in the southern colonies among Anglicans. Clearly, Middle Colony Presbyterians and Virginia Baptists proved to be important exceptions to this rule, but virtually all Anglican ministers in the Northern and Middle Colonies, where Anglicans often had to act the role of dissenters, became loyalists. A third of the Anglican clergy in Virginia and Maryland, where Anglicans held tax-supported pulpits, backed the Revolution, while elsewhere the correlation was stronger.[11]

In most colonies, the Revolution pitted a colonial political establishment against an expanding imperial administration, and the colonial clergy often owed more to the former than to the latter, even if the clergy involved were Anglican. The kind of politically active colonists who led the protest against British policy after 1763 usually supported the locally established church in colonies with state church systems; the established, tax-supported minister commonly supported the Revolution. Moreover, like the colonial political elites who used local government as a base from which to launch revolutionary-era protest and rebellion, ministers in the state churches used their fast and thanksgiving day sermons in the war against British policies. In this way, establishmentarian coercion, rather than Dissenting antiauthoritarian voluntarism, underwrote much of the American promotion of liberty and attack on Toryism.[12]

Roman Catholics and Baptists supported the Revolution. Catholics numbered only about 2,000 and lived among British Protestants in many ways still fighting the battles of the English Reformation. This was exacerbated by passage of the Quebec Act in 1774, which, as previously noted, gave neighboring Canadian Catholics, who recently came under British rule, the right to practice their religion openly. Catholics in the thirteen colonies were outsiders and widely discriminated against, and they were publicly ridiculed, often in biblical imagery reflecting the conflict of Christ and the Antichrist. Harvard College had its annual Dudleian Lecture, dedicated to publicly exposing Romish idolatry, wherein, in 1759, Jonathan Mayhew denounced Rome as a filthy prostitute and the mother of harlots. On Pope Day in Newport and Boston, mobs burned the pope in effigy, and when Parliament passed the Quebec Act, anti-Catholic hatred turned to fury.[13]

Nevertheless, American Catholics bought into American revolutionary ideology and supported the revolutionary cause, even in Maryland where the promise of religious freedom for Roman Catholics had been revoked. Catholic France provided loans, soldiers, and war material, in time becoming an official ally. With the urging of General George Washington and other leaders, anti-Catholic activity, if not sentiment, ceased, and Charles Carroll of Carrollton Manor in Maryland, a Catholic, signed the Declaration of Independence. In 1776, the Continental Congress sent Carroll's cousin, John, later first Catholic bishop in the United States, as part of a delegation to Canada in a failed effort to lure the Canadians into an alliance against England.[14]

The more numerous Baptists defined themselves as concerned first and foremost with salvation and the life to come, but they could not avoid taking political stands as well. Never being among the established, and almost always a persecuted minority, they struck out against the "standing order." By 1770, that translated into support for independence. In Massachusetts, for example, Isaac Backus not only protested religious taxes levied by the Congregational establishment on all denominations, but he also urged fellow Baptists to refuse to pay such taxes or to avail themselves of exemptions eventually offered them by the colonial legislature. Nevertheless, on November 22, 1774, Backus announced Baptist support for Massachusetts' resistance to Great Britain.[15]

Evangelical support for the Revolution

And finally there were the New Lights (and New Siders), those who, regardless of their denominational affiliation, were drawn toward independence by their evangelical fervor. The strength of the New Lights in the decades after the Great Awakening lay chiefly in their rediscovery and cultivation of an aesthetic feeling for the "beauty of union," the "communal piety of the saved." The beauty of union, they found, was the joy the awakened felt when they worshipped together.[16]

The New Lights found happiness in holiness, in revivals, in communion with fellow saints, and in the prospect of the kingdom to come. They longed for purity – the recognition that the power of God's light was directly proportional to the number of saints gathered in one place, and that it was correspondingly diminished by the number in fellowship who were unregenerate. The quest for perfection and union gave rise to millennialism, a natural outgrowth of the revival. God's power in the Awakening suggested that the pace of history was accelerating and that the Second Coming was close at hand.[17]

The Great Awakening raised the hopes of the evangelicals, and they shifted to the more optimistic postmillennial view: God's reign of a thousand years on earth would precede, not follow, Judgment Day. With this postponement, the New Lights could anticipate his coming with unmixed joy. Those who understood Edwards knew that the "good society" would begin simply with God's restoration to the Elect of the powers man lost at Adam's fall. Edwards envisioned, not destruction or reconstruction, but rather a massive renewal, a bigger and better revival. God would turn this world into Paradise, that is to say, into a Christian commonwealth.[18]

In that they believed the millennium would begin in America, New Light arguments were traditional and logical: Paradise was to be found in the west; according to scriptural prophecy on the "new day," the sun of righteousness would rise in the west; and logically, God would begin this great work in a new country and where his people were concentrated. It was not God's manner "to introduce a new excellence into the churches of an old, corrupt region."[19]

In assuming that America was the center of God's interest in the world, the New Lights were behaving like chosen people. They were returning to the Puritan conception of "a city on a hill." They would produce in the New World a better society than the Old World had ever known. They hoped to build on the Awakening, using various strategies to induce "heavenly showers," and to extend them to more people, so that the earthly kingdom – the better society – might be hastened. Blending this evangelical vision with the political ideology of the American Revolution, civil millennialism, resulted in a revolutionary millennialism shared by both groups. In sum, one way to hasten that better society was to gain American independence from the corrupt old world Great Britain.[20]

It is important to note that a point of contention among historians on the subject of evangelical ties to the American Revolution is focused primarily on the degree to which the evangelical influence was felt beyond New Light/New Side circles. Some have argued that the evangelical Calvinism that grew out of the Great Awakening provided revolutionary America with "a radical, even democratic, social and political ideology," that the "evangelical religion embodied, and inspired, a thrust toward American nationalism." Others have added that the Great Awakening, itself a movement against establishment authority, provided a "blueprint" or "practical model" for revolutionaries.[21] Jon Butler, however, was among the first to challenge the influence of the Great Awakening on the American Revolution by arguing that any link between the two was "virtually nonexistent" and that the Revolution was primarily a secular movement. Protestant liberals, he pointed out, were as supportive of the Revolution and employed the same rhetoric as evangelicals.[22]

The consensus to date meets these contending positions halfway, taking the position that the Great Awakening influenced, but did not cause, the Revolution. Although an unintended consequence, Gordon Wood has written: "By challenging clerical unity, shattering the communal churches, and cutting people lose from ancient religious bonds, the Great Awakening represented in one way or another, a massive defiance of traditional authority," thereby preparing the way for the Revolution. Others have supported this position, pointing out that the rhetoric of the Awakening made the Revolution's republican ideology more palatable to a "biblically minded people."[23]

Abstention from, and opposition to, the Revolution

It is important to note that most colonial ministers remained silent about politics during the upheavals of the 1760s and 1770s. Moravians and Quakers proved to be consistent pacifists, while Pennsylvania German Reformed and Lutheran clergy, as well as Scots-Irish clergymen serving frontier settlements, said or did little. In part, this may have resulted from their minority status and frequent tension with provincial elites who led the Revolution in Pennsylvania. But there was more to it. They and many of their clerical colleagues in other denominations saw the Revolution as a threat to Christianity. They agreed with the German Reformed Coetus's statement of May 1775, which stated that they lived "in precarious times, the like of which . . . has never been seen in America. The Lord knows what He has in store for us, and especially for our beloved Church." In 1777, the Coetus described the Revolution as a "sad war" that had uprooted "many a praiseworthy observance . . . especially in regard to the keeping of the Sabbath Day and Christian exercises in the families at home."[24]

Most members of the Presbyterian Synod of Philadelphia – Middle Colony Presbyterians being well represented among pro-Revolutionaries – refrained from public comment on the impending conflict. In a pastoral letter to its congregations in 1775, the Synod acknowledged that "it is well known . . . that we have not been instrumental in inflaming the minds of the people, or urging them to acts of violence and disorder." Indeed its ministers could not remember when "political sentiments have been so long and so fully kept from the pulpit," by which they meant sentiment supporting rebellion.[25]

The demand for obedience was as strong among colonial Presbyterians as it was among Anglicans, and the Presbyterian commitment had been tested only shortly before the Revolution. During the so-called Regulator Movement in North and South Carolina in the late 1760s, backcountry Presbyterian ministers, supported by German Lutheran and Anglican pastors, used their pulpits to denounce rebellion against colonial governments dominated by tidewater planter elites. A letter to the laity promulgated by the Synod in 1775 both instructed the laity on loyalty to George III and voiced support for Whig political principles. Synod members expressed their "attachment and respect to our sovereign King George," but they also expressed their regard for the "revolutionary principles by which his august family was seated on the British throne."[26]

The Presbyterian statement suggested why loyalism so frequently had a dual religious foundation and extended beyond the ranks of Church of England ministers, two-thirds of whom departed for England after the Revolution began. First, there was the traditional emphasis on authority and obedience in colonial preaching. As protest turned to independence for many ministers previously abstract fears that the flight from authority and obedience would turn everything upside down became a reality.[27]

A second reason centered on religious discrimination. The political elites who guided the American Revolution in so many places also had frequently mistreated religious minorities in earlier times. Scottish and Scots-Irish Presbyterians in North and South Carolina, English Baptists in Virginia, German Lutheran and German Reformed in Pennsylvania, Anglicans in New England, and others had all experienced religious discrimination that ranged from minor annoyances to governmental persecution. Most found the patriots' anti-Parliamentary protests ironic and even hypocritical. Some groups, like the Virginia Baptists, supported the Revolution anyway. But backcountry Presbyterians, German Lutherans and German Reformed settlers, and Middle and Northern Colony Anglicans often found themselves drawn to loyalism not only out of political principles but also because of antagonisms with settlers who had earlier used the government and the law against them.[28]

The revolution shapes American religion

The American Revolution shaped American religion, and it did so in complex ways. This complexity emerges even in the story of the decline and growth of various Christian denominations. The most serious erosion occurred in the Anglican congregations. In parish after parish Anglican ministers left because they openly supported the Crown, because they could not endure abuse by local patriots, or because they were no longer paid by either the Society for the Propagation of the Gospel or their vestries. Fifty Anglican priests were working in Pennsylvania, New York, and New England before the Revolution; only nine remained afterward. About a hundred of the 150 priests in the southern colonies also fled to England. As a result, 75 percent of the Church of England parishes, built up so carefully in the previous half-century, lost their clergymen and with them their principal leadership in sustaining public Christian worship.[29]

Between 1761 and 1776, the Philadelphia Baptist Association grew from twenty-nine congregations with 1,300 adult members to forty-two congregations with 3,000 members. But the Association's congregations quickly felt the sting of war. By 1781, the Association lost the membership gains and institutional growth achieved in the previous fifteen years. Its congregations declined in number to 26, and its membership from 3,000 to 1,400 adults. Many congregations disbanded, and even surviving congregations lost a fifth of their members. Between 1776 and 1781, average church membership declined from seventy-one to fifty-five adults.[30]

Other Protestant groups advanced during the American Revolution. South Carolina's Charleston Baptist Association experienced significant growth. In 1775, it counted 9 congregations, 7 ministers, and 529 members; in 1779, it counted 12 congregations, 12 ministers, and 890 members; and in 1783, it counted 13 congregations, 9 ministers, and 966 members. Presbyterian statistics described similar growth after the Revolution. In 1774, the Synod of Philadelphia reported 139 ministers, 153 churches with ministers (some serving more than one congregation), and 180 vacant pulpits. By 1788, the Presbyterians counted 177 ministers, 215 congregations with clergymen, and 206 congregations without clergy.[31]

Denominational statistics conveyed only part of the story, however. Methodism had the fewest difficulties in part because it had the least to lose. Methodist missionaries had worked in America less than a decade and all of them, except Francis Asbury, returned to England at John Wesley's command. Anglicans, in contrast, suffered the most because they had the most to lose in terms of both ministers and buildings. The physical destruction loosed on Anglican churches was reminiscent of sixteenth-century English anti-Catholic depredation. In parish after parish, supporters of the Revolution stripped Anglican churches of their royal coats of arms, although they usually left the buildings and other fittings intact.[32]

The rise of public religion

The association of society and government with Christianity was traditional in colonial political culture. But the American Revolution strengthened the demand to associate with Christianity in three ways: by revealing the previously shallow foundations of the association; by stressing a particular form of republicanism in government and society; and by stimulating a strong sense of cultural optimism that fitted certain religious themes, particularly American millennialism.

Many aspects of the American Revolution caused concern about America's religious future. The destruction of church buildings, the interruption of denominational organizations, the occasional decline in congregations and membership, the shattering of the Anglican Church, and the rise of secular pride in revolutionary accomplishments all weighed on American religious leaders. Even as the Revolution advanced, denominational leaders often bemoaned rather than celebrated America's moral fiber.[33]

Contemporaries agreed that a successful republican society and government depended on a virtuous people. This sentiment did not take root in a reborn Puritanism but in more modern eighteenth-century principles. Most equated republican longevity with widely inculcated moral virtue. The whole of society, not merely some of its parts, constituted the bedrock of the future. Massachusetts Colonial Governor John Winthrop's Puritan society had been ordered by means of hierarchical responsibilities assigned among the people, "some high and eminent in power and dignity; others mean and in subjection." The 1780 Massachusetts constitution, however, rested order on a broader foundation: "The happiness of a people, and the good order and preservation of civil government, essentially depend upon piety, religion, and morality." It did not mention the "high and eminent" or "others mean and in subjection."[34]

Optimism fueled the new republic, but much of postrevolutionary optimism was openly secular, not religious, and reflected the Founding Fathers' Enlightenment convictions. This was especially true of those often called the "old revolutionaries." Franklin, Washington, and Jefferson all professed beliefs in the supernatural. But their references to the supernatural were vague and ethereal, and their views of religion were far different from those of the Congregational, Baptist, Presbyterian, and Episcopalian clergymen who backed the Revolution. Franklin's god was a god of ethics, not revelation. Although he remained a Church of England vestryman, Washington was disinterested in theology, and Jefferson openly rejected sectarianism.[35] What all three Founding Fathers sought to replace orthodox Christianity with was what would later be called public religion.

The substance of American public religion was drawn from the Enlightenment, as it was realized in America. Its most visible statement was the Declaration of Independence, wherein "God" refers to the God of nature, rather than the God of Christian revelation. God emerges as "the Supreme Judge of the world" to whom Americans would appeal "for the rectitude of [their] intentions" and as "Divine Providence" in whom they would rely for protection. The words were Jefferson's, but Benjamin Franklin (see Figure 3.1) was the first

Figure 3.1 Benjamin Franklin

Source: Georgios Kollidas/Alamy Stock Photo

of his generation to call for public religion and fashion its design. Not surprisingly, what he proposed reflected his preference for an Age of Reason over an Age of Faith, of mind over the heart, of reason over revelation, of morals over miracles, and of public virtue over private salvation.[36]

Franklin issued his first call for public religion in his *Proposals Relating to the Education of Youth in Philadelphia*, which he published in 1749. Therein, he defended "the necessity of a public religion," arguing that such a faith would be useful to the public. It would be advantageous in promoting a religious character among private persons, and it would counter "the mischiefs of superstition," which he found in most denominations. Franklin's American public religion was not, however, to be anti-Christian; indeed, he insisted that it would show "the excellency of the Christian religion above all others ancient or modern."[37]

The seed that Franklin planted in 1749 grew over the next three decades leading to the Declaration of Independence, but not without mixed reactions. To many religious leaders, it was infidelity, deism, or a new heathenism. To philosophers, it was a homegrown American version of the Enlightenment. Proponents saw it as the "religion of the Republic," an entity Americans would later identify variously as civil faith, public piety, or civil religion.[38]

Franklin and the other founders of American public religion did not intend the end of individual denominations, but rather the cessation of sectarianism. They hoped to erect a tent over the various religious groups by means of a commonly agreed-upon universal creed. It would be essentially Protestant Christian, as were most Americans at the time, but by leaving to denominations theological specifics, public religion would serve a common morality.[39]

American millennialism

As noted earlier, American religious leaders attempted to absorb and redirect secular optimism. If claims measured God's approval, the clergy put the new nation in good stead. Providential rhetoric fixed God's sovereignty over the Revolution. Some clergymen even described the struggle in Manichean terms – the cause of heaven against the cause of hell – while many returned to the seventeenth-century motif of Americans as a chosen people.[40]

Millennialist rhetoric also expanded. Millennialism thrived on dramatic events such as the American Revolution. Providential rhetoric revealed God's approval of the Revolution, but millennialist rhetoric located it in sacred time. Thinking that Christ's Second Coming would occur in a specific historical setting, Ebenezer Baldwin, a Connecticut clergyman, thought that the American Revolution was "preparing the way for this glorious event." Samuel West, a New Hampshire minister, described the Revolution as fulfilling Isaiah's millennialist predictions. Some clergymen went further and suggested that the Revolution was a precursor to the beginning of the millennium and perhaps the "sixth vial" described in Revelation, which would destroy the Antichrist when it was emptied and usher in Christ's reign.[41]

Yet the very ubiquity of such predictions produced a bewildering variety of styles. No single millennialist vision emerged in the era of the American Revolution. Proponents variously predicted the coming of true liberty and freedom, a rise in piety, American territorial expansion and even freedom from hunger. Many propagandists hedged their predictions, just as their predecessors had done in the 1740s and 1750s. The few who provided definite dates for specific events usually developed different chronologies, and when Americans experienced political, social, and economic setbacks, some turned to darker visions of the world and the new nation's place in it.[42]

Apocalyptic thinking nevertheless declined in the revolutionary period. With the success of the Revolution, millennialism suited the American temperament better than apocalypticism, and in this regard, the Revolution profoundly shifted the colonial millennialist tradition. The Revolution was an event whose character and outcome seemed to have signaled the beginning of Christ's thousand-year reign, thus making the apocalypse either history or irrelevant.[43]

Millennialism had important political implications, as well. Millennialist rhetoric secured the allegiance of an unwilling and often perplexed society. It demanded lay adherence in a society where the people were now sovereign. When New Englanders sought a unicameral legislature and an elected executive, it did so on the ground that "the voice of the people is the voice of God." The rhetoric largely benefited the advancement of Christianity: a legislature that spoke for God should also listen to those who articulated Christian theology, morals, and ethics.[44]

The campaign against irreligion

The millennialist incorporation of secular optimism in the revolutionary period was accompanied by campaigns against irreligion in what was perceived to be its intellectual disguises of skepticism, atheism, and deism. Before the Revolution, clergymen had often endured derogatory remarks steeped in the doubts of the Enlightenment. The Revolution removed one source of this activity by stripping away the imperial elite of governors, magistrates and other officials who frequently supported such Enlightenment skepticism. But skepticism survived. Its most prominent representatives – Franklin, Jefferson, and Thomas Paine – seemed the apotheosis of the Enlightenment, and their support for it revealed a tolerance of skepticism many saw as altogether dangerous in a new republic.

The occasional charges of their critics notwithstanding, none of the previously noted Founding Fathers were atheists or even pure deists in most cases, but they did harbor deist sentiments. In general, allowing for individual variations, deism, which originated in Europe, is often referred to as a religion of nature, which grew out of the Enlightenment's emphasis on reason. Its proponents challenged the dominant belief that God played a direct and immediate role in the world. Instead, they maintained that God created the world and the natural laws by which it is governed, and that it operates without any further direct involvement by God. They were critical of any literal acceptance of revealed religion, or divine intervention, especially its miraculous and supernatural elements, which they argued were inconsistent with natural law.[45]

Franklin is a case-in-point. Born and raised in a still largely Calvinist Boston to a father who intended his son to become a minister, Franklin, while still an adolescent, began to question the faith of his father. As he wrote in his *Autobiography:*

> My parents had early given me religious impressions and brought me through my childhood piously in the Dissenting [Calvinist] way. But I was scarce fifteen, when, after doubting by turns of several points, as I found them disputed in the different books that I read, I began to doubt of revelation [revealed religion] itself. . . . Some books against

deism fell into my hands . . . [the unintended consequence of which was that the arguments of the deists] appeared to me much stronger than the refutations. I soon became a thorough deist.[46]

Nevertheless, after moving to Philadelphia, Franklin joined and maintained membership in the Presbyterian Church, which was akin to his New England religious heritage. As he also explained in his *Autobiography*, as an adult in Philadelphia, although he did not attend church regularly, "I was never without some religious principles. I never doubted, for instance, the existence of the Deity; that he made the world and governed it by his providence; that the most acceptable service of God was the doing of good to man; that our souls are immortal; and that all crimes will be punished and virtue rewarded, either here or hereafter."[47]

As he neared the end of his life, Franklin further explained: "As to Jesus of Nazareth . . . I think the system of morals and his religion, as he left them to us, the best the world ever saw or is likely to see; but I apprehend it has received various corrupting changes." He admitted to some doubts as to Jesus's divinity, but that he neither "dogmatized" upon it nor saw any harm in others believing it, if such belief had "good consequence."[48]

Deism became a chief object of attack in the war against irreligion. It had the attraction of being relatively new yet suspiciously commonplace among the new nation's political and social leaders. The word itself dated only from the seventeenth century and had achieved a place in common vocabulary only in the early eighteenth century. Most important, deism offered extraordinary opportunities to its critics to demonstrate the need for real religion, meaning orthodox Christianity, in the new republic. To its critics deism was the epitome of hypocrisy. It masqueraded as religion but was thoroughly irreligious. Deists admitted the justice of religious claims, opponents argued, but they attempted to make religion irrelevant to contemporary life. The deists' god was dead, they charged. At best, signs of his existence could be found only in the distant past.[49]

As Americans turned from war making to nation making, clergymen turned to deism to explain their postrevolutionary failures and crises. Deism served as a new and dangerous label under which a broad list of evils, old and new, could be assembled. Thomas Paine, and his *Age of Reason*, published in 1794, were among the critics' principal targets. It was for his religious writings that "the penman of the American Revolution" became "the very symbol of Infidelity," or, as President Theodore Roosevelt later called him, that "filthy little atheist."[50]

Four years after the American Revolution, in 1787, Paine visited his native England, where he was charged with seditious libel for his defense of the French Revolution, which included an attack on the British monarchy. Paine fled arrest to France, where he was welcomed by the revolutionary government then in power but later jailed when he opposed the Jacobin extremism that followed. Upon his release in 1794, Paine published Part One of *The Age of Reason* (Parts Two and Three followed in 1795 and 1807).

In his much vilified tract, Paine reiterated mainstream deist beliefs, but he did so in less than circumspect language. He explained that one of his reasons for writing *The Age of Reason* was to stop revolutionary France's "headlong" run into atheism. But in doing so, he charged Catholicism, and by implication, Christianity, with being in large part responsible for that movement, as well as one of the primary obstacles to the "age of reason." Among numerous other charges, he rejected biblical revelations as mere superstition and described the Old Testament as full of "glaring absurdities, contradictions, and falsehoods," as well as immoral acts.[51]

In 1798, while Paine was still abroad, the New England Congregationalist minister Jedidiah Morse explained why the deism Paine promoted should be so feared: "The existence of a God is boldly denied. Atheism and materialism are systematically professed. Reason and nature are deified and adored. The Christian religion, and its divine and blessed author, are not only disbelieved, rejected and condemned, but even abhorred."[52] In 1802, when Paine returned to the United States, the nation that once claimed him as a hero, shunned him. When he died, in 1809, he was refused burial in any consecrated cemetery.

Thomas Jefferson's try for the presidency in 1800 brought out critics of his religious views, as well. In that presidential campaign, he was denounced as an atheist and a "French infidel." It was particularly important because, as it was framed, the attack focused on the relationship between a president's personal religious views and the fate of the American republic. Jefferson's religious views were complex and defy absolute classification, especially because he kept his religious views to himself for the most part, choosing to share his thoughts only among friends. He harbored deist sentiments, but he was raised an Anglican and attended different churches in Philadelphia, Washington, and Charlottesville. He described himself as a Unitarian, but he has been labeled a theistic rationalist.

When challenged, Jefferson did not hesitate to turn the tables on his critics, no doubt inflaming them even more. When he was accused of attacking the reasonableness of Christianity, for example, he challenged the effect of Christianity's insistence on revelation, or revealed religion, and the mysteries of Scripture as giving "a great handle to atheism by its general dogma, that without revelation, there would not be sufficient proof of the being of God." God's existence, he countered, is subject to rational demonstration, observation, and reason, or by what has come to be known as the arguments from design and causality. Jefferson charged that such dogma flew in the face of "the revelatory character of nature and reason," the true basis for "private ethics and public order." And, he added, emancipation from religious and other forms of superstition would not only liberate the mind but also lead to the eradication of social and political oppression and even material want.[53]

Later in life, when he retired from public life and returned to the sanctuary of his beloved Monticello, Jefferson embarked on a spiritual quest, perhaps intended to more closely define his religious views. It was a personal search, which he kept hidden even from his immediate family. As part of that search, Jefferson read widely from sacred tests, but his attention to Christianity was particularly intense. At one point, he let it be known that he considered himself a Christian, but according to his own terms, which he added resulted in "a sect by myself." Jefferson rejected Christ's divinity, but like Franklin, he also expressed a quiet regard for Christ and Christian ethics, describing Jesus as "the great moral teacher of the ages" and Jesus's "system of morality . . . the most benevolent and sublime probably that has even been taught." But overriding all of this, he continued to reject religious coercion of any kind with a vigor that made some suspicious of his real religious views, despite the fact that evangelicals supported him for his efforts on behalf of religious freedom. As a result, Federalists linked Jefferson to anticlericalism and atheism in the notorious French Revolution, and many ministers denounced him from their pulpits, decrying the fate of the nation in the hands of a deist, an obvious agent of the Devil.[54] In the end, Jefferson withstood the attacks of his critics on matters of religion, but not so deism. By the early decades of the nineteenth century, however, deism would be eclipsed by the Second Great Awakening, but more on that in the next chapter.

The further separation of church and state

The final area in which the American Revolution affected American religion was in its move toward disestablishment, if, prior to 1789, only at the state level. (Church and state at the national level will be discussed in Chapter 4.) By 1763, pluralism and denominationalism had taken their toll. If the 13 colonies that were poised to become the United States of America had belonged to England for over 150 years, the Church of England had been established in only 5 of those colonies (Maryland, Virginia, North and South Carolina, and Georgia), all in the South, and in parts of New York. Three New England colonies (Massachusetts, Connecticut, and New Hampshire) had established Congregationalism, while the rest had no establishment at all.

How this state of affairs came about has already been considered in Chapter 2. The peculiar nature of that establishment that survived, however, merits some further consideration. In sum, all eight of those colonies wherein an establishment existed began breaking with European precedent by providing legal recognition and support for more than one church or denomination. As a general rule, those colonies taxed everyone for the support of religion but allowed most people's taxes to be remitted to the church of their choice. Establishment was coming to mean non-preferential establishment, or the financial support of religion – Protestant Christianity – by public taxation.[55] Massachusetts will serve as a case-in-point.

Massachusetts, the major and archetypal Puritan colony, did not provide for the establishment of the Congregational Church after 1692. In that year, its original colonial charter having been revoked and replaced by a less exclusive one bearing the influence of England's recently adopted Religious Toleration Act, the General Court (the Massachusetts legislature) provided for an establishment of religion on a town-by-town basis. It required every town to maintain an "able, learned and orthodox" minister, to be chosen by the voters of the town and supported by a tax levied on all taxpayers. As a matter of law, it was theoretically possible for several different denominations to benefit from the establishment.[56]

Because Congregationalists were the overwhelming majority in nearly every Massachusetts town, they stood to reap the benefits of establishment, with only a few exceptions. The act of 1692 exempted Boston because voluntary contributions there had successfully maintained the Congregational churches, making the compulsion of law unnecessary. The town of Swansea was dominated by Baptists. By 1693, it had two Baptist churches, and they became the official town churches, supported by public taxation. That, in turn, provoked an equally unusual response. Swansea Congregationalists sued in the county court under the pretext that the town, in establishing Baptist churches, had not provided for an "orthodox learned minister," in violation of the act of 1692. In 1708, the court ruled that religious taxes raised in Swansea must be divided equally between the two denominations, thereby setting the precedent in that colony for dual establishment.[57]

In a few towns, where Baptists and Quakers together constituted a majority, both successfully challenged the law. In those cases, however, they refused to pay the tax at all, arguing that the state had no jurisdiction over religion, which should be left to the voluntary support of believers. When they were granted exemptions both challenged the law colony-wide. Quakers argued their case before authorities in London on the grounds that the Massachusetts establishment violated the Toleration Act of 1689, and, in a partial victory for Dissenters, England's Privy Council ruled that Congregationalists could not impose ministerial taxes in towns where they did not constitute a majority.[58]

From 1727 until the end of the colonial period (and beyond), the Congregational Church was forced to retreat until the other denominations were on an equal footing with it. In 1727, Anglicans won the right to have their religious taxes turned over for the support of their own churches. In 1728, Massachusetts exempted Quakers and Baptists from all taxes for the payment of ministerial salaries. Then in 1731 and 1735, each denomination received an exemption from sharing the taxes for building new town churches.[59]

The American Revolution lent momentum to the movement toward disestablishment of religion in the states. The five colonies that had no establishment continued to avoid it as states. Joining their ranks was North Carolina. Provisions in the Pennsylvania state constitution of 1776 were typical of that group: No person, it read, "ought or of right can be compelled to attend any religious worship, or erect or support any place of worship, or maintain any ministry, contrary to, or against, his own free will and consent."[60]

Colonies that continued their church establishment as states made concessions to the growing sentiment against any establishment by moving toward multiple or non-preferential establishment. By and large, establishment of religion in those states, rather than being restricted in meaning to a state church, became instead a means by which to provide public support for several churches, with exclusive preference for none.[61] Massachusetts, once again, and Virginia, because of its major players, will serve as examples.

The Massachusetts' Constitution of 1780 ordered the legislature to authorize its towns "to make suitable provision, at their own expense, for the institution of the public worship of God, and for the support and maintenance of public Protestant teachers of piety, religion, and morality." It also empowered the legislature to make church attendance compulsory. Towns were to have the right of electing their ministers, however, and each taxpayer could designate the Protestant church of his choice to receive his church tax money, thereby creating a multiple establishment. Another clause provided that none of the Protestant churches mentioned earlier would ever be made subordinate to any other by law.[62]

In one regard, the Massachusetts Constitution of 1780 constituted a step backward from the liberalizing tendencies of the previous fifty years. It did not continue exceptions made in the colonial period for Baptists and Quakers, who because of their conscientious objections had enjoyed an exemption from religious taxes. They were forced to pay for the support of their own worship.[63]

The Virginia Constitution of 1776 avoided the issue of an establishment of religion, although it guaranteed the "free exercise of religion," thanks to the efforts of James Madison (see Figure 3.2). Madison failed, however, to win acceptance for his proposal, which would have ended any union of church and state. Baptists and Presbyterians protested the decision, but the dominant tidewater conservative element in the legislature remained convinced that republican government and society could not flourish without a religious establishment. As 1776 ended, the legislature repealed almost every statute that supported the establishment of the Church of England. Dissenters, for example, were to be exempt from church taxes. But under the law, and in administration of certain sacraments, particularly marriage rites, the Anglican establishment remained.[64]

In 1779, two conflicting bills were introduced in the legislature. Thomas Jefferson's *Bill for Religious Freedom* provided in part "that no man shall be compelled to frequent or support any religious worship, place, or ministry whatsoever." *A Bill Concerning Religion* proposed a general assessment, or tax, declared the Christian religion to be the established religion of Virginia, and provided articles of faith to which church members must subscribe in order to be incorporated as an established church and share in the church tax proceeds.[65] Neither bill could muster a majority for the next five years.

Figure 3.2 James Madison: Author of Virginia's Statute of Religious Freedom

Source: Archive Images/Alamy Stock Photo

In 1784, Patrick Henry introduced a new general assessment bill entitled *A Bill Establishing a Provision for Teachers of the Christian Religion.* It retained the substance of the earlier measure, but added the more liberal statement that all Christian denominations were equal before the law, none preferred over others. Eliminated were reference to established religion and proposed articles of faith.[66] James Madison rallied opposition to the bill, questioning the need for any form of establishment, and a final vote was postponed until the next session.

Henry's bill became a major issue in the intervening election, in response to which Madison published his *Memorial and Remonstrance against Religious Assessments.* Madison argued that religion is a private voluntary affair not subject to government in any way. A general assessment, he noted, was in fact an establishment of religion, and any establishment violated the free exercise of religion and threatened public liberty. To Madison, Christianity did not need government support; nor did government need the support of religion. Establishments, he argued, produced bigotry and persecution, defiled religion, corrupted government, and ended in spiritual and political tyranny.[67]

Others opposed general assessment, including Presbyterians, Baptists, and Quakers. A petition from the Presbyterian churches of Virginia echoed the sentiments of Baptists and Quakers in arguing that Christianity was most effective when left alone under God, "free from the intrusive hand of the civil magistrate." Religion and morality, the Presbyterians asserted, "can be promoted only by the internal conviction of the mind and its voluntary choice which such establishments cannot effect."[68]

The Virginia legislature let Henry's general assessment bill die and passed instead Jefferson's bill on disestablishment, reconstituted by James Madison in his *Statute of Religious Freedom*. Madison's statute declared in its preface that to compel anyone to support religious opinions he did not share was tyrannical and "that even forcing him to support this or that teacher of his own religious persuasion, is depriving him of the comfortable liberty" of giving his money as he pleased. The enabling provision stated "that no man shall be compelled to frequent or support any religious worship, place, or ministry whatsoever." The significance of the statute, Leonard Levy has written, "is not just that it broadened freedom of worship or of opinion in matters of religion but that it separated church and state in the context of protecting religious liberty."[69]

Summary

Religion played a major role in the American independence movement. The war shook existing churches to their core, but most recovered. The churches, though buffeted by a revolution whose battlefield exposed the tenuousness of popular Christian adherence and reinforced the vigorous secularity of its political principles, emerged with renewed vigor in the 1780s. Public, or civil, religion found its voice in America, as did a peculiar brand of national millennialism. All thirteen colonies that came to constitute the United States moved closer to the separation of church and state and free exercise of religion. Moreover, in the next half-century, American denominations would begin to master the new American environment by initiating a religious creativity that renewed spiritual reflection and perfected institutional power, all to serve Christian ends.

Review questions

1   What role did religion play in the movement for American independence?
2   What was "public religion," and what made it an important outgrowth of the independence movement?
3   How was American millennialism in the years leading up to American independence both an outgrowth, and supportive, of the American Revolution?
4   With what was the campaign against irreligion concerned during the era of the American Revolution?
5   How did the movement toward American independence impact the relationship between church and state?

Notes

1 Thomas S. Kidd, "The American Revolution," in *The Blackwell Companion to Religion in America*, ed. Philip Goff (Hoboken, NJ: Wiley-Blackwell, 2012), 17.
2 Jon Butler, *Awash in a Sea of Faith: Christianizing the American People* (Cambridge, MA: Harvard University Press, 1990), 194; Martin E. Marty, *Pilgrims in Their Own Land: 500 Years of Religion in America* (New York: Penguin Books, 1986), 131.
3 Carl Bridenbaugh, *Mitre and Sceptre: Transatlantic Faiths, Ideas, Personalities, and Politics, 1689–1775* (New York: Oxford University Press, 1962). See also: Arthur Lyon Cross, *The Anglican Episcopate and the American Colonies* (Hamden, CT: Archon Books, 1964); Thomas S. Kidd, *God of Liberty: A Religious History of the American Revolution* (New York: Basic Books, 2010), 57–74.
4 Butler, *Awash in a Sea of Faith*, 199.
5 Butler, *Awash in a Sea of Faith*, 200–1.
6 Marty, *Pilgrims in Their Own Land*, 134–5.
7 Marty, *Pilgrims in Their Own Land*, 135.
8 Epistle of Paul the Apostle to the Galatians 5:13.
9 Marty, *Pilgrims in Their Own Land*, 136–7.
10 Harry S. Stout, *The New England Soul: Preaching and Religious Culture in Colonial New England* (New York: Oxford University Press, 1986), ch. 14; Patricia U. Bonomi, *Under the Cope of Heaven: Religion, Society, and Politics in Colonial America* (New York: Oxford University Press, 1986), 209–10.
11 Stout, *New England Soul*, ch. 14; Butler, *Awash in a Sea of Faith*, 202.
12 Stout, *New England Soul*, ch. 14; Butler, *Awash in a Sea of Faith*, 202.
13 Marty, *Pilgrims in Their Own Land*, 140–2; Nathan O. Hatch, *The Sacred Cause of Liberty: Republican Thought and the Millennium in Revolutionary New England* (New Haven, CT: Yale University Press, 1977), 51–2.
14 Marty, *Pilgrims in Their Own Land*, 143–5. See also: Maura Jane Farrelly, *Papist Patriots: The Making of an American Catholic Identity* (New York: Oxford University Press, 2012).
15 Marty, *Pilgrims in Their Own Land*, 150–4; William G. McLoughlin, "Isaac Backus and the Separation of Church and State," *American Historical Review*, 73 (1968): 1392–413; Kidd, *God of Liberty*, 37–56.
16 Cedric B. Cowing, *The Great Awakening and the American Revolution: Colonial Thought in the 18th Century* (Chicago: Rand McNally, 1971), 201.
17 Cowing, *The Great Awakening*, 202.
18 Cowing, *The Great Awakening*, 202.
19 Cowing, *The Great Awakening*, 202–3.
20 Cowing, *The Great Awakening*, 203; Hatch, *The Sacred Cause of Liberty*, 21–2; Ruth H. Bloch, *Visionary Republic: Millennial Themes in American Thought, 1756–1800* (New York: Cambridge University Press, 1985), 75–7; Kidd, *God of Liberty*, 11–36.
21 Alan E. Heimert, *Religion and the American Mind from the Great Awakening to the Revolution* (Cambridge, MA: Harvard University Press, 1966), viii; Bonomi, *Under the Cope of Heaven*; Gary B. Nash, *The Unknown American Revolution: The Unruly Birth of Democracy and the Struggle to Create America* (New York: Viking Press, 2005).
22 Jon Butler, "Enthusiasm Described and Decried: The Great Awakening as Interpretive Fiction," *Journal of American History*, 69 (1982): 312, 324. See also: Butler, *Awash in a Sea of Faith*.
23 Gordon Wood, *The Creation of the American Republic, 1776–1787* (Chapel Hill: University of North Carolina Press, 1969), 187; Harry S. Stout, "Religion, Communications, and the Ideological Origins of the American Revolution," *William and Mary Quarterly*, 3rd sers, 34 (1977): 540; Mark A. Noll, "The American Revolution and Protestant Evangelicalism," *Journal of Interdisciplinary History*, 23 (1993): 628–30. See also: Jerome Mahaffey, *The Accidental Revolutionary: George Whitefield and Creation of America* (Waco, TX: Baylor University Press, 2011).
24 Butler, *Awash in a Sea of Faith*, 202–3.
25 Butler, *Awash in a Sea of Faith*, 203.
26 Mark Noll, *Christians in the American Revolution* (Grand Rapids, MI: Christian University Press, 1977), 65–8; Hatch, *The Sacred Cause of Liberty*, 22, 61; Butler, *Awash in a Sea of Faith*, 203.

27 Wallace Brown, *The Good Americans: The Loyalists in the American Revolution* (New York: Morrow, 1969), 56–8, 243–4, 253–4.
28 Bernard Bailyn, *Ideological Origins of the American Revolution* (Cambridge, MA: Harvard University Press, 1967), 312; John F. Woolverton, *Colonial Anglicanism in North America* (Detroit, MI: Wayne State University Press, 1984), 227–33.
29 Woolverton, *Colonial Anglicanism in North America*, 228–33.
30 Butler, *Awash in a Sea of Faith*, 207.
31 Butler, *Awash in a Sea of Faith*, 207.
32 Butler, *Awash in a Sea of Faith*, 207.
33 Wood, *The Creation of the American Republic*, 114–18, 344–89; Jack Richon Pole, *Foundations of American Independence, 1763–1815* (Indianapolis, IN: Bobbs-Merrill, 1972), 80–1.
34 Wood, *Creation of the American Republic*, 427.
35 Mark A. Noll, Nathan O. Hatch and George M. Marsden, *The Search for Christian America* (Westchester, IL: Crossway Books, 1983), 74–6; Paul Boller, *George Washington and Religion* (Dallas: Southern Methodist University Press, 1963); Marty, *Pilgrims in Their Own Land*, 160–1.
36 Marty, *Pilgrims in Their Own Land*, 155.
37 Marty, *Pilgrims in Their Own Land*, 155–6.
38 Marty, *Pilgrims in Their Own Land*, 156–7.
39 Marty, *Pilgrims in Their Own Land*, 156–7.
40 Ruth H. Bloch, *Visionary Republic*, ch. 3.
41 Bloch, *Visionary Republic*, 5, 9, 79–80; James West Davidson, *The Logic of Millennial Thought: Eighteenth-Century New England* (New Haven, CT: Yale University Press, 1977), 248–50.
42 Bloch, *Visionary Republic*, 105–10.
43 Butler, *Awash in a Sea of Faith*, 217.
44 Bloch, *Visionary Republic*, 80; Wood, *Creation of the American Republic*, 344–89.
45 Kerry S. Walters, *Rational Infidels: The American Deists* (Durango, CO: Longwood Academic, 1992), x.
46 Benjamin Franklin, *Autobiography* (New York: Vintage Books, 1990), 55.
47 Franklin, *Autobiography*, 78–9.
48 John Bigelow, ed., *The Life of Benjamin Franklin* (Philadelphia: Lippincott, 1905), vol. 3, 457–9.
49 Henry F. May, *The Enlightenment in America* (New York: Oxford University Press, 1976), 20–3, 116–32.
50 Martin E. Marty, *The Infidel: Freethought and American Religion* (New York: Meridian Books, 1961), 24, 181.
51 Walters, *Rational Infidels*, 2, 4; Jay E. Smith, "Thomas Paine and the Age of Reason's Attack on the Bible," *The Historian*, 58 (1996): 745–61.
52 Butler, *Awash in a Sea of Faith*, 219; For more on Paine's religious ideas, in the context of his thought on other subjects, see: Craig Nelson, *Thomas Paine: Enlightenment, Revolution and the Birth of Modern Nations* (New York: Penguin Books, 2006), 260–72.
53 Walters, *Rational Infidels*, 164; Marty, *The Infidel*, 30; Annette Gordon-Reed and Peter Onuf, *"Most Blessed of the Patriarchs": Thomas Jefferson and the Empire of the Imagination* (New York: Liveright Publishing Corporation, 2016), ch. 9. Jefferson's views on Jesus are best expressed in his compilation of extracts from the New Testament, *The Philosophy of Jesus of Nazareth* (1804) and *The Life and Morals of Jesus of Nazareth* (1819).
54 Fawn Brodie, *Thomas Jefferson: An Intimate History* (New York: W. W. Norton, 1974), 431–2; Steven Waldman, *Founding Faith: Providence, Politics, and the Birth of Religious Freedom in America* (New York: Random House, 2008), 185–6; Edwin S. Gaustad, *Faith of the Founders: Religion and the New Nation 1776–1826*, 2nd edn. (Waco, TX: Baylor University Press, 2004), 99; Gordon-Reed and Onuf, *"Most Blessed of the Patriarchs,"* 273–82, 295–9.
55 Leonard W. Levy, *The Establishment Clause: Religion and the First Amendment* (New York: Macmillan Publishing Company, 1986), 8–9.
56 Levy, *Establishment Clause*, 15.
57 Levy, *Establishment Clause*, 15–6; William G. McLoughlin, *New England Dissent 1630–1833: The Baptists and the Separation of Church and State* (Cambridge, MA: Harvard University Press, 1971), 1: 136–48, 160.
58 McLoughlin, *New England Dissent*, 1: 165–99.

59 McLoughlin, *New England Dissent*, 1: 217, 225–43.
60 Levy, *Establishment Clause*, 25.
61 Levy, *Establishment Clause*, 26.
62 Levy, *Establishment Clause*, 27; Thomas J. Curry, *The First Freedoms: Church and State in America to the Passage of the First Amendment* (New York: Oxford University Press, 1986), 163–4.
63 McLoughlin, *New England Dissent*, 2: 1092.
64 Thomas E. Buckley, *Church and State in Revolutionary Virginia, 1776–1787* (Charlottesville: University of Virginia Press, 1977), 19; Levy, *Establishment Clause*, 52–3; Curry, *First Freedoms*, 135–6.
65 Buckley, *Church and State in Revolutionary Virginia*, 47–62; Curry, *First Freedoms*, 139–41.
66 Buckley, *Church and State in Revolutionary Virginia*, 189–91.
67 Levy, *Establishment Clause*, 55; Curry, *First Freedoms*, 143.
68 Levy, *Establishment Clause*, 56–7; Curry, *First Freedoms*, 144.
69 Levy, *Establishment Clause*, 60; Curry, *First Freedoms*, 146. For more on Virginia's quest for religious liberty see: John Fea, *Was America Founded as a Christian Nation? A Historical Introduction* (Louisville, KY: Westminster John Knox Press, 2011), 137–40.

Recommended for further reading

Bloch, Ruth H. *Visionary Republic: Millennial Themes in American Thought, 1756–1800*. New York: Cambridge University Press, 1985.
Bonomi, Patricia U. *Under the Cope of Heaven: Religion, Society, and Politics in Colonial America*. New York: Oxford University Press, 1986.
Curry, Thomas J. *The First Freedoms: Church and State in America to the Passage of the First Amendment*. New York: Oxford University, 1986.
Fea, John. *Was America Founded as a Christian Nation? A Historical Introduction*. Louisville, KY: Westminster John Knox Press, 2011.
Gaustad, Edwin S. *Faith of the Founders: Religion and the New Nation 1776–1826*, 2nd edn. Waco, TX: Baylor University Press, 2004.
Gordon-Reed, Annette and Peter Onuf, *"Most Blessed of the Patriarchs": Thomas Jefferson and the Empire of the Imagination*. New York: Liveright Publishing Corporation, 2016.
Lambert, Frank. *The Founding Fathers and the Place of Religion in America*. Princeton, NJ: Princeton University Press, 2003.
Levy, Leonard W. *The Establishment Clause: Religion and the First Amendment*. New York: MacMillan Publishing Company, 1986.
Sanford, Charles B. *The Religious Life of Thomas Jefferson*. Charlottesville: University Press of Virginia, 1984.
Wood, Gordon. *The Creation of the American Republic, 1776–1787*. Chapel Hill: University of North Carolina Press, 1969.

Chapter 4

Religion and the Early Republic

Religion in the Early Republic

In 1787, in the constitution by which the new nation would operate, the United States of America committed itself to securing "the blessings of liberty to ourselves and our posterity." Among the liberties to which the new republic committed itself was freedom of religion, and that freedom was spelled out four years later in the First Amendment to the US Constitution: "Congress shall make no law respecting an establishment of religion, or prohibiting the free exercise thereof."

The Early Republic witnessed a second series of religious revivals, the Second Great Awakening, and an unprecedented democratization of religion. As Nathan Hatch has written: "The wave of popular religious movements that broke upon the United States in the half-century after independence did more to Christianize American society than anything before or since."[1] The overall rate of religious adherence, the percentage of the entire population that belonged to a church, doubled from 17 percent to 34 percent, while the denominational landscape changed dramatically. In 1776, Congregationalists claimed 20.4 percent of all religious adherents; by 1850, they encompassed only 4 percent. Episcopalians dropped from 15.7 percent to 3.5 percent and Presbyterians from 19 percent to 11.6 percent. Baptists, however, grew from 16.9 percent to 20.5 percent of all adherents, while Methodists exploded from 2.5 percent to 34.2 percent.[2]

Disestablishment and free exercise of religion at the national level

The Founding Fathers, in establishing a new nation, struggled with the question of whether the United States should, or even could, be organized around a single religious creed drawn from one or several churches. The Declaration of Independence made reference to God (although not necessarily by that name, as in "nature's God," Creator," or "Supreme Judge of the World"), but nothing else.

The Articles of Confederation, by which the nation was governed from 1781 to 1789, said little more. Religion was commonly referenced in most documents issued by the Confederation Congress. The Northwest Ordinance of 1787, for example, established a bill of rights for the Northwest Territory intended to extend "the fundamental principles of civil and religious liberty," upon which the states to be created therein, their laws, and constitutions were to be created. Article I declared: "No person, demeaning himself in a peaceable and orderly manner, shall ever be molested on account of his mode of worship, or religious sentiments, in the said territory." Nevertheless recognizing the importance of religion to the new nation, linking it to morality and education, the authors added in Article III: "Religion, morality, and knowledge being necessary to good government and the happiness of mankind, schools and the means of education shall be encouraged."[3] But the Articles of Confederation, in itself, did not assume or delegate any authority in religious matters to the federal government.

The Constitutional Convention of 1787 paid only slight attention to the subject of religion. The Constitution contains no reference to God, or even to religion, except for a prohibition of religious tests as a qualification for federal office-holders. They would be bound "by oath or affirmation" to support the Constitution, "but no religious test shall ever be required as a qualification to any office or public trust under the United States" (Article VI). The federal test oath clause was adopted with little debate. Luther Martin was one of the few to even comment on it:

> [The test oath clause] was adopted by a great majority of the convention, and without much debate; however, there were some members so unfashionable as to think, that a belief of the existence of a Deity and of a state of future rewards and punishments would be some security for the good conduct of our rulers, and that, in a Christian country, it would be at least decent to hold out some distinction between the professors of Christianity and downright infidelity or paganism.[4]

During the state ratification debates, Connecticut Federalist Oliver Ellsworth defended the federal ban on religious tests as a means toward securing "the important right of religious liberty." A religious test oath, he explained, was "the parent of hypocrisy, and the offspring of error and the spirit of persecution." Isaac Backus, a Baptist and anti-Federalist delegate to the Massachusetts convention, decided to support the Constitution in part because of its prohibiting religious oaths. Imposing such oaths, Backus reasoned, violated a principle evident by reason and Scripture, "that religion is ever a matter between God and individuals."[5]

The delegates to the Constitutional Convention did not adopt a bill of rights. That omission did not reflect any opposition on their part to personal liberties or to religious freedom. They simply regarded such measures as superfluous. They reasoned that the new national government possessed only expressly enumerated powers, and no power had been granted to legislate on any such subject that would be the concern of a bill of rights. Because no such power existed, none could be exercised, and therefore all provisions against that possibility were unnecessary.[6]

When Congress submitted the Constitution to the states for ratification, it met with a firestorm of criticism that nearly brought about its premature demise. Opponents of ratification feared that the centralizing tendencies of a consolidated national government would extinguish the rights of the states and individuals unless protected by a bill of rights. Thomas Jefferson, then in France, wrote in support of a bill of rights that would protect freedom of religion, while Richard Henry Lee explained that while contemporary America suffered little religious turmoil, a constitution made for the ages should proclaim the right to "the free exercise of religion."[7]

In the end, six of the thirteen original states added to their votes for ratification of the Constitution recommendations for amendments, some of which would secure specific fundamental personal liberties including freedom of religion. In response to those recommendations, on June 8, 1789, as one of the Congress's first orders of business, Representative James Madison proposed for the House a series of amendments to the Constitution. The section on religion read: "The civil rights of none shall be abridged on account of religious belief or worship, nor shall any national religion be established, nor shall the full and equal rights of conscience be in any manner, or on any pretext, infringed."[8]

The term "national" proved troublesome. To some it meant that the federal government could not establish, or prefer, one denomination over another. To others it precluded any preference for any number of, or even all, denominations. Madison agreed to the following rewording of his proposed amendment: "No religion shall be established by law, nor shall the equal rights of conscience be infringed." When the proposed amendment was debated by the House, Madison reported that he understood the words to mean that Congress would be prohibited from establishing "a religion, and enforce the legal observation of it by law." Neither should Congress be allowed, he continued, "to compel men to worship God in any manner contrary to their conscience." The House version finally sent to the Senate read: "Congress shall make no law establishing religion or prohibiting the free exercise thereof, nor shall the rights of conscience be infringed."[9]

The Senate entered into a similar debate between those who favored a more narrow versus a broader construction of the proposed amendment, taking up and then rejecting various rewordings of the House's proposal: (1) "Congress shall not make any law establishing one religious sect or society in preference to others"; (2) "Congress shall not make any law infringing the rights of conscience, or establishing any religious sect or society"; and (3) "Congress shall make no law establishing any particular denomination of religion in preference to another." The failure of these and other motions suggests that the Senate too rejected any attempt at narrowing the amendment's intent, preferring a ban on federal involvement in religion of any kind, even in a non-preferential manner. Nevertheless, its proposed amendment differed from the House's: "Congress shall make no law establishing articles of faith or a mode of worship, or prohibiting the free exercise of religion."[10]

When the House rejected the Senate's version of the proposed amendment, the measure went to a joint conference, where the following wording was adopted: "Congress shall make no law respecting an establishment of religion, or prohibiting the free exercise thereof." The United States Supreme Court did not offer its interpretation of those words until 1947, when, in *Everson* v. *Board of Education*, it ruled:

> The 'establishment of religion' clause of the First Amendment means at least this: Neither a state nor the Federal Government can set up a church. Neither can pass laws which aid one religion, aid all religions, or prefer one religion over another.[11]

Much clearer is that those who framed the First Amendment meant its language, like that of the rest of the Bill of Rights, to apply only to the national government. The United States Supreme Court in *Permoli* v. *Municipality No. 1* of New Orleans (1845) pointed out that the First Amendment explicitly levies a ban on Congress. In 1789, James Madison proposed an amendment to the Constitution prohibiting the states from violating "the equal rights of conscience." Had that amendment been adopted, the federal government could easily have construed it to prohibit the states from maintaining establishments of religion.[12] A rule of constitutional interpretation known as the incorporation doctrine posits that the Fourteenth Amendment, ratified in 1868, incorporates the rights protected by the First Amendment, including religion. But it was not until 1940 that the Supreme Court incorporated the free exercise of religion clause into the Fourteenth Amendment and not until 1947 before it did the same for the establishment clause. Until then, in matters of religion at least, the states stood apart from the guarantees of the First Amendment and proceeded according to their own constitutions and bills of rights.

Disestablishment and free exercise of religion at the state level

At the formation of the new nation, seven states retained a church establishment. None was affected by the First Amendment to the United States Constitution, except perhaps by the influence of its words. Nevertheless, by 1833, all state establishments collapsed. The case of Virginia has been considered in Chapter 3. As Massachusetts was the last to relinquish its establishment, it will provide one last example of how disestablishment finally came about, moving from a multiple establishment, to a non-preferential establishment, and, finally, to no establishment at all.

A Massachusetts state Supreme Court decision of 1811 reaffirmed its 1785 ruling against the constitutional right of unincorporated religious societies to secure the rebate of their members' taxes. That decision could have had the effect of enhancing significantly the Congregational advantage over the less numerous unincorporated non-Congregational churches. It was initiated by a Universalist minister, who had sued the parish of Falmouth (in what is now Maine) for the monies paid by members of his unincorporated congregation, only to have the supreme judicial court sustain the claim of the parish that the state constitution authorized only the ministers of incorporated religious societies to obtain tax rebates.[13] Rather than silencing the opposition, however, it only encouraged them.

Outraged opponents of the decision, whose churches were rapidly increasing in number, orchestrated a public campaign for relief and fashioned an alliance with the Republican Party to defeat the Federalists, who backed the courts, in the elections of 1811. The result was the Religious Freedom Act of 1811, which authorized any religious society, whether incorporated or not, to receive the taxes of its members. After 1811, the basic law of the state confirmed and expanded its commitment to a multiple establishment of religion among Protestant denominations.[14]

By 1820, when Massachusetts held a new constitutional convention, the rapid growth of non-Congregationalists and a schism within Congregationalism foreshadowed the unviability of even this multiple church-state relationship. At the convention, Congregationalists staved off radical changes in the relevant sections of the old constitution. Delegates recommended modest changes, such as use of "Christian" instead of "Protestant," a concession to the growing Roman Catholic population; abolition of the requirement of compulsory public worship, already a dead letter; and constitutional recognition of the Religious Freedom Act of 1811. But they added nothing to the existing rights of unincorporated religious societies. Resentful voters overwhelmingly withheld ratification, but a decision by the state's high court in early 1821 produced unforeseen results that nevertheless transformed the church-state relationship.[15]

Baker v. Fales (1821) became notorious as "the Dedham case," by which a state court assisted Unitarians in "plundering" the old Congregational churches. Unitarianism was largely born of schism within Congregational ranks between Unitarians and Trinitarians, the First Congregational Church in Dedham being typical in that regard. A majority of the parish had become Unitarian, as a result of which the more orthodox church members seceded. Both groups claimed title to the church, but the state's high court held unanimously that those members that remained constituted the church and retained the rights and property belonging to it.[16]

Nearly ten years after the Dedham decision, the state's Supreme Court decided the Brookfield case, *Stebbins* v. *Jennings* (1830). During the preceding decade, there had been at least thirty Congregational schisms. In most of the cases, the seceders were Trinitarians, and in all cases, the seceders lost the properties of the churches involved. In 1830, with a new chief justice at the head of the court, the entire issue was reargued and Chief Justice Lemuel Shaw reaffirmed the principle of the Dedham decision.[17]

Massachusetts Congregationalists finally understood that establishment – which they had created and supported for so long – could work against them. Shortly after the Brookfield decision, they abandoned their historic position and joined with Baptists, Quakers, and even Unitarians in opposition to any establishment of religion. On November 11, 1833, Massachusetts voters by a ten-to-one majority ratified an amendment to the state constitution mandating disestablishment. Massachusetts may have been the last state to end its establishment, but the process by which it occurred had been replicated, by and large, in nearly all of those states that had preceded it in that decision.[18]

A summary view of the founding fathers on church and state

Chapter 3, on religion and the American Revolution, opens with a quote from Thomas Kidd. He writes that "no subject in American religious history is as ideologically freighted as the role of religion in the American founding era," in that whatever historical perspective one takes "holds implications in today's debates about religion's place in America's public sphere." Indeed, the question, as it is often put, "Was America founded as a Christian nation?" has been one of the most hotly debated questions in American history, for which there is no easy answer.

There is no doubt that, at its founding, Americans were overwhelmingly Christian. Further, although one of the most diverse Christian populations in the world, Christianity was at the heart of the new nation, shaping American beliefs and character. But if there is little debate over that point, the relationship between government and religion was a point of contention. In the search for an answer, participants in this debate commonly seek the original intent of the US Constitution, only to find, as suggested earlier, that the matter is hardly addressed therein, except to clearly leave it to the states. Moreover, if the nation's founding document distanced the national government from matters of religion, a position insisted upon by the states during the ratification debates, how those same states addressed the subject varied greatly and changed over the next several decades.

As a last resort, searching for an answer to this question commonly resorted to quoting the Founding Fathers. But even there, it is impossible to reduce the various views of the Founding Fathers on church and state to one, non-contradictory position. What to make, for example, of John Adams, who, on the one hand, in the United States Treaty with Tripoli of 1797 insisted that "the government of the United States is not, in any sense, founded on the Christian religion." But who wrote to Thomas Jefferson in 1813 that "the general principles on which the Fathers achieved independence," and that were "the only principles [to] which the beautiful assembly of gentlemen could unite," were "the general principles of Christianity"?[19]

Franklin's and Jefferson's "Divine Providence" was the god of nature, but for most of the other authors of the Declaration of Independence, it was the God of Scriptures.[20] Nevertheless, it is possible to group the Founding Fathers into three categories: enlightened separationists, political centrists, and pietistic separationists. All three were committed to the ideal of religious liberty, but they approached the issue from different perspectives.

Both enlightened and pietistic separationists worked to separate church and state in an institutional sense. Those deeply influenced by the Enlightenment, such as Thomas Paine and Thomas Jefferson, adhered to anticlerical views and focused on insulating government from religious domination. Madison shared this view, but tempered it with a concern for protecting the purity of religious belief and practice as well. Those Founders espousing pietistic separation, like Isaac Backus, inherited the emphasis of Roger Williams and William Penn on protecting religion from the corrupting effect of governmental interference, while political centrists such as George Washington and John Adams approached the issue of church and state in more pragmatic terms. Less concerned than the separationists with the specific means of attaining religious liberty, they regarded religion as an essential source of personal and social morality and when in office, they repeatedly recognized its importance in the nation's public life.[21]

If there is one relative certainty upon which to conclude this subject, it is that, regardless of their particular religious beliefs, the great majority of the Founding Fathers agreed with Washington and Adams that the Republic could not survive without religion's moral influence. Consequently, regardless of where they stood on the relationship between church and state, they did not envision a secular society but rather one receptive to voluntary religious expression.

George Washington, once again, in his Farewell Address, explained: "Of all the dispositions and habits which lead to political prosperity, religion and morality are indispensable. . . . Whatever may be conceded to the influence of refined education on minds of peculiar structure, reason and experience forbid us to expect that national morality can prevail in exclusion to religious principles." And then there was Thomas Jefferson, the deist, who in his *Notes on the State of Virginia*, wrote: "Can the liberties of a nation be thought secure when we have removed their only firm basis, a conviction in the minds of the people that these liberties are the gift of God?" Thus, we are left to agree with historian Frank Lambert:

> By no means did the separation of church and state mean that Americans were not a religious people. Nor did it preclude the possibility that the nation was already or could become a Christian nation; that would be determined by the voluntary decisions of men and women in free religious market, not by government coercion.

What Lambert was referring to was what we inherited from the Founding Fathers – that which distinguished us from other Western nations – namely denominationalism.[22]

The New England theology

In his book, *Awash in a Sea of Faith: Christianizing the American People*, Jon Butler provided an excellent bridge between the previous section of this chapter, which concludes with the Founding Fathers' belief in the importance of religion to the new republic, and the expansion of religious activity, which is the subject of the pages to follow. He identified three attempts on the part of religious leaders to "stamp Christian values and goals" on the newly independent nation, wherein, unlike other Western nations, there was no established church. The first was to provide a Christian explanation for the Revolution, covered in Chapter 3, as was the attack on irreligion, the second attempt. The third attempt, yet to be addressed, was the Americanization of denominations with European roots and the creation of new religious groups with distinctively American principles.[23]

As noted in Chapter 3, liberal Christianity traces its American roots to colonial New England. The central doctrinal characteristic of the movement was God's role as architect and governor of the universe, but without the wrath associated with God by Puritan Calvinists. Benevolence became the deity's chief characteristic, and people were no longer consigned to heaven or hell irrespective of their actual beliefs or willful deeds. Man became a free agent. God's grace continued to be necessary for salvation, but liberals showed much greater confidence in man's ability to effect his own salvation.[24]

In 1787, King's Chapel in Boston became the first Unitarian Church in America. For two decades, it stood alone, but both the number of Unitarians and their authority grew. With the election of John Thornton Kirkland President of Harvard, in 1810, the College became a bastion of liberal Unitarian theology. By 1820, William Ellery Channing, Minister of the Federal Street Church in Boston, became the leading Unitarian theologian. In 1825, he helped organize the American Unitarian Association, which brought 125 churches under its banner.[25]

Still active in New England during the Early Republic were old Calvinists, who continued to honor the traditional doctrine and polity of New England as it had gradually adjusted to changing circumstances. Like the liberals, they renounced the excesses of revivalism. But in contrast to liberals, they did not repudiate the Puritan conviction that regeneration was essential to the Christian life, nor did they cease to hope that the Holy Spirit would descend with special favor on whole communities and nations. The Old Calvinists had among them several prominent figures, like Jedediah Morse, Minister in Charlestown, Massachusetts; David Tappan, Professor of Divinity at Harvard; Joseph Willard, President of Harvard; and Thomas Clap, President of Yale. Nevertheless, as a whole, the moderates were undistinguished in strictly theological enterprises, and they won few recruits to succeed them in their ministry.[26]

The New Divinity men were more successful. They acknowledged Jonathan Edwards as their hero, and they sought to establish their churches on strict principles of regenerate membership and on new, but sharply defined, standards of doctrinal orthodoxy. Almost all were graduates of Yale, and most of them were settled over churches in Connecticut and the Connecticut River Valley. Although they defended revivals and sought to fan the fires of religious fervor anew, their concern with doctrine and metaphysics tended to hinder those efforts. Their churches were often beset by declining membership, factional troubles, or open schism. Moderates and liberals often dismissed them as a "metaphysical school," yet they persisted, and, at the end of the century, though it was not directly of their doing, they were rewarded by a Second Great Awakening.[27]

The New Divinity men's contribution to American religious history was almost entirely in the realm of ideas. Building on the older Puritan divinity as it had been enlivened in the Awakening and set on a new course by Edwards, they maintained and extended the New England theology. As such, Sydney Ahlstrom has written, they "contributed creatively to the single most brilliant and most continuous indigenous theological tradition that America has ever produced." Among the leading contributors were Samuel Hopkins; Jonathan Edwards, Jr. (Jonathan's son); and Nathanael Emmons. Joseph Bellamy provided the movement with its theological foundation.[28]

Bellamy, the first and most undeviating of Jonathan Edwards's disciples, trained for a time in Edwards's home. Not surprisingly, then, most of what Bellamy espoused was consistent with what Edwards had taught, although Bellamy did introduce some important shifts in emphasis. Among Bellamy's innovations was his concept of God as Moral Governor. As we have seen, this idea was already widespread in the Early Republic, but in his hands, it was prefatory to most other revisions of the Reformed tradition to be proposed by the New Divinity men. One of those revisions, and possibly the fundamental one, was the exoneration of God as the cause of sin through an emphasis on the divine permission of sin as the necessary means of achieving the greatest good in this best of all possible worlds. This was followed quite naturally by less emphasis on Edwards's argument for mankind's unity with Adam, which in turn led to a turning away from the idea of the imputation of Adam's sin. For Bellamy, man was sinful because he sinned.[29]

A corollary was Bellamy's redefinition of reprobation, according to which God's punishment of sin was not seen as an expression of holy wrath, but rather as an essential means of maintaining the authority of God's Law. But perhaps best known of all was Bellamy's reinterpretation of the atonement, whereby God was no longer considered an offended party receiving Christ's death as satisfaction for man's infinitely evil ways and limited in its effect only to the elect. Bellamy took Christ's sacrifice as an outworking of God's love accomplished for the well-being of the universe.[30]

Historians have given the New Divinity movement mixed reviews. Some have found it to be "one of the most intricate and pathetic exhibitions of theological reasonings which the history of Western thought affords." "Modern Protestants," one concluded, are "so thankful to be rid of the Puritan incubus that they point to these post-Edwardseans as the death agony of a monstrous theology which should never have been born." Another wrote, "The profound tragedy of Edwards's theology was transformed into a farce by his would-be disciples, who used his language and ignored his piety."[31]

Other scholars have viewed the New Divinity movement differently, praising Edwards's successors as building on that tradition in meaningful ways and as existing at the summit of nineteenth-century theology.[32]

Sydney Ahlstrom provided a more balanced assessment. Ahlstrom offered praise but in the context of the time. The extenuating circumstance for the New Divinity men was that they existed during the Enlightenment, when the country was more concerned with political matters – government, law, trade, war, and nation building – not theology. Nevertheless, he points out, "they succeeded in doing what almost no one else in the Reformed tradition was then doing creatively." They maintained and even developed a theological rigor in the face of both revivalistic and rationalistic challenges.

The Second Great Awakening in New England

The years since the First Great Awakening were hard to understand for some. In fact, in the face of what some perceived as the growing threat of deism, skepticism, infidelity, or at least spiritual lethargy, God seemed almost to have withdrawn his blessing from New England. There had been occasional local revivals, especially in the years 1763–1764, but, until the end of the century, little followed, although the number of New Divinity men had grown from a small band to over a hundred. The first phase of the Second Great Awakening in New England took place between 1797 and 1801, when many towns from Connecticut to New Hampshire felt "refreshing showers." "I saw a continued succession of heavenly sprinklings," wrote Edward Dorr Griffin, "until, in 1799, I could stand at my door in New Hartford, Litchfield County, and number fifty or sixty contiguous congregations laid down in one field of divine wonders." In 1801, the Awakening came to Yale, where one-third of the students were converted. And soon after, Bennet Tyler, one of the revival's leaders, wrote:

> God, in a remarkable manner, was pouring out his Spirit on the churches of New England. Within the period of five or six years . . . not less than one hundred and fifty

churches in New England were visited with times of refreshing from the presence of the Lord.[33]

Until it began to be influenced by the Great Awakening in the West, the New England Awakening was remarkably uniform in almost all of its appearances. Revivals came to the parishes of the New Divinity men with a consistency that they could interpret only as a sign of divine favor. In the words of the Edwardseans, it was the preaching of "plain gospel truths, with which the people had long been acquainted, and had heard with indifference." These "plain gospel truths" were God's absolute sovereignty, man's total depravity, and Christ's atoning love.[34]

The revivals were without the hysteria and commotion that had brought the First Great Awakening into disrepute in many quarters and that was arousing similar opposition in the West. That people were calm was something for which the New England ministers thanked God. They were not marked by "outcries, distortions of the body, or any symptoms of intemperate zeal." Indeed, they reported, "you might often see a congregation sit with deep solemnity depicted in their countenances, without observing a tear or sob during the service." Nevertheless, the fruits of conversion were incontestable, the New England ministers insisted. They could be seen in the renewed spiritual seriousness and reformation of morals among the converted.[35]

Whereas the First Great Awakening was heavily reliant on itinerants, the Second Great Awakening in New England was largely conducted by settled ministers within their own congregations. Prominent among the leaders of the Second Awakening were Timothy Dwight, Nathaniel William Taylor, and Lyman Beecher. Dwight, grandson of Jonathan Edwards and President of Yale from 1795 to 1817, is often hailed as first among this select group of leaders. His primary crusade was against deism. Whether he was an old Calvinist or a New Divinity man has been much debated, but to a large extent, he was neither. As the founder of the New Haven Theology, as it came to be known, he started a new trend that was carried to completion by Nathaniel William Taylor.[36]

Taylor, arguably the best theologian of his time in New England, was both Dwight's most devoted student and the real architect of the New Haven Theology. Taylor ministered to the First Church of New Haven from 1811 to 1822, but his most important services were rendered as Professor of Theology at the Yale Divinity School. From that platform, he became the Edwards of the Second Great Awakening, and his influence extended far beyond his own region and denomination.[37]

In spirit, the New Haven Theology remained distinctly Reformed, for Taylor would never concede that he had departed from the Westminster Confession, Dwight, or Edwards. But he did gather together the innovations of the intervening New Divinity, based them firmly and knowledgeably on Scottish Philosophy, and propounded a plausibly rationalistic revival theology for mid-nineteenth-century America. Taylor condemned liberal Christianity for its overestimation of human reason, goodness, and educability, but he also sought to modify orthodox Calvinism's doctrine of the total inability of man to effect his own salvation. He insisted that no man becomes depraved but by his own act, for the sinfulness of the human race does not pertain to human nature as such. "Sin is in the sinning," and therefore "original" only in the sense that it is universal. Though inevitable, it is not – as Edwards argued – causally necessary. Man always had, in Taylor's famous phrase, "power to the contrary."[38]

And finally there was Lyman Beecher, the self-asserting apostle of Taylorism. No other figure sums up better in his own life the many facets of the Second Great Awakening and its enormous consequences for American history. Beecher was the most methodical and pragmatic of the New England evangelicals, and his carefully organized techniques have been well documented. Within a movement that generally frowned upon itinerants as they were employed in the First Great Awakening, Beecher enlisted regular clergy in parishes that had experienced revivals into pulpit exchanges with those who had not. He organized new converts into voluntary associations for organized missionary activities. When necessary, he emphasized or not principal points of Calvinism:

> I believe that both the doctrines of dependence and moral accountability must be admitted. . . . [But] I also believe that greater or less prominence should be given to the one or the other of those doctrines according to the prevailing states of public opinion.[39]

While pursuing his career as a revivalist, Beecher brought to fullness the conception that most distinguishes the evangelistic resurgence of the next half-century: the intimate association of evangelism in its broadest sense with moral reform and social benevolence. As a reformer, he was especially active in the temperance movement. When he was called in 1826 to Boston's Hanover Street Congregational Church, he brought the tactics of revivalism to the service of conservatism against liberals and Unitarians. In 1832, he moved west to become president of Lane Theological Seminary.[40]

A concluding note on the Second Great Awakening in New England

Two points should be made to conclude this section on the Second Great Awakening in New England. Along with the redefinition of free moral agency, theologians of the Second Great Awakening in New England revised the concept of limited atonement. If, as they allowed, all men have free will, Christ could not have died for only a few predestined elect, but for whoever would accept God's offer of salvation. Further, they played down the idea that the atonement of Christ was a punishment he suffered for Adam's sin. Instead, they suggested that Christ came to earth to suffer as a man because he wished to sacrifice himself for the love of mankind.[41] It was a voluntary act of self-sacrifice that served both as a stimulus and as an example for believers, which relates to the second point.

The Second Awakening created a new kind of religious institution, the voluntary association of private individuals for missionary, reformatory, or benevolent purposes. Usually these societies were chartered and governed independently, even when they had a nominal relation to some church body. Their membership grew wherever interest could be created, often on an interdenominational basis. Their activities were carried on without church or state controls, and in most cases, they were focused fairly sharply on one specific purpose. This will be further explored in the Chapter 5.

The Great Awakening in the West

In 1814, on the occasion of the Yale commencement, Lyman Beecher addressed the leadership of New England's Second Great Awakening. Beecher informed his audience of the unprecedented number of new ministers required to serve the young nation, and he challenged them to provide financial assistance for worthy candidates. Declaring that the entire nation could boast only 3,000 educated ministers, he called for 5,000 new recruits, men who could train at a place such as Yale and rescue the people of America from another kind of religious leader who presumed to speak about divine matters:

> There may be, perhaps, 1500 besides who are nominally ministers of the Gospel. But they are generally illiterate men, often not possessed of a good English education, and in some instances unable to read or write. By them, as a body, learning is despised.[42]

Beecher went on to spell out the effects of people being "exposed to the errors of enthusiastic and false teachers." Illiterate teachers could not stand as pillars of civilization and moral influence, he explained, nor could they command the attention of that "class of the community which is above their own," wielding "that religious and moral literary influence which it belongs to the ministry to exert." "Illiterate men have never been the chosen instruments of God," Beecher argued, explaining that the twelve disciples were instructed by Christ himself for three years "to supply the deficiency of an education."[43] Beecher, of course, was referring to those ministers who served as the vanguard of the Second Great Awakening in the West.

As is true of most other such events, it is difficult to date the beginning of the Second Great Awakening in the West. Most historians agree, however, that it began between the late 1780s and 1800s. When the American Revolution ended, Americans moved west rapidly and in large numbers. They surged ahead of all trappings of civilization, including church and community. Bringing religion to them would require extraordinary measures, including the camp meeting. The camp meeting became the pre-eminent symbol of the Awakening in the West, which at least in its outward manifestation was quite different from the revivals in New England.[44]

The earliest major figure in the western Awakening was the Presbyterian minister James McGready, a bold and uncompromising Scots-Irishman. McGready ministered in North Carolina until 1796, when he took charge of three parishes in southwestern Kentucky. At the Gasper River Church in July 1800, he organized the first camp meeting. Joining McGready was another Presbyterian, Barton W. Stone. Born in Maryland, Stone moved into western North Carolina, where he was converted under McGready. In 1800, he was serving the small Cane Ridge and Concord Churches in Bourbon, Kentucky. In August 1801, Stone organized a camp meeting at Cane Ridge that attracted a crowd of people estimated at from 10,000 to 25,000, when nearby Lexington, the state's largest city, barely exceeded 2,000.[45]

The Cane Ridge Revival lasted from six to seven days and would likely have lasted longer were it not for the failure of provisions for the unexpected crowd. When it was over, contemporaries referred to it as "the greatest outpouring of the Spirit since Pentecost." Historians have variously described these camp meetings as "holy fairs," or religious festivals, and referred to them, collectively, as a watershed in American religious history. But what happened nearly defies description. Barton Stone put it as simply as any:

> Many things transpired there [at Cane Ridge], which were so much like miracles, that if they were not, they had the same effects as miracles on infidels and unbelievers; for many of them by these were convinced that Jesus was the Christ, and bowed in submission to him.[46]

Historians have described the Cane Ridge crowd as including hardened, tobacco-chewing, tough-spoken, and notoriously profane farmers, famous for their alcoholic thirst, who were joined by their "scarcely demure wives and large broods of children," all attracted in anticipation of participating in so large a social occasion in an otherwise lonely frontier farmer's life.[47]

William McLoughlin has argued that women in particular were drawn to camp meetings, because they bore the heaviest burdens of pain, sickness, sorrow, unremitting labor, and old age. "For their labors there were few social rewards and no public victories." They were excluded from most frontier pastimes, save joining religious institutions should they find their way into their communities. But then, Christian fellowship was an important source of security for men and women: "It gave regularity and order to life; it offered a source of strength beyond the self."[48]

The most controversial element of the Cane Ridge Revival was the outward, physical manifestations of those overcome by religious emotions. Once again, we turn to Barton Stone's personal account:

> The bodily agitations or exercises, attending the excitement in the beginning of this century, were various and called by various names. . . . The falling exercise was very common among all classes. . . . The subject of this exercise would, generally, with a piercing scream, fall like a log on the floor, earth, or mud, and appear as dead. . . .
>
> The jerks cannot be so easily described. Sometimes the subject of the jerks would be affected in some one member of the body, and sometimes the whole system. . . .
>
> The dancing exercise . . . generally began with the jerks, and was peculiar to the professors of religion. The subject, after jerking awhile, began to dance, and then the jerks would cease.
>
> The barking exercise (as contemptuously called it), was nothing but the jerks. A person affected with the jerks, especially in his head, would often make a grunt, or bark, if you please, from the suddenness of the jerk. . . .
>
> The laughing exercise was frequent, confined solely with the religious. It was a loud, hearty laughter, but . . . it excited laughter in none else. The subject appeared rapturously solemn, and his laughter excited solemnity in saints and sinners. . . .
>
> The running exercise was nothing more than . . . persons feeling something of these bodily agitations, through fear, attempt[ing] to run away, and thus escape from them; but it commonly happened that they ran not far, before they fell, or became so greatly agitated that they could proceed no farther. . . .

Stone concluded this chapter with a description of the singing exercise, wherein the subject in a very happy mind would "sing most melodiously." Such music, Stone concluded, "silenced everything, and attracted the attention of all. It was most heavenly. How could you ever be tired of hearing it?" There were "many eccentricities and much fanaticism in this excitement," he offered in closing, but "the good effects were seen and acknowledged in every neighborhood."[49]

Perhaps the most important figure to appear in the Second Great Awakening in the West was the Presbyterian revivalist Charles Grandison Finney (see Figure 4.1). As the leading prophet of revivalism and perfectionism, he provides a transition to Chapter 5. Further, because Finney's work was largely in the old Northwest, he, more than most frontier revivalists, came into contact with New Englanders of the Taylor/Beecher school. Indeed Taylor and Beecher and their disciples both feared and learned more from Finney than any other competitor. Under Finney, the revivalism of the old Northwest, now the Midwest, constituted the culmination of the northern phase of the Awakening. After 1830, however, Finney brought

Figure 4.1 Charles Grandison Finney

Source: North Wind Picture Archives/Alamy Stock Photo

his revival methods back east to New England, New York City, Philadelphia, and even the British Isles.[50]

Reports in New England portrayed Finney's revivals as fanatical affairs, and fearing the ridicule they might bring on their own efforts, Taylor and Beecher arranged to meet Finney in New Lebanon, New York, in 1827. Taylor and Beecher hoped to persuade Finney to tone down his enthusiasm, but they failed. Finney simply countered that as he and his followers were winning so many converts it made no sense to change their ways. Finney agreed to discourage "audible groaning," shouting, fainting and other convulsions, but little else.[51]

Finney largely repudiated Calvinism. He did not become a rationalist, but he did come to believe that "reason was given us for the very purpose of enabling us to justify the ways of

God," and that "the will is free and . . . sin and holiness are voluntary acts of mind." Conversion, Finney declared, is not a miracle or dependent on a miracle. "It is purely a philosophical result of the right use of constituted means." Therefore, a revival is not a miracle; rather "it consists entirely in the right exercise of the powers of nature." Drawing a parallel between bringing about a revival and raising a crop of wheat, Finney insisted that as the laws governing revivals were so clear and simple, anyone following them could obtain the desired results.[52]

Finney developed a new concept of professional mass evangelism and demonstrated that it could be used as effectively in the cities as in rural camp meetings. He helped make revivalism a profession and popularized the practice of protracted meetings – three- or four-day revivalistic gatherings. Finney sometimes held these meetings in tents, sometimes in large churches or auditoriums or even theaters, and in contrast to most other revivalists, his meetings were interdenominational, often sponsored by all the churches in a town. In that regard, Finney and the professional revivalists that would follow in his footsteps served to supplement, rather than compete with, the regular ministry, thereby becoming, as William McLoughlin put it, "the most powerful engine in the process of American church growth, frontier acculturation, and benevolent reform."[53]

Historians associate three major consequences with the Great Awakening in the West. First, because of that Awakening, revivalism became both symbol and impetus for the century-long process by which the greater part of American evangelical Protestantism became revitalized. The organized revival became a major mode of church expansion. Second, it in large part determined the country's denominational expansion, most notably among Baptists and Methodists. And third, it helped advance the democratization of Christianity in America.[54]

The democratization of Christianity in America

Between the American Revolution and 1845, the population of the United States grew from 2.5 million to 20 million. This unprecedented growth was due in large part to a high birth rate and the availability of land, although heavy immigration would begin in the 1830s. Nevertheless, the United States remained overwhelmingly rural, the ratio of people to land barely doubling, while the number of Americans expanded tenfold. Amidst this population boom, American Christianity became a mass enterprise. The 1,800 Christian ministers serving in 1775 swelled to nearly 40,000 by 1845. The number of preachers per capita more than tripled, and the colonial legacy of 1 minister per 1,500 inhabitants became 1 per 500. This greater preaching density was remarkable given the spiraling population and the restless movement of people to occupy land beyond the reach of any church organization.[55]

The sheer number of new preachers in the Early Republic was not a predictable outgrowth of religious conditions in the British colonies. Rather, their sudden growth indicated a profound religious upsurge and resulted in a vastly altered religious landscape. Twice the number of denominations competed for adherents, and insurgent groups enjoyed the upper hand. One new denominational cluster, the Christians or the Disciples of Christ, for example, had an estimated 4,000 preachers, equaling the number of clergy serving Presbyterian denominations. The Congregationalists, who had twice the clergy of any other American church in 1775, could not muster one-tenth the preaching force of the Methodists in 1845.[56]

The Disciples, Methodists, and Baptists constituted mass movements and were led by young men of relentless energy, who went about movement-building as self-conscious outsiders. They shared an ethic of unrelenting toil, a passion for expansion, hostility to orthodox belief and style, a zeal for religious reconstruction, and a systematic plan to realize their goals. Further, however diverse their theologies and church organizations, they all offered common people compelling visions of individual self-respect and collective self-confidence.[57]

As common people became significant actors on the religious scene, there was increasing confusion and angry debate over the purpose and function of the church. A style of religious leadership that the public deemed "untutored" and "irregular" as late as the First Great Awakening became overwhelmingly successful, even normative, in the Second. Ministers from different classes vied with each other to serve as divine spokesmen, and democratic or populist leaders associated virtue with ordinary people and exalted the vernacular in word, print, and song.[58]

Faced with problems beyond the ordinary experiences of easterners, westerners often rushed to biblical prophecy for help in understanding the troubled times that were upon them. Some demanded a return to revivals, the likes of those of the eighteenth century, while others felt free to experiment with new forms of organization and belief. By the end of the first decade of the nineteenth century, Nathan Hatch has argued, it became anachronistic to speak of dissent in America as if there were still a commonly recognized center against which new or emerging groups defined themselves. New groups were already vying to establish their identity as a counterestablishment.[59]

In at least three respects, the popular religious movements of the Early Republic articulated a profoundly democratic spirit. First, they denied the age-old distinction that set the clergy apart as a separate order of men, and they refused to defer to learned theologians and traditional orthodoxies. Second, they associated virtue with ordinary people rather than with elites, and exalted the vernacular in word and song as the hallowed channel for communicating with and about God. And third, they rejected the past as a repository of wisdom. In these ways, they reconstructed the foundations of religion in keeping with the values and priorities of ordinary people.[60]

These popular religious movements empowered ordinary people by taking their deepest spiritual impulses at face value rather than subjecting them to the scrutiny of orthodox doctrine and clergymen. Preachers from a wide range of new religious movements openly fanned the flames of religious ecstasy, and what had been defined as "enthusiasm" was increasingly advocated from the pulpit as an essential part of Christianity. Such a shift in emphasis, accompanied by rousing gospel singing rather than formal church music, reflected the common people's success in defining the nature of faith for themselves.[61]

The Christian Movement

Characteristically, participants in the Christian Movement simply called themselves Christians. They followed the lead of Elias Smith, a New England Jeffersonian, who sought a radical simplification of the gospel. Smith became a central figure in a loose network of religious radicals who between 1790 and 1815 chose the name Disciples of Christ. They demanded, in the light of the American Revolution, a new dispensation free from the restrictions of history, a new kind of church based on democratic principles, and a new form of biblical authority calling for common people to interpret the New Testament for themselves. Other major figures in the movement included James O'Kelly in Virginia, Barton Stone in Kentucky, and Alexander Campbell in Pennsylvania. A Calvinist Baptist, a Methodist, and two Presbyterians, all found traditional sources of authority anachronistic and moved toward similar definitions of egalitarian religion.[62]

From Portsmouth, New Hampshire, Smith, ordained a Baptist minister and launched the first religious newspaper in the United States, the *Herald of Gospel Liberty*, which he edited from 1808 to 1818. From that forum, and in scores of pamphlets and sermons, he and a band of fifty or so itinerants launched a blistering attack on Baptists, Congregationalists, Methodists, and Federalists of any religious persuasion. By 1815, the newspaper had 1,400 subscribers.[63]

In Virginia, James O'Kelly's Republican Methodists, founded in 1794, were taking the same route, undoing the "ecclesiastical monarch" of the Methodist Church. An early leader among Virginia Methodists, O'Kelly could not abide the bishopric of Francis Asbury and withdrew with over 30 ministers to form a church that had as many as 20,000 members when it merged with Smith's Christians in 1809. "As a son of America, and a Christian," he declared to Asbury, "I shall oppose your political measures and contend for the Savior's government. I contend for Biblical government, Christian equality, and the Christian name."[64]

Barton Stone embarked upon the same pilgrimage in the wake of the Cane Ridge Revival in Kentucky in 1802, wherein he resolved that he could no longer live under Presbyterian doctrine or church organization. A year later he and five other ministers proclaimed that it was not just the Presbyterians who were wrong, but all churches. Signing a document entitled "The Last Will and Testament of the Springfield Presbytery," they vowed to follow nothing but the Christian name and the New Testament. "It was not without deep connotation," Nathan Hatch has pointed out, "that Stone characterized his break with the Presbyterians as the 'declaration of our independence.'"[65]

Finally, there was Alexander Campbell, Scottish immigrant, the only college graduate of the four, and the only one not to participate in the American Revolution. Campbell found himself following the same trajectory of his fellow American Christians. By 1830, his quest for primitive Christianity led his movement, the Disciples of Christ, to unite with Stone's Christians. By 1860, their denomination claimed about 200,000 adherents, the fifth largest Protestant body in the United States. The Christians hammered relentlessly at the simple themes of sin, grace, and conversion. They organized fellowships that resisted social distinctions and welcomed spontaneous experience, and they denounced any religion that seemed bookish, cold, or formal. Further, the Christians espoused reform in three areas. First, they called for a revolution within the church to place laity and clergy on an equal footing and to exalt the conscience of the individual over the collective will of any congregation or church organization. Second, they rejected the traditions of learned theology and called for a new view of history that welcomed inquiry and innovation. Finally, they advocated the inalienable right of every person to understand the New Testament for him- or herself.[66]

The Methodists

The Methodists grew out of a reform movement in the Church of England led by John and Charles Wesley in the 1740s. Emphasizing a personal experience of religious conversion, the Wesley's rejected the Calvinist insistence on human depravity and predestination, instead adopting the Arminian belief in "the completeness of Christ's sacrifice for all" and that salvation was possible through God's freely given grace and individual conversion.[67]

The Methodists began arriving in colonial America in the 1760s led by Francis Asbury (see Figure 4.2). Their earliest successes occurred in the 1770s in Virginia, where Methodist preachers sparked revivals that set the tone for those to follow. As one Methodist preacher reported: "It was common for sinners to be seized with a trembling and shaking, and from that to fall

Figure 4.2 Francis Asbury

Source: Chronicle/Alamy Stock Photo

down on the floor as if they were dead; and many of them have been convulsed from head to foot, while others have retained the use of their tongues so as to pray for mercy, while they were lying helpless on the ground." But the Methodists story begins in earnest in the half-century following American independence, during which they were successful in separating themselves from any association with the Church of England and moving to the fore of the Second Great Awakening.[68]

In 1806, Bishop Francis Asbury sent a report to his English colleague, Thomas Cooke, in which he expressed his growing confidence in the role of the Methodists in converting the

New World. He spoke of the hundreds of gospel ministers under his charge, of the 8,273 new members added during the last year, and of the pervasive sense that God's work was accelerating at an unprecedented rate. In particular, he delighted in the success of American camp meetings, describing the overwhelming power of a four-day meeting twenty miles northeast of New York City, which, he estimated, 3,000 lay people and 100 preachers had attended. Five years later, he boasted that these occasions brought together as many as four million Americans annually – an estimated one-third of the total population.[69]

In the very years that Methodist leadership in Great Britain seemed willing to forgo numerical growth as their primary goal, even accepting numerical losses in order to preserve discipline, American Methodists remained ruthlessly committed to arousing a following and creating new societies. Increasingly, Methodist leaders were sent out to call churches into existence, not to wait for churches to call them. Both roving evangelists and propagandists, they went from house to house looking for anyone who would listen, taking Francis Asbury's first discipline seriously: "You have nothing to do but to save souls. Therefore, spend and be spent in this work.[70]

The Methodist Church was not the most democratic movement of the day, organizationally. Even under Francis Asbury's leadership, the church refused to share ecclesiastical authority with the laity. Asbury was continually criticized for this by his more democratic competitors, but he never apologized for it or for its cadre of itinerant preachers being bound together by strict rules and discipline under one leader. Instead, he defended his own authority by linking it directly to the apostolic age, transcending the corruptions of the intervening centuries. More than another church, Asbury insisted that the Methodists had restored the "primitive order" of the New Testament, "the same doctrine, the same spirituality, the same power in ordinances, in ordination, and in spirit."[71]

While the structure of the Methodist Church may seem out of accord with the democratic stirrings of the times, the vital spring of Methodism under Asbury was to make Christianity a faith of the people. It was the church's duty, he said "to condescend to men of low estate." From Asbury and preachers like him, people were invited to join a movement promising them dignity of choice and the possibility of becoming a class leader, exhorter, local preacher, and circuit rider. Lay preaching became the hallmark of American Methodism and "served as a powerful symbol that the wall between a gentlemen and commoner had been shattered."[72]

The Baptists

American Baptists have always viewed the General Missionary Convention in Philadelphia in 1814 as a watershed event in their history. The meeting was the first step in creating a national denomination out of hundreds of autonomous Baptist churches scattered along the Atlantic seaboard. For the thirty-two delegates at the organizing session of the Triennial Convention, this national undertaking was an important sign that the Baptist movement was coming of age. Baptist membership had grown tenfold since the American Revolution, and its 2,000 churches, 1,600 ministers, and 100 associations could no longer be overlooked. Already Baptists had begun to taste a measure of respectability and to look forward to a day when they would not have to bear the reproach of inferior social position.[73]

At least one prominent Baptist, however, took exception to this quest for respectability. John Leland was one of the most popular and controversial Baptists in America. He was most famous as an advocate of religious freedom in Virginia, but he was primarily a preacher and an itinerant evangelist. Leland was a persistent critic of clerical professionalism, which he believed was at the core of American Protestant denominations. He denounced the oppression of "a hierarchical clergy-despotic judiciary – [and] an aristocratic host of lawyers," the mechanical operations of theological seminaries, the tyranny of formal structures, and the burden of credalism – "this Virgin Mary between the souls of men and the Scriptures."[74]

Leland's opposition to creeds and confessions was a function of his firm identification with a popular audience, an instinct that even his radical predecessor Isaac Backus did not appreciate. Backus had defended his positions with learned tracts addressed to civil and religious elites. He opposed "high and new things" in religion and was suspicious of rallying popular opinion. Leland relished a common audience, peppering his speeches and writings with blunt common sense and earthy humor. The greatest difference between Backus and Leland, however, was their contrasting view of the social order. While Backus never doubted the right of all to worship as they pleased, he was unconvinced that laymen could articulate their own theology. Leland rejected the idea of natural inequality in society, that some were set apart to lead and others to follow. He depicted the typical clergyman as venal and conniving, rather than capable of rising above self-interest. Like Jefferson, he perceived the organized church as corrupted by "priestcraft," which he defined as the clerical quest for "self-advantage."[75]

Leland was a diligent publicist whose ideas had broad circulation, thereby assuring his legacy within the Baptist Church. That legacy consisted of a twofold persuasion that operated powerfully in the hinterland of Baptist church life: an aversion to central control and a quest for self-reliance. Whatever success others had in building central institutions, their way was dogged at every step by serious defections to the antiformalist appeals of Leland and his successors. Thus, Baptists had the advantage not only of the peculiar rite of adult baptism but also of a democratic congregational polity, in which the members of each local church were subject to no higher ecclesiastical authority. Ordinary people gladly championed the promise of personal autonomy as a message they could understand and a cause to which they could subscribe in God's name.[76]

Summary

American churches' profound commitment to their audience in the early decades of the nineteenth century shaped the way religious thinking was organized and carried out. When the commoner rose in power, people of ideas found their authority circumscribed. As a result, Nathan Hatch has argued, democratic America has never produced another theologian like Jonathan Edwards, just as it has never elected statesmen of the caliber of Johns Adams, Thomas Jefferson, and James Madison. Insurgent religious leaders were not so much anti-intellectual as intent on destroying the monopoly of classically educated and university-trained clergymen. The insurgents considered people's common sense more reliable, even in theology, than the judgment of an educated few.[77]

This shift involved a new faith in public opinion as an arbiter of truth. Common folk were no longer thought to be irresponsible and willful. Rather they were deemed ready to embrace truth, if only it was retrieved from academic speculation and the heavy hand of the past. These new ground rules flattened out uncomfortable complexity and often resolved issues by a simple choice of alternatives in the free market-place of ideas.

Review questions

1   Was America founded as a Christian nation?
2   Did passage of the First Amendment to the Constitution institutionalize the separation of church and state and guaranteed the free exercise of religion in America?
3   How would you compare the religious views of the Founding Fathers included in this chapter?
4   How would you compare the initial impulses of the First and Second Great Awakening?
5   How did the Second Great Awakening influence both the course of American religion and growth of American democracy?

Notes

1   Nathan O. Hatch, *The Democratization of American Christianity* (New Haven, CT: Yale University Press, 1989), 3.
2   Roger Finke and Rodney Stark, *The Churching of America, 1776–1990: Winners and Losers in Our Religious Economy* (New Brunswick, NJ: Rutgers University Press, 1994), 16, 55.
3   Arlin M. Adams and Charles J. Emmerich, *A Nation Dedicated to Religious Liberty: The Constitutional Heritage of the Religion Clauses* (Philadelphia: University of Pennsylvania Press, 1990), 10–1.
4   Adams and Emmerich, *Nation Dedicated to Religious Liberty*, 14.
5   Adams and Emmerich, *Nation Dedicated to Religious Liberty*, 15.
6   Leonard W. Levy, *Emergence of a Free Press* (New York: Oxford University Press, 1985), 220–36; Leonard W. Levy, *The Establishment Clause: Religion and the First Amendment* (New York: Macmillan Publishing Company, 1986), 65–6. See also: Isaac Kramnick and Robert Laurence Moore, *The Godless Constitution: The Case against Religious Correctness* (New York: Norton, 1996).
7   Thomas J. Curry, *The First Freedoms: Church and State in America to the Passage of the First Amendment* (Oxford, NY: Oxford University Press, 1986), 195.
8   Levy, *Establishment Clause*, 66; Curry, *First Freedoms*, 199.
9   Levy, *Establishment Clause*, 75–7, 81.
10 Levy, *Establishment Clause*, 82; Curry, *First Freedoms*, 207.
11 Curry, First Freedoms, 207. See also: Martin Marty, *The One and the Many: America's Struggle for the Common Good* (Cambridge, MA: Harvard University Press, 1997).
12 Adams and Emmerich, *Nation Dedicated to Religious Liberty*, 19–20; Curry, *First Freedoms*, 199, 204–5.
13 Levy, *Establishment Clause*, 32–3.
14 William G. McLoughlin, *New England Dissent 1630–1833: The Baptists and the Separation of Church and State*, 2 vols. (Cambridge, MA: Harvard University Press, 1971), 2: 1088–106; Levy, *Establishment Clause*, 32–3.
15 McLoughlin, *New England Dissent*, 2: 1160–85.
16 Levy, *Establishment Clause*, 35.
17 Levy, *Establishment Clause*, 37.
18 Levy, *Establishment Clause*, 38. For a brief overview of disestablishment in other states, see: John Fea, *Was America Founded as a Christian Nation? A Historical Introduction* (Louisville, KY: Westminster John Knox Press, 2011).
19 Fea, *Was America Founded as a Christian Nation*, 3.
20 Steven Waldman, *Founding Faith: Providence, Politics, and the Birth of Religious Freedom in America* (New York: Random House, 2008), 87.
21 Adams and Emmerich, *Nation Dedicated to Religious Liberty*, 31.
22 Frank Lambert, *The Founding Fathers and the Place of Religion in America* (Princeton, NJ: Princeton University Press, 2003), 240–1. See also: Edwin S. Gaustad, *Faith of the Founders: Religion and the New Nation, 1776–1826*, 2nd edn. (Waco, TX: Baylor University Press, 2004); Peter W. Williams, *America's Religions: From Their Origins to the Twenty-First Century*, 3rd edn. (Urbana: University of Illinois Press, 2008), 5, 9.

23 Jon Butler, *Awash in a Sea of Faith: Christianizing the American People* (Cambridge, MA: Harvard University Press, 1990), 212.

24 Conrad Wright, *Beginnings of Unitarianism in America* (Hamden, CT: Archon Books, 1976), 59–186; Daniel W. Howe, *The Unitarian Conscience* (Cambridge, MA: Harvard University Press, 1970); Charles H. Lippy, *Seasonable Revolutionary: The Mind of Charles Chauncy* (Chicago: Nelson-Hall, 1981); David Robinson, *The Unitarians and the Universalists* (Westport, CT: Greenwood Press, 1985), 9–23.

25 Wright, *Beginnings of Unitarianism in America*, 252–80; Conrad Wright, "Institutional Reconstruction in the Unitarian Controversy," in *American Unitarianism, 1805–1865*, ed. Conrad Wright (Boston: Massachusetts Historical Society and Northeastern University Press, 1989), 3–29; Robinson, *Unitarians and the Universalists*, 30–8; Arthur W. Brown, *Always Young for Liberty: A Biography of William Ellery Channing* (Syracuse, NY: Syracuse University Press, 1956).

26 William G. McLoughlin, *Revivals, Awakenings, and Reform: An Essay on Religion and Social Change in America, 1607–1977* (Chicago: University of Chicago Press, 1978), 98–101.

27 Sydney E. Ahlstrom, *A Religious History of the American People* (New Haven, CT: Yale University Press, 1972), 404–5; McLoughlin, *Revivals, Awakenings, and Reform*, 101; Charles Roy Keller, *The Second Great Awakening in Connecticut* (New Haven, CT: Yale University Press, 1942).

28 Ahlstrom, *Religious History of the American People*, 405–7.

29 Ahlstrom, *Religious History of the American People*, 407.

30 Ahlstrom, *Religious History of the American People*, 407.

31 Herbert W. Schneider, *The Puritan Mind* (Ann Arbor: University of Michigan Press, 1958), 208; Joseph Haroutunian, *Piety versus Moralism: The Passing of the New England Theology* (New York: Henry Holt, 1932), 71, 96, 127, 130, 176.

32 Frank H. Foster, *A Genetic History of the New England Theology* (Chicago: University of Chicago Press, 1907); George N. Boardman, *History of the New England Theology* (Chicago: University of Chicago Press, 1899), 14.

33 Griffin is quoted in Keller, *Second Great Awakening in Connecticut*, 37–8; Ahlstrom, *Religious History of the American People*, 416; Bennet Tyler, *The New England Revivals from Narratives First Published in the Connecticut Evangelical Magazine* (Boston: Massachusetts Sabbath Society, 1846), v.

34 Tyler, *New England Revivals*, 59.

35 Ahlstrom, *Religious History of the American People*, 417.

36 McLoughlin, *Revivals, Awakenings, and Reform*, 109–10; Kenneth Silverman, *Timothy Dwight* (New York: Twayne Publishers, 1969).

37 McLoughlin, *Revivals, Awakenings, and Reform*, 111, 118.

38 Ahlstrom, *Religious History of the American People*, 419–20; McLoughlin, *Revivals, Awakenings, and Reform*, 114–15; Sidney E. Mead, *Nathaniel W. Taylor* (Chicago: University of Chicago Press, 1942).

39 McLoughlin, *Revivals, Awakenings, and Reform*, 111–14

40 Ahlstrom, *Religious History of the American People*, 422; Lyman Beecher, *Autobiography*, ed. Barbara Cross (Cambridge, MA: Harvard University Press, 1961).

41 McLoughlin, *Revivals, Awakenings, and Reform*, 119–20.

42 Lyman Beecher, *An Address to the Charitable Society for the Education of Indigent Pious Young Men for the Ministry of the Gospel* (New Haven, CT: no publisher, 1814), 5–8.

43 Beecher, *Address to the Charitable Society*, 5–8.

44 Catherine C. Cleveland, *Great Revival in the West, 1797–1805* (Chicago: University of Chicago Press, 1916), 54; Charles A. Johnson, *Tire Frontier Camp Meeting: Religion's Harvest Time* (Dallas, TX: Southern Methodist University Press, 1955), 43–51. See also: John Boles, *The Great Revival, 1787–1805: The Origins of the Southern Evangelical Mind* (Lexington: University of Kentucky Press, 1972).

45 Ahlstrom, *Religious History of the American People*, 432–3; Johnson, *Frontier Camp Meeting*, 32; McLoughlin, *Revivals, Awakenings, and Reform*, 132.

46 Barton W. Stone, "A Short History of the Life of Barton W. Stone Written by Himself," in *Voices from Cane Ridge*, ed. Rhodes Thompson (St. Louis, MO: Bethany Press, 1954), 68. On the camp meeting revivals as "holy fairs," see: Leigh Eric Schmidt, *Holy Fairs: Scotland and the Making of American Revivalism*, 2nd edn. (Grand Rapids, MI: William B. Eerdmans, 2001).

47 Ahlstrom, *Religious History of the American People*, 433.
48 McLoughlin, *Revivals, Awakenings, and Reform*, 133.
49 Stone, "Short History of the Life of Barton W. Stone," 69–72; Johnson, *Frontier Camp Meeting*, 55–62.
50 McLoughlin, *Revivals, Awakenings, and Reform*, 122–3; Johnson, *Frontier Camp Meeting*, 172; Charles E. Hambrick-Stowe, *Charles G. Finney and the Spirit of American Evangelicalism* (Grand Rapids, MI: William B. Eerdmans, 1996), 22–45; Whitney R. Cross, *The Burned-Over District: The Social and Intellectual History of Enthusiastic Religion in Western New York, 1800–1850* (Ithaca, NY: Cornell University Press, 1950).
51 McLoughlin, *Revivals, Awakenings, and Reforms*, 124–6; Hambrick-Stowe, *Charles G. Finney*, 65–72.
52 Hambrick-Stowe, *Charles G. Finney*, 32; McLoughlin, *Revivals, Awakenings, and Reform*, 125.
53 McLoughlin, *Revivals, Awakenings, and Reform*, 127; Hambrick-Stowe, *Charles G. Finney*, 228–36; William G. McLoughlin, *Modern Revivalism: Charles Grandison Finney to Billy Graham* (New York: Ronald Press, 1959).
54 Ahlstrom, *Religious History of the American People*, 435–6.
55 Hatch, *Democratization of American Christianity*, 3–4.
56 Hatch, *Democratization of American Christianity*, 3–4.
57 Hatch, *Democratization of American Christianity*, 4–5.
58 Hatch, Democratization of American Christianity, 5.
59 Hatch, *Democratization of American Christianity*, 7; Ruth H. Bloch, *Visionary Republic: Millennial Themes in American Thought, 1756–1800* (New York: Cambridge University Press, 1985); Donald G. Mathews, "The Second Great Awakening as an Organizing Process," *American Quarterly*, 21 (1969): 23–43.
60 Joyce Appleby, *Capitalism and a New Social Order: The Republican Vision of the 1790s* (New York: Oxford University Press, 1984), 79; Olivia Smith, *The Politics of Language, 1791–1819* (New York: Oxford University Press, 1984).
61 George A. Rawlyk, *Ravished by the Spirit: Religious Revivals, Baptists, and Henry Alline* (Kingston, ON: McGill-Queens University Press, 1984), 14; Richard L. Bushman, *Joseph Smith and the Beginnings of Mormonism* (Urbana: University of Illinois Press, 1984), 59.
62 Hatch, *Democratization of American Christianity*, 68–9.
63 McLoughlin, *New England Dissent*, 2: 45–9.
64 Charles Francis Kilgore, *The James O'Kelly Schism in the Methodist Episcopal Church* (Mexico City: Casa Unida de Publicaciones, 1963); Edward J. Drinkhouse, *A History of Methodist Reform*, 2 vols. (Baltimore, MD: Board of Publication of the Methodist Protestant Church, 1899), especially volume one; Milo T. Morrill, *A History of the Christian Denomination in America, 1794–1911* (Dayton, OH: Christian Publishing Association, 1912).
65 "The Last Will and Testament of the Springfield Presbytery" (1847), in John Rogers, *The Biography of Elder Barton Warren Stone* (Paris, KY: Cane Ridge Preservation Project, 1972), 1–3; Robert Marshall and Barton W. Stone, *An Apology for Renouncing the Jurisdiction of the Synod of Kentucky* (Lexington, KY: Joseph Charles, 1804); Hatch, *Democratization of American Christianity*, 70–1.
66 Robert Richardson, *Memories of Alexander Campbell* (Cincinnati, OH: Standard Publishing Company, 1913), 1: 438, 465–6; Alexander Campbell, "An Oration in Honor of the Fourth of July, 1830," in *Popular Lectures and Addresses*, ed. Alexander Campbell (Philadelphia: J. Challen, 1863), 374–5; Hatch, *Democratization of American Christianity*, 71, 73.
67 Jon Butler et al., *Religion in American Life: A Short History*, 2nd edn. (New York: Oxford University Press, 2011), 80.
68 Thomas S. Kidd, *God of Liberty: A Religious History of the American Revolution* (New York: Basic Books, 2010), 189; Butler, *Religion in American Life*, 80–1.
69 Francis Asbury, *The Journal and Letters of Francis Asbury*, ed. Elmer C. Clark, J. Manning Potts and Jacob S. Payton (Nashville, TN: Abingdon Press, 1958), 3: 341–5, 453; Elizabeth Nottingham, *Methodism and the Frontier Indiana Proving Ground* (New York: Columbia University Press, 1944).
70 David Hempton, *Methodism and Politics in British Society 1750—1850* (Stanford, CA: Stanford University Press, 1984), 73; Mathews, "The Second Great Awakening," 36.

71 Asbury, *Journal and Letters*, 3: 475–8, 492.
72 Hatch, *Democratization of American Christianity*, 8.
73 Hatch, *Democratization of American Christianity*, 93–5; James A. Rogers, *Richard Furman: Life and Legacy* (Macon, GA: Mercer University Press, 1985), 179, 293–5; Robert G. Torbet, *History of the Baptists* (Chicago: Judson Press, 1963), 310.
74 McLoughlin, *New England Dissent*, 2: 915–38; Byron Cecil Lambert, *The Rise of the Anti-Mission Baptists: Sources and Leaders, 1800—1840* (New York: Arno Press, 1980), 116–52; John Leland, *An Oration Delivered at Cheshire, Massachusetts, July 5, 1802, on the Celebration of Independence* (Hudson, NY: Charles Holt, 1802), 12.
75 Hatch, *Democratization of American Christianity*, 99.
76 Hatch, *Democratization of American Christianity*, 101. See also: Lambert, *Rise of the Anti-Mission Baptists*.
77 Hatch, *Democratization of American Christianity*, 162.

Recommended for further reading

Butler, Jon. *Awash in a Sea of Faith: Christianizing the American People*. Cambridge, MA: Harvard University Press, 1990.

Fea, John. *Was America Founded as a Christian Nation? A Historical Introduction*. Louisville, KY: Westminster John Knox Press, 2011.

Gaustad, Edwin S. *Faith of the Founders: Religion and the New Nation, 1776–1826*, 2nd edn. Waco, TX: Baylor University Press, 2004.

Hambrick-Stowe, Charles E. *Charles G. Finney and the Spirit of American Evangelicalism*. Grand Rapids, MI: W. B. Eerdmans, 1996.

Hatch, Nathan O. *The Democratization of American Christianity*. New Haven, CT: Yale University Press, 1989.

Lambert, Frank. *The Founding Fathers and the Place of Religion in America*. Princeton, NJ: Princeton University Press, 2003.

Levy, Leonard W. *The Establishment Clause: Religion and the First Amendment*. New York: Macmillan Publishing Company, 1986.

Sehat, David. *The Myth of American Religious Freedom*. New York: Oxford University Press, 2011.

Waldman, Steven. *Founding Faith: Providence, Politics, and the Birth of Religious Freedom in America*. New York: Random House, 2008.

Wigger, John H. *Taking Heaven by Storm: Methodism and the Rise of Popular Christianity in America*. New York: Oxford University Press, 1998.

Chapter 5

Religion and the age of reform

The great age of American reform

Nineteenth-century reformers commonly believed they were heeding God's will and appealed to God as the ultimate authority for their crusade. Buoyed by the prospects of the prosperous new nation, middle-class Americans became inspired by a postmillennial perfectionism and set out to create the "city on a hill" John Winthrop had promised two centuries earlier. The earliest efforts at reform grew out of the missionary impulses of evangelical Protestant churches but in time moved beyond the churches. Similarly, women served as the rank and file of the reform movement, seeking to transform the nation but in the process transformed their role in American society and American religion.

American Transcendentalism

American Transcendentalists resisted any attempt to be labeled. As a result, many historians have resorted to describing what the group represented as a loosely organized literary or intellectual movement. But Transcendentalism was first and foremost a religious movement. In fact, American Transcendentalism developed in the 1830s as a revolt against what Ralph Waldo Emerson called "the corpse-cold Unitarianism of Harvard College and Brattle Street." Seventeen of the Transcendental Club's twenty-six members were Unitarian ministers, and they hoped to use their belief in the intuitive perception of spiritual and moral truth to restore Unitarianism's idealism and pietism without losing its freethinking and individualism and without resorting to the excesses of emotional revivalism.[1]

American Transcendentalism was but a distinctive phase of a far larger movement that existed in Western civilization. It was part of the Romantic Movement, which was itself a successor to the Enlightenment and in part a revolt against eighteenth-century rationalism. Thus, American Transcendentalism's impulses came from abroad, especially in the works of English Romantics such as Scott, Wordsworth, Coleridge, and Carlyle and in the English translations of French and German writers like Cousin, Kant, Fichte, and Schleiermacher. To a lesser extent, ideas from the Orient were influential as well.[2]

Scholars often date the beginning of American Transcendentalism to 1836, the year the Transcendental Club met for the first time. It was also the year Emerson published his classic, *Nature*, wherein he presented the Transcendental prescription for losing one's egotistical self and becoming one with God. Through nature, Emerson argued, it becomes possible for man to enjoy firsthand contact with God. When contemplating nature, he wrote: "I become a transparent eyeball; I am nothing; I see all; the currents of the Universal Being circulate through me; I am part or parcel of God."[3]

Perhaps the principal event in the religious history of the American Transcendental Movement, however, was Ralph Waldo Emerson's "Divinity School Address" delivered at Harvard on July 15, 1838. Asked by members of the graduating class to address them at their commencement, Emerson decided to take the opportunity to express opinions about religion that he had been considering ever since leaving the ministry in 1832. As Donald Koster has put it, Emerson's address "proved to be an intellectual grenade exploded in the very halls of authority."[4] His address touched off an acrimonious controversy, but it also became one of the basic documents of the movement and a profound influence on American religion in the nineteenth century.

Emerson began his address by celebrating what he called "moral sentiment," or intuitive insight into moral and spiritual laws that could never be received secondhand. Everybody, he explained, possesses this sentiment. It represents the "indwelling Supreme Spirit" in all men and women and it is "the essence of all religion." The Christian church, Emerson continued, had come to neglect the moral sentiment and in doing so had fallen into two serious errors: (1) It exaggerated the personal and miraculous authority of Jesus Christ; and (2) it looked upon revelation itself as past and dead and confined to biblical times. The "assumption that the age of inspiration is past, that the Bible is closed," Emerson argued, and "the fear of degrading the character of Jesus by representing him as a man, indicate with clearness the falsehood of our theology."[5]

Erroneous views of miracles and of revelation, said Emerson, were responsible for a decaying church and waning belief. The only remedy for the erosion of faith was to recognize the reality of the moral sentiment and our ability, through it, to achieve "eternal revelation in the heart" today, as Jesus did centuries ago. Avoid secondary knowledge, Emerson advised the would-be ministers. Dare to love God without mediator or veil and in preaching try to acquaint people firsthand with God. It was the office of a true teacher, he declared, to "show us that God is, not was; that He speaketh, not spake."[6]

Andrews Norton attacked Emerson's address in the Boston *Daily Advertiser.* Norton was the leading Unitarian theologian of the time. Recently retired as Professor of Sacred Literature in the Harvard Divinity School, he had just published (in 1837) the first volume of his three-volume *Evidences of the Genuineness of the Gospels.* In that volume, Norton found the basic evidence for the Christian religion in Jesus's miracles. When Emerson called them into question, Norton charged him with weakening the very foundation of Christian theology and with calling into question whether he believed in God at all.[7]

George Ripley attacked Norton for writing off as unbelievers all who shared Emerson's views. To do this, he wrote, was to enforce the exclusive principle that Calvinists had applied to Unitarians earlier in the century, when the latter cast overboard the Trinity and other orthodox Christian doctrines. Ripley recalled that Norton had once been a champion of intellectual freedom and had formerly reprimanded the orthodox for being so presumptuous as to define Christianity in such a way as to exclude Unitarians.[8]

Theodore Parker, Unitarian minister in West Roxbury, followed the controversy surrounding Emerson's "Divinity School Address." He found the address to be "the noblest and most inspiring strain I ever listened to," but he was also amused by the commotion it had created. "It is thought that chaos is coming back," he told a friend, and that the world was coming to an end. "For my part," he added, "I see that the sun still shines, the rain rains, and the dogs bark, and I have great doubts whether Emerson will overthrow Christianity at this time."[9]

Parker's entry into the fray created an especially difficult situation for Norton and his group because, unlike Emerson and Ripley, Parker remained in the church. In fact, the most controversial of his remarks on Emerson's address came in an ordination sermon he delivered in South Boston on May 19, 1841. He chose as his topic "A Discourse on the Transient and Permanent in Christianity," the title of which was drawn from an essay by David Strauss, whose *Life of Jesus*, published in Germany in 1835, was regarded as outlandish by liberal as well as orthodox Christians.[10]

Parker argued that Christian forms, rites, creeds, doctrines, theology, and even the church itself, were transitory. Only the great truths intuited by Jesus had enduring value for the human race. In this regard, Parker quickly dismissed the infallible inspiration of both the Old and New Testaments, as well as the personal authority of Jesus. "It is hard to see," he wrote, "why the great truths of Christianity rest on the personal authority of Jesus, more than the axioms of geometry rest on the personal authority of Euclid or Archimedes." Even if Jesus had never lived, said Parker, the truths he taught would stand firm, though, of course, the world would have lost the example of his "beautiful character."[11]

The uproar over Parker's ordination sermon was even greater than that over Emerson's "Divinity School Address." He was ostracized publicly by most of his fellow-ministers, all but a handful refusing to allow him in their pulpits. "As far as the ministers are concerned," lamented Parker, "I am alone, ALL ALONE." This was especially true after Parker delivered a series of lectures in Boston in 1841 and 1842, subsequently published as *A Discourse of Matters Pertaining to Religion* (1842), in which he announced: "If Christianity be true at all, it would be just as true if Herod or Catiline had taught it."[12]

The Boston Association of Unitarian ministers held a special meeting in January 1843, wherein they tried unsuccessfully to persuade Parker to resign. They could not muster the votes to expel him, but he remained a virtual pariah in the Unitarian community. In 1853, the executive committee of the American Unitarian Association, "in a denominational capacity," separated itself from the errors of Transcendentalism and declared its faith in "the Divine origin, the Divine authority, [and] the Divine sanctions of the religion of Jesus Christ." Nevertheless, several of the younger ministers rallied to Parker's cause, and the breach was never sealed. Even when Parker lay near death in Italy in 1859, the Boston Association turned down a resolution to express sympathy for him in his suffering.[13]

Emerson's, Ripley's, and Parker's critiques of miracles and Christ pulled the props out from under historical Christianity, but none of the three ever ceased to admire Jesus as a moral leader. Some Transcendentalists thought Emerson's view of religion was focused too much on the individual believer. Ripley, for example, believed that the purpose of Christianity was to redeem society as well as the individual from sin, and after resigning his pastorate, he organized an experimental community at Brook Farm. William Henry Channing founded a church for workers in New York City in 1836 and experimented with several independent churches dedicated to social reform in New York and Boston. And Orestes Brownson wrote *New Views of Christianity, Society, and the Church* (1836), in which he argued that a kind of transcendentalized Unitarianism, uniting spiritual Christianity with material social reform, could bring about the Kingdom of God on earth.[14]

Religion and reform

Once the War of 1812 ended, a combination of theological and economic developments led many men and women to assume that the world did not have to be the way it was and that individual efforts mattered. These were the articles of faith for middle-class Americans with their confidence in progress and human will. They were encouraged by the religious revivalism of the period, which taught that good deeds were the mark of godliness and that the millennium was near.[15]

Reform took place in a period that seemed much in need of reform. In the course of a half-century, the nation had been transformed in ways unanticipated and not entirely welcome. Immigration, urbanization, and industrialization had begun to change the social and cultural landscape. During the 1830s, approximately 600,000 people came to the United States, a four-fold increase over the 1820s. In the next decade, the figure rose to 1.7 million and then to 2.6 million in the 1850s. At the same time, the proportion of Americans working in manufacturing and commerce and living in cities rose. New cities sprang up and old ones boomed. In 1810, there were 46 urban areas (defined as places with 2,500 or more population). In 1860, there were 393, including two cities – New York and Philadelphia – with over 500,000 residents.[16]

Cities were ripe for moral crusades. Reformers regarded them as dismal swamps of vice, disease, and misery. But increasingly, reformers turned their attention to slavery. Located almost entirely in the North, they came to see the South's peculiar institution as a relic of barbarism, and their own way of life as representing the course of civilization and progress. In this way, economic differences strongly reinforced moral judgments.[17]

America's increased prosperity meant that there were more numerous middle-class men and women with education, income, and leisure to devote to social causes. New technologies put powerful weapons in the hands of such people. The same transportation revolution that brought goods to distant markets also carried lecturers to widely dispersed audiences reformers could not have reached a generation before. Innovations reduced the cost of printing to the point where reformers could produce newspapers, pamphlets, and even books for a national readership.

Finally, the age of reform was marked by significant changes in the nature of politics. Not only had the Age of Jackson arrived, wherein the United States became more democratic and engaged in more democratic rhetoric, but a new style of politics emerged. With a rapidly increasing electorate and number of offices open to election, politicians began to court potential voters. Reformers reacted to this by complaining that a degraded and sinful majority was being manipulated by political machines, but many reformers nevertheless designed their crusades with politics in mind. If everything worked according to plan, temperance, Sunday schools, and public education would produce a morally responsible electorate. Evangelical Protestants lobbied Congress in 1828 to stop postal employees from working on Sunday, and in the next decade, abolitionists mounted a petition campaign urging Congress to take a stand against slavery. Ultimately, some reformers began to run their own candidates for political office.[18]

The missionary impulse

Antebellum reform was directly linked to the Second Great Awakening. Whether it came in camp meetings or from the pulpit of the local church, the evangelical message was proclaimed across the land and the public responded with explosions of spiritual zeal. Evangelicals both celebrated American freedom and economic prosperity and cautioned the American people against the potential such a new world presented for loss of commitment to God and community. At the same time that they shared in the nation's faith in progress, their sermons were filled with the rhetoric of sin, damnation, and salvation. Reformers shared this bifurcated world-view. Moreover, revivals provided reformers with techniques for organizing and propagandizing.[19]

A MILLERITE PREPARING FOR THE 23ʳᵈ OF APRIL.
"Now let it come! I'm ready."

Figure 5.1 William Miller seated in a well

Source: Granger Historical Picture Archive/Alamy Stock Photo

Evangelical clergy and laymen engaged in moral crusades of their own and appeared in the lead of secular ones like temperance and antislavery. Such revivalistic institutions as Lane Seminary and Oberlin College were breeding grounds for reformers, many of whom had been inspired by Charles Grandison Finney and Lyman Beecher. In regions like the Western Reserve of Ohio and the "burned-over district" of New York, reform movements followed close on the heels of revivals, while even reform political parties, like the abolitionist Liberty Party, did best in areas where religious enthusiasm had run high.[20]

The American Revolution and the Second Great Awakening prompted a renewal of millennialism as seen in providential rhetoric that revealed God's approval of both. Premillennialists continued to hold that the return of Christ, the Day of Judgment, and an end to history were imminent. The best known of the premillennialists of the pre-Civil War period was William Miller (see Figure 5.1), a farmer from Low Hampton, New York, who underwent a conversion experience and became a Baptist. By his interpretation of the Bible, Christ was to return in 1843, a prediction widely disseminated by the Boston minister Joshua Hines. The result, by several estimates, was tens of thousands of Americans preparing for the Second Coming.[21]

Miller initially predicted Christ's return in March 1843. When that did not happen, he recalculated the date as March 1844 and then October 22 of the same year. Reports circulated that many Millerites abandoned their jobs and property and gathered on hilltops to await the Second Coming. At the very least, many gathered and prayed in expectation. Not surprisingly, scores of the disillusioned abandoned Miler, but many continued to believe that the Second Coming was imminent. Some found a home among the Seventh-Day Adventists, founded on the teachings of Ellen G. White, herself a Miller convert. Others would find the premillennialist teachings of Charles Taze Russell more to their liking, which would provide the basis for the Jehovah's Witnesses.[22]

Postmillennialists, however, were more numerous and of greater significance in antebellum reform. They may have disagreed over whether the reign of God was near or far, whether it would begin cataclysmically or quietly, but they agreed that it would be a real historical era occurring before the Final Judgment and that it would consist of a thousand years of peace, prosperity, harmony, and Christian morality. Their vision of the ideal society made the imperfections of their own day stark by comparison. Moreover, it assured them that a better world was possible, thereby spurring antebellum crusaders into action.[23]

Millennial optimism merged with a belief that the United States was chosen by God to fulfill a great mission to defeat the forces of irreligion and evil, thereby "setting the stage for the triumph of virtue and righteousness," an old notion given new life in the antebellum period by territorial expansion and religious revivals. This idea of national destiny – manifest destiny – was a driving force in the conquest of a continent, but it was also employed by reformers. They claimed that America's special place in God's design not only justified their attempts to dominate lands and people in the West morally and physically, but it also meant that its sins were more heinous than those of other countries and that their reforms were urgently needed. The divine plan, indeed the millennium, depended on it.[24]

Millennialism's missionary impulse would not have been so strong if clergymen had not told mankind it could help God usher in his kingdom. When nineteenth-century preachers made that claim, they were abandoning a line of theology stretching from John Calvin through early American Congregationalism and Presbyterianism. Calvinists maintained that human beings were innately sinful and could, of their own free will, do nothing pleasing to God. By the early years of the nineteenth century, clergy such as Charles Grandison Finney repudiated those propositions.[25]

Finney developed the concept of "disinterested benevolence," which he saw as the sum of all holiness or virtue. The phrase itself had an honorable history in American Protestantism going back to Jonathan Edwards. Finney, however, took any trace of Calvinism out of it and turned it into an inspiration for reformers. Finney was certain that people could act virtuously if they wanted to, so he tried to persuade them of the "utility of benevolence." Using reasoning more reminiscent of Ben Franklin than John Calvin, Finney insisted that men and women not only could, but also should, "set out with a determination to aim at being useful in the highest degrees." Of true Christians, Finney wrote: "To the universal reformation of the world they stand committed."[26]

Central to Finney's theology was a doctrine of perfectionism, the idea that individuals could become sanctified while on earth. He and the majority of evangelicals accepted a modern form of this doctrine, while staunchly rejecting a dangerous implication in it – the possibility that sanctified persons could do no wrong. Thus, perfectionism became an energizing principle, giving inspiration to people who wanted to impose absolute moral integrity upon their own lives and upon a changing world. Perfectionists believed that anything short of millennial standards should not be tolerated and that belief was manifested in abolitionism, temperance, and other reform movements, as well as in attempts to construct new social orders, or utopias.[27]

Reform movements

Most of the early nineteenth-century Protestant voluntary organizations clustered in New England and the Mid-Atlantic States. A few of them aimed at specific "sins," but others were quite general in scope, like the Connecticut Society for the Reformation of Morals, established in 1813. Such groups drew upon local clergy and pious laymen, who acted as a kind of moral police, pointing out immorality and law-breaking that elected officials preferred to ignore.[28]

The largest Protestant voluntary associations were dedicated to missionary activity. The first national association was the American Board of Commissioners for Foreign Missions, begun by Congregationalists in 1810. The American Bible Society came into existence in 1816, with the goal of putting the Scriptures into the hands of every family in the nation, while the American Sunday School Union (1824) established a similar goal for children. The most significant of all, however, was the American Tract Society, formed in 1825, which issued a never-ending stream of publications. By 1830, voluntary associations covered the country with the printed word and had thousands of auxiliaries contributing to the cause. Firmly revivalistic, but also reformist, these groups preached against lack of faith as well as for moral causes.[29]

By 1830, Protestant voluntary associations constituted a loosely interconnected "benevolent empire." Although formally distinct from each other, these evangelical organizations propagated the same world-view, tapped the same financial resources, and had many of the same people on their boards of directors. They often held their conventions at the same times and in the same cities, thereby permitting a measure of coordinated action. In 1829, they mounted an especially energetic campaign in the West.[30]

The agencies of the benevolent empire had other things in common besides ideology, membership, and sources of revenue. Many of them were interdenominational. The managers of the Sunday School Union and the Bible Society, for example, included Presbyterians, Congregationalists, Methodists, Episcopalians, Baptists, Dutch Reformed, and a few Moravians and Quakers. And the laity played a crucial role in such organizations. Clergy were never absent, but what is striking is the time, money, and administrative skill contributed by laymen. People like Arthur and Lewis Tappan, wealthy New York merchants, were at the center of nearly every one of the major religious and secular reforms of the day: antislavery, pacifism, temperance, health, education, and women's rights, to name just a few.[31]

Religious communitarianism

Since the War of 1812, John Humphrey Noyes wrote in 1870, "the line of socialistic excitements lies parallel with the line of religious revivals." Noyes had in mind the experiments in living attempted by small groups of antebellum reformers, many of which grew out of the millennial impulse discussed earlier. These were little utopias carved out of the American countryside, dedicated to one or another social or religious theory and designed to serve as models for the rest of the world. Noyes pointed to the failings of revivalists and utopians: Revivalists "failed for want of regeneration of society," and utopians "failed for want of regeneration of the heart." The unwillingness of the two to unite "their two great ideas" was all the more tragic, he continued, because they had so much in common. They shared a faith in the perfectible nature of mankind and a belief that the millennium was at hand. Both desired "to bring heaven on earth."[32]

Over a hundred communitarian societies were built in the nineteenth century prior to the Civil War; the exact number is uncertain. The greatest wave of enthusiasm for utopian ventures came in the 1840s in the aftermath of the revivals of the 1820s and 1830s. Most communities lasted no more than a few years and involved only a small number of active members, but their importance as expressions of antebellum reform transcends such statistics. Communitarians aimed at creating a totally new order rather than improving the old one. As Noyes recognized, it was the ultimate expression of perfectionist and millennialist logic.[33]

It is difficult at first to see much coherence in anything so varied as antebellum communalism. The communities themselves ranged from highly structured to utterly unstructured, from theological to freethinking, from celibate to "free love." To make sense out of the diversity, historians have developed different classifications. The simplest approach divides the communities between those that were primarily organized around religious doctrines and those that were primarily secular. We shall concentrate on the former.

Utopias of European origin

Some of the largest and most stable utopian societies in antebellum America were neither antebellum nor American in origin. These ventures represent a particular kind of religious communalism, best labeled pietistic. The communities themselves were in the United States but not especially of it. Several traced their ancestry to German sects, the rest to other seventeenth- or eighteenth-century European religious splinter groups. The most notable of the German-speaking communities – Ephrata, Harmony, Zoar, and Amana – were especially adept at keeping their Old-World character in the midst of a rapidly changing new world. We shall consider only the first two and the Shakers.

1   Ephrata was not quite the first, nor was it the largest, utopian society in North America, but by the antebellum period, it was the oldest. Ephrata's founder, Conrad Beissel, left the Palatinate in 1720 apparently with the idea of joining Woman in the Wilderness, a mystical community of German Pietists who gathered in the Pennsylvania forest to await the millennium. By the time Beissel arrived, most members of the Woman in the Wilderness had scattered or died. Beissel remained, however, and spent much of the next twelve years in hermit-like spiritual contemplation. In 1724, he joined the Dunkers, a German sect, but in 1728, he published a work contradicting some of their doctrines. He attracted a few followers, and in 1732, he established Ephrata, near Lancaster, Pennsylvania, as a communitarian society or cloister.[34]

     The days of those who lived at Ephrata were filled with work and worship. Their diet was sparse and vegetarian, and their dress was homespun. Men lived in one large building, women in another, and little in those dwellings distracted them from spiritual thoughts. The rooms were small and Spartan, and the residences were constructed and furnished without the use of metal, in imitation of Solomon's temple.[35]

     For all its plainness and religiosity, Ephrata did not have absolutely rigid rules on two matters quite crucial to later communitarians: sexual relationships and private property. Beissel did not insist upon chastity, but he encouraged it, and most of his followers were celibate in the mid-eighteenth century, when their numbers reached 300. The community punished "the untimely intercourse of some of the brethren," but over the years, there was a decline in celibacy as well as in membership. By 1800, most of the Ephratans were married. Beissel also did not demand that all property be held in common, although the community as a whole owned whatever was donated to Ephrata or produced by its residents. Those who valued worldly goods simply left the cloister, took housing nearby, and became "'outdoor" members, over whom Beissel and his successors exercised less rigorous discipline.[36]

By the early nineteenth century, Ephrata was a relic. Beissel died in 1768. Peter Miller, his successor, survived him by twenty-eight years, leaving no one with his or Beissel's intellect and personal power to carry on. Ephrata inspired interest and at least one imitator in the nineteenth century, but by then, it was not even the most vital of the German pietistic communities, an honor that more properly belonged to George Rapp's Harmony Society.[37]

2   In 1791, Rapp, a 33-year-old German farmer, told an official investigating his religious beliefs, "I am a prophet and called to be one." Rapp had been in conflict with the established Lutheran Church of Württemberg, and in 1803, that conflict caused him and several hundred disciples to leave for the United States. He purchased land in western Pennsylvania, and in February 1805, he incorporated the Harmony Society.[38]

Although living conditions were primitive at first, the Harmonists were steady and industrious. In a decade, they cleared and cultivated over 2,000 acres of land, and as early as 1807, they were selling goods to the outside world. In 1815, dissatisfied with the climate, the soil, and the difficulty of getting their products to market, the Harmonists sold their Pennsylvania property and moved to Indiana, where they continued to grow and prosper, but, for reasons that are not clear, the society moved again in 1825. It sold everything to Robert Owen, the wealthy British social theorist, and returned to Pennsylvania to land north of Pittsburgh. The society's third home was named Economy. At first, the Harmonists did well, despite a slow drop in their population, but by 1874, they closed several factories for lack of a labor force. By 1900, the society had fewer than ten members.[39]

Harmony was a worldlier place than Ephrata, yet the two had some similar characteristics. Each was the creation of a vigorous and compelling founder. Rapp's control over his followers, although occasionally challenged, remained firm until his death in 1847, at age 90. Each community was millennialistic. Rapp informed an inquirer in 1822 that Harmonists "believe without doubt that the kingdom of Jesus Christ [is] approaching near." If anything, Harmonists were more consistent in banning private ownership of property than Ephratans had been, but like the Ephratans, Harmonists generally remained celibate. Rapp had advocated sexual abstinence as early as 1791, but he did not make it policy until 1807, and even then, he made exceptions. Celibacy and unwillingness to proselytize non-Germans, however, had the same effect on the Harmony Society as on Ephrata. The membership grew old, died, and left none to keep the faith.[40]

3   The American career of the Shakers was rooted in the spiritual experiences of Ann Lee, the illiterate daughter of a Manchester (England) blacksmith. Born in 1736, she took to factory and menial labor at an early age. While still a young woman, she married Abraham Stanley, a blacksmith, like her father. It was an unhappy match. Ann Lee apparently felt repugnance at sexual intercourse and suffered through the birth and premature loss

of four children. Before marrying Stanley, she had joined the Shakers, a small sect tracing its lineage to seventeenth-century France and so named for the convulsive dance that was part of their ritual. Fired with zeal, she preached, prayed, and went into trances. She was also persecuted by mobs and by authorities, who occasionally threw Ann Lee and fellow-Shakers into prison. While in jail in 1770, she had a revelation and upon her release began to attract followers, who accepted her as "Mother in Christ." In 1774, another revelation directed her and eight followers to take passage to America. Her husband accompanied her but abandoned her soon after they arrived in New York.[41]

Mother Ann and her tiny flock moved to Watervliet, New York, where they endured difficult times both because of the hardships of making a living and because of the hostility of neighbors, who suspected them of pro-British sympathies in the American Revolution. She died in 1784, three years before the sect formed its first true communal settlement in Mount Lebanon, New York.[42]

The Shakers began to grow after 1799, when a Baptist revival swept the country around Mount Lebanon. In what would prove to be a persistent pattern, they gathered in men and women who had been awakened by evangelical preaching but not satisfied by it. The Shakers took advantage of revivals going on in the West by sending out preachers of their own. The result was another rich harvest of converts and formation of half a dozen new communities. At their height in the 1830s, the Shakers numbered around 6,000.[43]

Although Mother Ann was central to their theology, the Shakers owed their organizational success to her successors. In 1787, Joseph Meacham and Lucy Wright became the first American-born leaders. In 1836, Frederick W. Evans became an elder, a position he held for fifty-seven years. All three proved to be effective administrators and propagandists for the Shakers. For all their ability, however, much of the Shakers' strength was in their distinctive and compelling way of life.[44]

Mother Ann Lee had taught that God was both male and female in nature, with Jesus representing the masculine side. Since Mother Ann represented the feminine side, her coming marked completion of God's revelation and the beginning of the Kingdom of Heaven on earth. This was a variety of millennialism and an assertion of the spiritual equality of men and women. Both sexes shared authority throughout the sect's hierarchy, from its "Head of Influence" at Mount Lebanon to the "families" (or smaller groups of men and women) that were the basic unit within each community. There were few places in American society where females were so emancipated from their usual roles as wives and mothers and granted so much genuine influence. Thus, it is not surprising that by the middle of the nineteenth century most Shakers were women.[45]

Shaker men and women lived in chastity as well as relative equality. Mother Ann made "Virgin Purity" a pillar of her faith and insisted that her followers be celibate. Shakers believed that sexuality was an animal passion belonging to a lower, less spiritual order of existence. Even though many non-Shakers shared that belief, few antebellum Americans went to the extreme of trying to ban sexual intercourse altogether, and Shakerism struck many observers as being cold and contrary to human nature.[46]

Yet one of the secrets of Shakerism's appeal was the way it alternated self-denial with emotional release. Much of a Shaker's day was spent in silence, hard work, and emotional restraint. Various rituals, however, provided moments of sheer ecstasy. The most curious of these, and the best known, was the dance that was part of Shaker services. The dance and its accompanying music changed over time, but it always was a performance in which both sexes participated, parading in what visitors described as odd, regimented movements, sometimes dignified, sometimes spasmodic. The Shakers also went through periods of special enthusiasm, as in the late 1830s and early 1840s, when each of their communities was swept by spiritualism, mystical experiences, and speaking in tongues. The Shakers gave regular expression to evangelical emotionality and made it all the more intense by mixing it with asceticism.[47]

Finally, on the matter of private property, the Shakers were among the most radical of utopians. They did away with distinctions in "temporal blessings" about as completely as any American commune ever has. But theirs was "Christian Communism," to use Ronald Walters's phrase, not the modem, secular variety. "They shared their possessions because they did not did not value them much; their eyes were on heaven."[48]

American communitarianism

Although pietistic societies were beginning to fade as early as the 1820s, they had lessons to teach later communitarians. The pietistic communities had begun the process of breaking away from conventional notions of family relationships and private property. Their pacifism, millennialism, and ability to survive provided a model and inspiration. American communitarians after 1825 generally operated within the Christian tradition, just as eighteenth-century Pietists did, but each took different components from it, which in turn led to different modes of behavior. The Pietists drew upon the communalism, monasticism, and mysticism of the primitive church. Later utopians lived out a Social Gospel, bringing Protestant principles to bear upon the wider world around them, as well as within the community. Brook Farm and Oneida provide two instructive examples of the latter group.

1   Brook Farm, begun in 1844 and located in West Roxbury, Massachusetts, was a product of New England culture. Compared to communities like Hopedale, Brook Farm was not as infused with reform zeal; if anything, it was more individualistic. But it was also religious in inspiration. Elizabeth Peabody spoke of an early plan for it as "Christ's Idea of Society," and it originated in conversations between two Unitarian ministers, William Ellery Channing and George Ripley. In 1841, Ripley and some colleagues purchased land and began the community.[49]

Brook Farm is sometimes characterized as a "Transcendentalist Utopia," but what it owed to Transcendentalism is not completely clear. Transcendentalism itself was not a coherent set of doctrines. It was more a sensibility and a set of attitudes about mankind and nature. Ripley may have found in Transcendentalism a belief in the limitless potential of human beings, but as Ronald Walters has pointed out, other communitarians got the same belief from evangelical Protestantism, through its perfectionist strain. Reform was at the heart of American Transcendentalism, and in communities like Brook Farm, members sought "a life free of the debasing materialism of the spiritually bankrupt conventions of American society." But there was no hope of social betterment, from the Transcendentalist point of view, unless people took their cues from the "great inward Commander." Thus, Ralph Waldo Emerson, for one, agonized over whether to join Brook Farm and finally convinced himself that he was more valuable preserving his autonomy and remaining unaffiliated.[50]

Brook Farm encouraged serious self-development. George Ripley had hoped "to insure a more natural union between intellectual and manual labor than now exists." Accordingly, the community was organized so that all members not only worked with their hands but also had the means "for intellectual improvement and for social inter-course, calculated to refine and expand." Some, like Nathaniel Hawthorne, were not enchanted by having to do farm chores, but others were enthusiastic about the other arts. "The weeds," George William Curtis recalled fondly, "were scratched out of the ground to the music of Tennyson and Browning." And whatever the effect upon weeds, Brook Farm's cultural ferment was unparalleled among American utopian societies. In 1845, Brook Farm took over publication of the *Phalanx*, a New York Fourierist periodical, renamed it the *Harbinger*, and made it into an important weekly journal. Brook Farm's schools were well staffed and remarkably flexible for the times. They had a broad liberal arts curriculum, broke with the practice of rote memorization, and attempted to combine learning with doing.[51]

From its beginnings, Brook Farm was economically marginal. It was organized as a dividend paying joint-stock venture, but it was too Transcendental to be profit-making. The founders hoped to make "the acquisition of individual property subservient to upright and disinterested uses." They nonetheless sought to "reserve sufficient private property, or means of obtaining it, for all purposes of independence." The result was a muddle of community and private interests, which would have been troublesome if Brook Farm had been prosperous. As it was, the real problem was making ends meet. In 1846, after a brief period or reorganization as a Fourieristic Phalanx, a disastrous fire swept the expensive and uninsured new main building. The community closed and the remaining property was sold in 1849.[52]

2   Where Brook Farm was shaped by Ripley's Unitarianism and Transcendentalism, Oneida was a product of evangelical Protestantism. Its founder was John Humphrey Noyes, a Vermonter by birth; a Dartmouth College, Andover Theological Seminary, and Yale Divinity School man by education; and a lawyer and clergyman by training. He had what was probably the most original mind of any American communitarian.[53]

While at Yale Divinity School, Noyes came to believe that once a person was saved, he or she became perfect, that is, incapable of sinning. He believed he had reached that state on February 20, 1834. In 1837, Noyes first voiced his unorthodox sexual ideas. Abigail Merwin, an early convert whom Noyes loved, spurned both him and his doc-trines, and married another man. Much grieved, Noyes wrote to a follower that "when the will of God is done on earth as it is in heaven there will be no marriage." Among those who become perfect, all will belong to each other; there will be no exclusive attachments. Thus, Merwin would be his bride in spirit, even if she was another man's under human law.[54]

In June 1838, Noyes married Harriet Holton and the couple settled in Putney, Ver-mont, where Noyes's tiny congregation of disciples printed his works and developed his doctrines and practices. In 1841, the group began to organize and to pool its resources, and three years later Noyes, his brother George and two of his brothers-in-law created a financial partnership, which they soon opened to anyone who cared to invest in it. By 1846, the Putney perfectionists were evolving the legal and economic structure of a communal society, but they also were beginning the marital experiments that would cause them to be driven from Vermont. That spring, John and Harriet Noyes and George and Mary Cragin began a system of "complex marriage," maintaining that it was not a sin for any sanctified man and woman to have intercourse. Noyes's two sisters and their husbands joined the complex marriage, and by the end of 1846, the central members of the Putney group declared themselves a community of persons as well as of property.

By the fall of 1847, Noyes fled to New York City to avoid prosecution on charges of adultery, and shortly after, he and some of the Putney group joined a communal settlement begun by fellow-perfectionists in Madison County, New York. Together they formed the Oneida Association.[55]

In addition to complex marriages, Noyes's program at Oneida involved birth control and planned reproduction. Of the few methods available in the early 1840s, Noyes chose male continence, or intercourse without ejaculation. He promoted male continence for various reasons, including health: It freed women from pregnancy and spared men the expenditure of seminal fluid, which Noyes, like many nineteenth-century Americans, believed was debilitating. He also added theological arguments. Male continence, he maintained, was part of God's design. It would "give speed to the advance of civilization and refinement." With fear of pregnancy banished, sexual intercourse would become "a joyful act of fellowship" or even a religious ritual.[56]

Sexual encounters at Oneida were subject to a variety of rules and regulations. By the 1860s, all requests for intercourse had to be made through a third party and were duly recorded in a ledger. In 1869, the community began to experiment with planned reproduction, or "stirpiculture." A committee approved, even suggested, "scientific combinations" of community members to become parents. Since Noyes believed moral characteristics were passed on to children, the men, and women selected were supposed to be the most spiritually advanced in the community, but some attention was given to physical conditions as well. During the next decade, fifty-eight children were born at Oneida, thirteen conceived accidentally and forty-five as stirpiculture babies. Nine of the children were fathered by Noyes.[57]

Oneida flourished in spite of the hostility its sexual practices aroused. Noyes attributed the community's endurance to what he saw as two of the essential features of stable utopian societies: community ownership of property and an emphasis on manufacturing and commerce rather than agriculture. By the 1870s, however, younger members absorbed new ideas from their college education on the outside. The result was an undercurrent of questioning of the old ways and a decline in religious fervor. Noyes's failing leadership was an even greater problem. Although he clearly was the driving force of Oneida, he was too often absent. In 1875, he tried to impose his son Theodore, a Yale-trained physician, as head of the community. The community balked, however, and Noyes faced open rebellion.[58]

In 1879, a quarrel erupted over the question of which male ought to act as "first husband" to virgin females in the community, a duty Noyes had taken upon himself. Noyes feared being charged with statutory rape and fled to Canada. Like many other communal ventures, Oneida depended on the personal power of its central figure. With him gone, with the leadership divided, and with a group of local clergymen attacking the community, Oneida's governing council reluctantly decided that the system of complex marriage had to be abandoned. On January 1, 1881, Oneida ceased to be a community and became a joint-stock company.[59]

Women, reform, and religion

In the colonial period, especially but not limited to Puritan New England, the family, the community, and the church were patterned after a gender based hierarchical structure. In the community, that was reflected in a traditional, preindustrial sexual division of labor consistent with a world of farms, small shops, and cottage industries, where male and female, as well as young and old, played a role. In the home, the structure was based on what has been termed an "affectionate, hierarchical marriage," which defined the relationship between husbands, wives, and children. And that, in time, served as a model for the social order of church and community. As to the church, which was the central institution in the community, women constituted the majority of most congregations. Indeed, for women, the church became part of their community and personal identity. They were excluded from leadership positions, but they nevertheless exercised authority through informal networks. As Ann Braude has put it, women became the "backbone of the church," meaning they were "invisible" but essential" to the well-being of the church and community.[60]

In the midst of the American War for Independence, revolutionary rhetoric raised unsettling questions regarding the proper role of women in the new republic, while economic development after 1800 widened the range of careers available, at least in theory, to both men and women. What resulted was a conservative assertion of redefined and separate spheres for both. The best of the new opportunities were reserved for males and required spending long hours away from the rest of the family. The home increasingly became a female domain, cut off from business and public affairs. If she were middle class, a woman no longer worked in ways society recognized as "work." Further, as we shall see, her role in the church changed as did the nature of American religion.[61]

Antebellum images of masculinity and femininity both reflected those social changes and helped shape them. Men, according to most writers, were naturally strong in body and mind, aggressive and sexual. Women were innately weak, passive, emotional, religious, and chaste. These were complementary virtues and vices – men supported women, and women provided the sensitivity men lacked. Such stereotypes, Ronald Walters has pointed out, reassured each sex that it belonged where it was: "Woman was too fair a flower to survive in business or politics, where man's cunning and intellect were prime virtues; in the home she was protected, her goodness blossomed, and she refined man's coarseness."[62]

A level of ambivalence resulted from those gender roles. On the one hand, republican ideology called for a new role for women, Republican Motherhood, comprised of a sufficiently educated female citizenry to educate future generations of sensible republicans. On the other hand, domestic tradition viewed highly educated women as unnatural and "perverse threats to family stability." At least from a twentieth-century perspective, such notions implied female inferiority. Nevertheless, many antebellum commentators suggested that females had a great social role to play, if not in politics and the professions, then through their influence over men and children in the home. Although a woman "may never herself step beyond the threshold," one clergyman commented, "'she may yet send forth from her humble dwelling, a power that will be felt round the globe."[63]

That sort of rhetoric – labeled the "cult of domesticity" – may have described only some lives. To poor women, who often worked outside the home, it represented, at best, a standard to which they might aspire; at worse, it was a measure of their failure. Some females, however, discovered that the common assumptions about them could justify activities other than being a housewife. Reform was one of these. If woman's influence was so beneficial, why should it be kept at home? Why not bring to the outside world all those feminine virtues necessary to counteract masculine vices? The first step involved women, a majority in many church congregations, participating actively in early-nineteenth-century religious and charitable enterprises. By the 1830s, they moved into more secular causes: health reform, temperance, antislavery, and campaigns to redeem prostitutes and curb licentiousness. Many joined the nation's first women's rights movement, while a few became interested in communitarian ventures and talked about rearranging relations between the sexes.[64]

Few of the first generation of female reformers posed any direct challenge to the *status quo*. By mid-century, however, that was no longer the case, and resistance to their efforts grew proportionately. By the 1850s most reformers, including women, began to realize that moral suasion, which had been at the heart of their involvement in the public sphere, had failed to transform American society. Increasingly, reformers turned to electoral means, which had largely excluded women.[65]

As early as 1840, there was talk of creating a formal institutional structure to advance the cause of women. In that year, Elizabeth Cady Stanton was in London with her abolitionist husband, a delegate to a World's Antislavery Convention. After an acrimonious debate, female representatives were excluded from the Convention, and Stanton's indignation at the insult coincided with her discovery of those whom she later called "the first women I had ever met who believed in the equality of the sexes." Among them was an American Quaker and abolitionist, Lucretia Mott. The two became close friends and resolved to hold a convention as soon as they returned home. That convention was held in Seneca Falls, New York, in July 1848.[66]

For the opening of the Seneca Falls Convention, Stanton, Mott, and others prepared a Declaration of Sentiments modeled on the Declaration of Independence. Reminding Americans of the natural rights ideology of the American Revolution, their Declaration began with the premise that "all men and women are created equal" and substituted "man" for King George as the tyrant. They submitted "to a candid world" a bill of indictment against male domination, just as their forefathers had done against the British seventy-two years earlier.[67]

Stanton and her collaborators accused man of endeavoring, "in every way that he could, to destroy her [woman's] confidence in her own powers, to lessen her self-respect, and to make her willing to lead a dependent and abject life." They specifically objected to the lack of the vote and educational and professional opportunities for women, as well as to laws depriving wives of control over property and awarding children to fathers in cases of divorce. They included eleven resolutions asserting sexual equality, advocating a single moral standard for males and females, and urging women not simply to stay at home but to "move in the enlarged sphere which her great Creator has assigned her." They added a resolution calling for "the overthrow of the monopoly of the pulpit, and for the securing to woman an equal participation with men in the various trades, professions, and commerce."[68]

The importance of the women's rights movement that produced the Seneca Falls Convention should not be underestimated. Its immediate accomplishments may have been few, but, as Robert Abzug has argued, any understanding of the drive toward sexual equality in America must begin with recognition of what happened in the debate over women in the antebellum period, in which reformers articulated the most dynamic vision of womanhood in American history. The women's rights movement began when they served reform in other areas of American society. By the 1840s, realizing inequities within their own lives, they sought to improve their own lot as well. They began by exercising their newly gained power in the family and in the church, and then entered the world beyond.[69]

The feminization of American religion

Women played a major role in the reform movement in antebellum America. Indeed, the abolitionist, temperance, and peace societies depended on women for their existence, and, in terms of their place in American society, women, especially middle-class women, benefitted from their participation. Women increased their influence on American religion – American Protestantism, in particular – thereby altering the course of American religious history so significantly as to have historians point to their efforts as causing "the feminization of American religion."[70]

In the period following the American Revolution, the previously mentioned political and economic activities were deemed critically important to the nation and therefore more masculine, more competitive, more aggressive, and more responsive to shows of force and strength. Religion and the family – America's official and conventional cultural life itself – were not as important and so became the property of the ladies. Religion entered a process whereby it became more domesticated, more emotional, softer, and more accommodating, or more feminine.[71]

Although it would not last, at the height of the evangelical democratization of the Second Great Awakening, some women became preachers, especially among Methodists, Baptists, and Congregationalists. Thereafter, women and ministers became allies in opposition to that from which they had been excluded. The hierarchy of ministers, limited to males, remained unchanged, but those same male ministers, operating in a world where persuasion had replaced coercion, found themselves answerable to a larger degree to the women who filled their pews than the men, who remained members in name only. Cut off from their masculine heritage, they feminized their teachings, de-emphasizing harsher Calvinist doctrines such as those related to original sin and emphasizing family morals and the concept of superior female morality.[72]

Observers of the American scene frequently made note of this development. Frances Trollope referred to the women-filled pews and remarked that:

> it is only from the clergy that the women of America receive that sort of attention which is so dearly valued by every female heart throughout the world. I never saw, or read, of any country where religion had so strong a hold upon the women, or a slighter hold upon the men.

When Orestes Brownson complained about a "female religion," he was referring to the prominent role women were playing in the congregations and revivals. He caricatured ministers as domesticated pets of those women, fit only "to balance teacups and mouth platitudes." Brownson's solution was to join the Catholic Church, as yet a holdout against such changes.[73]

The "male principle," as it has been called, came under attack in antebellum American Protestant churches. It continued to be the case that God was referred to as male, but there was an increasing tendency to elevate the importance of femaleness, which is to say the idea of a Father-Mother God, and even the concept of a male-female Savior, exemplified in the figure of Mother Ann Lee and Shaker theology. In contrast to his Calvinist counterpart, the new Christ – the feminized Christ – was the exemplar of meekness and humility, the sacrificial victim. If Christ assumed the role of a human dominated by love, sacrificing himself for others, asking nothing but giving everything, and forgiving his enemies in the bargain, he was playing the same role as the true woman.[74]

Summary

In nineteenth-century America, religion was given over to women in its content and in its membership. In the process, religion became the repository for those female values that were seen as having no place outside the home and church in the business of building a nation.

Women and virtue became almost synonymous. In order to do this, it was necessary first to assign certain virtues to women and then to institutionalize those virtues. The family, popular culture and religion were the vehicles by which feminine virtues were institutionalized. Barbara Welter may have summarized all of this best, when she wrote that:

> religion in its emphasis on the brotherhood of man developed in women a conscious sense of sisterhood, a quality absolutely essential for any kind of meaningful women's movement. The equality of man before God, expressed so effectively in the Declaration of Independence, had little impact on women's lives. However, the equality of religious experience was something they could personally experience, and no man could deny it to them.[75]

Review questions

1   In what ways was America's first great age of reform an outgrowth of the American Revolution?
2   Although commonly seen as a literary movement, how was American transcendentalism both a religious and reform movement?
3   What common elements existed among the sampling of reform movements discussed in this chapter? In what ways were they different?
4   How did the role of women in American religion change in the first half of the nineteenth century?
5   What was meant by, and what led to, what some historians consider "the feminization of American religion"?

Notes

1   Perry Miller, ed., *The Transcendentalists: An Anthology* (Cambridge, MA: Harvard University Press, 1960), ix, 8; Henry David Gray, *Emerson: A Statement of New England Transcendentalism as Expressed in the Philosophy of Its Chief Exponent* (New York: Frederick Ungar Publishing Co., 1917; rpt. 1958), 7; Walter G. Muelder, Laurence Sears and Anne V. Schlabach, eds., *The Development of American Philosophy: A Book of Readings* (Boston: Houghton Mifflin Company, 1960), 109; Paul Boller, Jr., *American Transcendentalism, 1830–1860: An Intellectual Inquiry* (New York: G. P. Putnam's Sons, 1974), xix; Octavius Brooke Frothingham, *Transcendentalism in New England: A History* (Gloucester, MA: Peter Smith, 1876; rpt. 1865), 114; William G. McLoughlin, *Revivals, Awakenings, and Reform: An Essay on Religion and Social Change in America, 1607–1977* (Chicago: University of Chicago Press, 1978), 102.
2   See: Merle Curti, *The Growth of American Thought* (New York: Harper, 1951); Donald N. Koster, *Transcendentalism in America* (Boston: Twayne Publishers, 1975); Arthur E. Christy, *The Orient in American Transcendentalism: A Study of Emerson, Thoreau, and Alcott* (New York: Columbia University Press, 1932).
3   Ralph Waldo Emerson, *Nature in Emerson: The Selected Writings of Ralph Waldo Emerson*, ed. Brooke Atkinson (New York: The Modern Library, 1950), 6.
4   Koster, *Transcendentalism in America*, 36.
5   Ralph Waldo Emerson, "The Divinity School Address," in *Theology in America: The Major Protestant Voices from Puritanism to Neo-Orthodoxy*, ed. Sydney E. Ahlstrom (Indianapolis, IN: The Bobbs-Merrill Company, 1967), 298, 311.
6   Emerson, "Divinity School Address," 311–16.
7   Boller, *American Transcendentalism*, 8–9.
8   Boller, *American Transcendentalism*, 12–13.
9   Boller, *American Transcendentalism*, 15–16.
10 Boller, *American Transcendentalism*, 17–18; Miller, *Transcendentalists*, 106.

11 Theodore Parker, "A Discourse on the Transient and Permanent in Christianity," in *The Development of American Philosophy: A Book of Readings*, ed. Walter G. Muelder, Laurence Sears and Anne V. Schlabach (Boston: Houghton Mifflin Company, 1960), 112–13.

12 Boller, *American Transcendentalism*, 19.

13 Sydney E. Ahlstrom, *A Religious History of the American People* (New Haven, CT: Yale University Press, 1972), 607; Boller, *American Transcendentalism*, 20–1.

14 Boller, *American Transcendentalism*, 27–9.

15 Clifford Stephen Griffin, *The Ferment of Reform, 1830–1860* (Arlington Heights, IL: Harlan Davidson, 1967), 1–8; Robert H. Abzug, *Cosmos Crumbling, American Reform and the Religious Imagination* (New York: Oxford University Press, 1994), 3–8.

16 Ronald G. Walters, *American Reformers, 1815–1860* (New York: Hill and Wang, 1978), 5.

17 Walters, *American Reformers*, 6; Timothy L. Smith, *Revivalism and Social Reform: American Protestantism on the Eve of the Civil War* (Nashville, TN: Abington Press, 1957), 34–44, 148–62; Griffin, *Ferment of Reform*, 21–7. See also: Avery O. Craven, "The Northern Attack on Slavery," in *Antebellum Reform*, ed. David Brion Davis (New York: Harper and Row, 1967), 19–37; Clifford S. Thistlewaite, "The Anglo-American World of Humanitarian Endeavor," in *Antebellum Reform*, ed. David Brion Davis (New York: Harper and Row, 1967), 81–96; Charles C. Cole, *The Social Ideals of the Northern Evangelists* (New York: Columbia University Press, 1954).

18 Walters, *American Reformers*, 7–8; Alice Felt Tyler, *Freedom's Ferment: Phases of American Social History from the Colonial Period to the Outbreak of the Civil War* (New York: Harper Torchbooks, 1962), 21–2; Richard Carwardine, *Transatlantic Revivalism: Popular Evangelism in Britain and America, 1790–1865* (Westport, CT: Greenwood Press, 1978), 1–132. See also: Daniel Walker Howe, "The Evangelical Movement and Political Culture in the North during the Second Party System," *The Journal of American History*, 77 (1991): 1216–39.

19 Catherine A. Brekus, *Strangers and Pilgrims: Female Preaching in America, 1740–1845* (Chapel Hill: University of North Carolina Press, 1998), 12–15; Donald G. Mathews, "The Second Great Awakening as an Organizing Process, 1780–1830," *American Quarterly*, 21 (1969): 23–43.

20 Walters, *American Reformers*, 23; Smith, *Revivalism and Social Reform*, 45–62, 103–13. See also: John R. Bodo, *The Protestant Clergy and Public Issues, 1812–1848* (Princeton, NJ: Princeton University Press, 1954); Whitney R. Cross, *The Burned-Over District: The Social and Intellectual History of Enthusiastic Religion in Western New York, 1800–1850* (Ithaca, NY: Cornell University Press, 1950).

21 Steven Mintz, "The Promise of the Millennium," in *Critical Issues in American Religious History: A Reader*, ed. Robert R. Matheson (Waco, TX: Baylor University Press, 2006), 194–214.

22 Mintz, "Promise of the Millennium," 205.

23 Smith, *Revivalism and Social Reform*, 225–37; Tyler, *Freedom's Ferment*, 23–45. See also: James H. Moorhead, "Between Progress and the Apocalypse: A Reassessment of Millennialism in American Religious Thought, 1800–1880," *The Journal of American History*, 71 (1984): 524–42.

24 Walters, *American Reformers*, 26; Mintz, "Promise of the Millennium," 204. See also: William R. Hutchison, *Errand to the World: American Protestant Thought and Foreign Missions* (Chicago: University of Chicago Press, 1987).

25 Walters, *American Reformers*, 26–7; Smith, *Revivalism and Social Reform*, 148–62; Abzug, *Cosmos Crumbling*, 30–76.

26 Walters, *American Reformers*, 27; Charles E. Hambrick-Stowe, *Charles G. Finney and the Spirit of American Evangelicalism* (Grand Rapids, MI: William B. Eerdmans, 1996), 183–6.

27 Walters, *American Reformers*, 28; Hambrick-Stowe, *Charles G. Finney*, 183–6. See also: Hardman, *Charles Grandison Finney*; William G. McLoughlin, *Modern Revivalism: Charles Grandison Finney to Billy Graham* (New York: Ronald Press, 1959).

28 Walters, *American Reformers*, 30–1; Smith, *Revivalism and Social Reform*, 80–94.

29 Walters, *American Reformers*, 31–2; Tyler, *Freedom's Ferment*, 31–5.

30 Walters, *American Reformers*, 33.

31 Walters, *American Reformers*, 33. See also: Bertram Wyatt-Brown, *Lewis Tappan and the Evangelical War against Slavery* (Cleveland, OH: Case-Western Reserve University Press, 1969).

32 Walters, *American Reformers*, 39; John Humphrey Noyes, *Strange Cults and Utopias of Nineteenth Century America* (formerly titled: *History of American Socialisms*) (New York: Dover Publications, 1870; rpt. 1966), 2–4.

33 Walters, *American Reformers*, 40; Noyes, *Strange Cults and Utopias of Nineteenth Century America*, 10–20.

34 Walters, *American Reformers*, 41; Tyler, *Freedom's Ferment*, 111.

35 Tyler, *Freedom's Ferment*, 114; Mark Holloway, *Heavens on Earth: Utopian Communities in America* (New York: Dover Books, 1966), 45–6.

36 Noyes, *Strange Cults and Utopias of Nineteenth Century America*, 133–4; Holloway, *Heavens on Earth*, 47–8.

37 Tyler, *Freedom's Ferment*, 114–15.

38 Walters, *American Reformers*, 42–3; Tyler, *Freedom's Ferment*, 121; Holloway, *Heavens on Earth*, 89.

39 Tyler, *Freedom's Ferment*, 121–5; Holloway, *Heavens on Earth*, 90–2.

40 Walters, *American Reformers*, 43–4; Tyler, *Freedom's Ferment*, 121–5; Noyes, *Strange Cults and Utopias of Nineteenth Century America*, 135. See also: Karl J. R. Arndt, *George Rapp's Harmony Society, 1785–1847* (Philadelphia: University of Pennsylvania Press, 1965).

41 Marguerite Fellows Melcher, *The Shaker Adventure* (Cleveland, OH: The Press of Western Reserve University, 1941; rpt. 1960), 3–16; Holloway, *Heavens on Earth*, 55–9.

42 Melcher, *Shaker Adventure*, 16–40.

43 Walters, *American Reformers*, 40–5; Melcher, *Shaker Adventure*, 57–83.

44 Melcher, *Shaker Adventure*, 52–3, 56, 79–80, 179, 255, 276.

45 Walters, *American Reformers*, 46; Tyler, *Freedom's Ferment*, 148–9.

46 Melcher, *Shaker Adventure*, 9–10; Holloway, *Heavens on Earth*, 65–7.

47 Tyler, *Freedom's Ferment*, 155–60; Holloway, *Heavens on Earth*, 75–7.

48 Walters, *American Reformers*, 47.

49 Noyes, *Strange Cults and Utopias of Nineteenth Century America*, 104–6; Koster, *Transcendentalism in America*, 17.

50 Walters, *American Reformers*, 51; Koster, *Transcendentalism in America*, 101–7; Abzug, *Cosmos Crumbling*, 18–20. See: William R. Hutchison, *The Transcendentalist Ministers: Church Reform in the New England Renaissance* (New Haven, CT: Yale University Press, 1959).

51 Walters, *American Reformers*, 52; Tyler, *Freedom's Ferment*, 177–82; Noyes, *Strange Cults and Utopias of Nineteenth Century America*, 109–13.

52 Walters, *American Reformers*, 52–3; Tyler, *Freedom's Ferment*, 183–4; Koster, *Transcendentalism in America*, 21–2.

53 Noyes, *Strange Cults and Utopias of Nineteenth Century America*, 614–15; Robert David Thomas, *The Man Who Would Be Perfect: John Humphrey Noyes and the Utopian Impulse* (Philadelphia: University of Pennsylvania Press, 1977), 1–41.

54 Thomas, *Man Who Would Be Perfect*, 20–41, 86–90, 92–3.

55 Tyler, *Freedom's Ferment*, 187–9; Noyes, *Strange Cults and Utopias of Nineteenth Century America*, 624–33, 638–40; Thomas, *Man Who Would Be Perfect*, 105–11, 143–5.

56 Walters, *American Reformers*, 57; Thomas, *Man Who Would Be Perfect*, 101–5.

57 Walters, *American Reformers*, 57; Thomas, *Man Who Would Be Perfect*, 173–5.

58 Tyler, *Freedom's Ferment*, 190–1; Noyes, *Strange Cults and Utopias of Nineteenth Century America*, 641–5; Thomas, *Man Who Would Be Perfect*, 167–76.

59 Holloway, *Heavens on Earth*, 194–6; Thomas, *Man Who Would Be Perfect*, 176. See also: Maren Lockwood Carden, *Oneida: Utopian Community to Modern Corporation* Baltimore, MD: Johns Hopkins University Press, 1969.

60 Amanda Porterfield, *Female Piety in Puritan New England: The Emergence of Religious Humanism* (New York: Oxford University Press, 1992), 3–4.

61 Linda K. Kerber, *Women of the Republic: Intellect and Ideology in Revolutionary America* (Chapel Hill: University of North Carolina Press, 1980), 7. See: Ann Braude, *Sisters and Saints: Women and American Religion* (New York: Oxford University Press, 2007), ch. 1 "Women Are the Backbone of the Church"; Laurel Thatcher Ulrich, *Good Wives: Image and Reality in the Lives of Women in Northern New England, 1650–1750* (New York: Vintage Books, 1991).

62 Walters, *American Reformers*, 102–3; Barbara Welter, "The Cult of True Womanhood: 1820–1860," *American Quarterly*, 18 (1966): 151–74.

63 Kerber, *Women of the Republic*, 10, 269; Abzug, *Cosmos Crumbling*, 183–203; Walters, *American Reformers*, 103.

64 Kerber, *Women of the Republic*, 111; Glenda Riley, *Inventing the American Woman: A Perspective on Women's History* (Arlington Heights, IL: Harlan Davidson, 1987), 75–6, 96–8; Barbara Welter, "The Feminization of American Religion," in *Religion in American History: A Reader*, ed. Jon Butler and Harry S. Stout (New York: Oxford University Press, 1998), 160.
65 Lori D. Ginzberg, "Moral Suasion Is Moral Balderdash: Women, Politics, and Social Activism in the 1850s," *The Journal of American History*, 73 (1986): 601–22.
66 Walters, *American Reformers*, 106–7.
67 Walters, *American Reformers*, 107.
68 Walters, *American Reformers*, 107–8.
69 Abzug, *Cosmos Crumbling*, 184–5.
70 Barbara Welter, *Dimity Convictions: The American Woman in the Nineteenth Century* (Athens: Ohio University Press, 1976), 83; Welter, "Feminization of American Religion," 158.
71 Welter, *Dimity Convictions*, 84; Ann Douglas, *The Feminization of American Culture* (New York: Anchor Press, 1988), 17–19; Riley, *Inventing the American Woman*, 26–7, 51–2, 75–6.
72 Riley, *Inventing the American Woman*, 76; Douglas, *Feminization of American Culture*, 7–9, 42–3; Brekus, *Strangers and Pilgrims*, chs. 3–6. See: Nathan O. Hatch, *The Democratization of American Christianity* (New Haven, CT: Yale University Press, 1989). Though forced out of leadership and preaching roles in mainstream denominations, women would continue to find both in marginal groups such as the Shakers and Universal Friends. Susan Juster, *Disorderly Women: Sexual Politics and Evangelicalism in Revolutionary New England* (Ithaca, NY: Cornell University Press, 1994).
73 Frances Trollope, *Domestic Manners of the Americans* (New York: Random House, 1831; rpt. 1949), 7; Welter, *Dimity Convictions*, 86, 221 FN9.
74 Welter, *Dimity Convictions*, 87–8; Welter, "Feminization of American Religion," 161. See also: Eliza W. Farnham, *Woman and Her Era* (New York: A. J. Davis, 1964).
75 Welter, *Dimity Convictions*, 102.

Recommended for further reading

Braude, Ann. *Sisters and Saints: Women and American Religion*. New York: Oxford University Press, 2007.
Cross, Whitney R. *The Burned-Over District: The Social and Intellectual History of Enthusiastic Religion in Western New York, 1800–1850*. Ithaca, NY: Cornell University Press, 1950.
Douglas, Ann. *The Feminization of American Culture*. New York: Anchor Press, 1988.
Hardman, Keith J. *Charles Grandison Finney, 1792–1875: Revivalist and Reformer*. Syracuse, NY: Syracuse University Press, 1987.
Holloway, Mark. *Heavens on Earth: Utopian Communities in America*. New York: Dover Books, 1966.
Hutchison, William R. *The Transcendentalist Ministers: Church Reform in the New England Renaissance*. New Haven, CT: Yale University Press, 1959.
Kerber, Linda K. *Women of the Republic: Intellect and Ideology in Revolutionary America*. Chapel Hill: University of North Carolina Press, 1980.
McLoughlin, William G. *Revivals, Awakenings, and Reform: An Essay on Religion and Social Change in America, 1607–1977*. Chicago: University of Chicago Press, 1978.
Rose, Anne C. *Transcendentalism as a Social Movement, 1830–1850*. New Haven, CT: Yale University Press, 1981.
Walters, Ronald G. *American Reformers, 1815–1860*. New York: Hill and Wang, 1978.

Chapter 6

A people apart

Traditional African religion

Twenty Africans arrived aboard a Dutch slave ship in Jamestown, Virginia, in 1619. As laws providing for slavery did not exist, they were sold as indentured servants. By the end of the century, that changed as laws providing for the institution were adopted and human cargos of Africans became more frequent and spread throughout the colonies. Enslaved Africans came primarily from West Africa, and much like Native Americans, they belonged to many different tribes, that possessed their own practices, rituals, gods, and beliefs, all of which were an integral part of their identity as a people. Although both suffered through similar hardships, what set African Americans apart from Native Americans were the unique circumstances of their involuntary passage to America and their enslavement.[1]

Unlike the monotheistic and highly structured religions in the West, the religions of the enslaved Africans had little organizational structure and no formal statement of beliefs, relying almost entirely on orally transmitted traditions from one generation to the next. As diverse as the practitioners of traditional African religions were, however, they shared certain elements. For one, they shared a common belief in the continuity of life between current generations and those of the past, who remained a vital part of the lives of the living. They practiced elaborate burial ceremonies followed by lengthy and reoccurring periods of mourning to recall the memory of, and pay homage to, the deceased. They believed that their ancestors still lived. Those who led unworthy lives were relegated to a barren, desert-like land, where they were largely ignored. But the good ascended to a heaven-like place, where they were venerated by their descendants (often at family shrines) and served as guardians and intermediators between the gods and their descendants. They could intervene for good or ill in the lives of their descendants, providing or withholding fertility or good or bad health, rewarding or punishing their descendants, or serving as sources of supernatural power. The deceased could even become gods themselves.[2]

Traditional African religions shared a similar understanding as to what determined the ultimate fate of individuals. The Yorubas, for example, who constituted a significant segment of enslaved Africans in America, believed that humans were made up of a physical and a spiritual component. Before they were born, humans chose a destiny commonly determined with an ancestor, but that was forgotten upon birth. That destiny was not necessarily unalterable, but changes could not be made until the person recovered knowledge of its character. That could be accomplished through the intervention of a diviner, who established contact with the ancestor in the supernatural world who could reveal the preordained destiny and provide advice as to how to proceed.[3]

In addition to being pantheists and animists, Africans were polytheists, meaning they believed in multiple gods, some of whom were specific to particular tribes. Most believed in one creator god, whose stature was superior to the rest and who exercised ultimate authority over creation. That god generally did not intervene in affairs of the world. That was left to a host of lesser divinities, many of whom were associated with local villages and over which they were seen as exercising considerable influence. Priests were believed to have special powers, or gifts, in communicating with, supplicating, and engaging those deities upon whom the people depended. Most were commonly associated with natural phenomenon, like thunder or rain, but, again much like Native Americans, they may also have been associated with animals or insects. No matter their association, few were entirely good or bad, but rather were capable of either, depending on the situation and their relationship with the humans involved. Also like Native Americans, they had their tricksters – a wide range of animals and insects, who variously caused chaos and confusion but also occasionally positive change.[4]

Stories concerning the gods were commonly handed down orally from one generation to the next, often modified in the telling to reflect the circumstances of the moment. Animals were sacrificed to the gods, and divination employed, which included rituals, often with music and dance, intended to access the will of the gods by dissolving any barrier between the real and the spirit world. Closely related were the practices wherein priests accessed those powers that belonged in the spirit world, bringing them into the ordinary world for purposes of good or ill. They could heal someone or inflict harm, enhance the powers of warriors to be successful in war or destroy the enemy, bring about a bountiful harvest or ruin someone's crops, assure or block a woman's fertility, and so on.[5]

Some of the best-known practices along these lines were conjuring and voodoo and Santeria, all of which had roots in Africa but were transformed in important ways in America. Originating as a practice engaged in by West African priest-healers, but assumed in American by root-doctors, these spiritually gifted individuals engaged in "root-work" that brought extraordinary powers from the spirit world to bear on daily life. They commonly used special herbs and other substances in a conjure bag, which when brought into contact with humans brought about the desired effect, casting out evil spirits or casting spells. Voodoo had its roots in vodun, or vodou, a West African religion that flourished in the West Indies before making its mark in Louisiana following the migration of Afro-Caribbeans after the Haitian Revolution of 1804. Santeria arrived in the United States via Cuba. Both came to include Christian elements, as well.[6]

Enslaved African Muslims

The obvious exception to what has just been described were enslaved African Muslims. Until fairly recently, enslaved African Muslims received little attention from historians, this despite the vast scope of research on slavery. Nevertheless, documentation points to a significant presence among the new arrivals in the British colonies of North America and the United States, perhaps 10 to 15 percent of all Africans brought to this area prior to 1808, when the American Atlantic slave trade ended. The greatest concentration of African Muslims during this period was along the Georgia and South Carolina coasts, including the Georgia Sea Islands. Charleston, South Carolina and Savannah, Georgia were major slave ports, and they were in close proximity to rice and indigo growing areas, whose planters preferred slaves from the area of West Africa where inhabitants were familiar with those types of cultivation and, coincidentally, had heavier concentration of Muslims. And the evidence further suggests that, despite being far outnumbered by Christians and African practicing various traditional religions, enslaved African Muslims "preserved a distinctive lifestyle built on religious cohesiveness, cultural self-confidence, and discipline."[7]

Various sources identify Muslims as generally being better educated than others among the enslaved. Some Muslim slaves came from privileged families and arrived in Americas literate, reading and writing Arabic. This was largely due to the emphasis placed on the ability to read the *Koran* (*Qur'an*), a charge that did not exist among those who followed traditional African religions. That religious influence – promoted by thousands of Koranic schools in West Africa – soon led to the production of religious materials by American Muslims, several examples of which have survived over the years. These include passages from the *Koran*; personal accounts of their lives in Africa and America, that included testimonials to their faith as Muslims; and even a Muslim slave manuscript that after nearly a century of analysis and controversy concerning its content has been determined to consist of excerpts from a "message," or Risala, an Islamic legal work dating to the tenth century and a Tunisian legal scholar.[8]

African Muslims, as well as other African slaves in America, authored autobiographies. According to one source, between 1703 and World War II, about 6,000 slave narratives were recorded in North America, about half of which were written during slavery. Among these, however, very few were written by native born Africans. And of the ten identified as true African narratives, only five were born and raised as Muslims. Among the most interesting of these narratives for their reflections on slavery were by Omar ibn Said and Abu Bakr al Siddiq (also known as Abu Bakr Said). Both appeared at roughly the same time, 1831 and 1834, from men who came from neighboring areas in West Africa and served as slaves for twenty-four and thirty years, respectively. Further, both are quite similar in their content, avoiding reminiscences of parents, siblings, wives, and children, as was stock in most other slave narratives. Instead, both wrote at great length about the extent of literacy in their native lands and their own religious education, including where they were educated and by whom. They concluded their narratives by highlighting the main principles of Islam, as if to properly explain them to unbelievers, thereby establishing that they were men of faith and accomplishments, who had not always been mere beasts of burden but intellectuals before they were enslaved.[9]

For Muslims, the most important way to maintain their identity and integrity was to retain their faith while in captivity. They often regarded Christians with disdain, as "infidels" or "ignorant heathens," largely because of the Christian slave traders who enslaved them. But to maintain their faith they had to find ways to adhere to the Five Pillars of Islam – the profession of faith, prayers five times a day, almsgiving, an annual month-long fast, and even a pilgrimage to Mecca – as well as traditional Muslim dress and diet, all of which was not easy, or even possible, in a hostile world. Their owners often saw any Muslim practices – which they called "Muhammadanism" – as pagan, as well as threatening and therefore not to be tolerated. Nevertheless, existing evidence suggests that enslaved African Muslims strove to continue to practice their faith as best they could, but commonly in private. When interviewed by Works Progress Administration workers in the 1930s, descendants of African Muslims in Georgia recalled their families praying, marking religious holidays, engaging in religious rituals and professions of faith, and wearing Muslim garb while in captivity.[10]

The higher level of education most African Muslims possessed led to their distinguishing themselves among their fellow slaves, who paid them respect. Such knowledge could also cause them to be suspect by their owners as slave revolts throughout the Americas, including the US, were commonly led by better-educated slaves. But it could also lead to their personal advancement and their being given more responsibility, privileges, and, very occasionally, freedom. Still, there is no evidence to suggest that anything less than the vast majority of African Muslims remained enslaved throughout their lifetime.[11]

Despite the resistance to enculturation, African Islam, as practiced by the slaves did not survive in the US. Indeed their numbers declined rapidly beginning with second-generation slaves and all but disappeared by the early years of the nineteenth century. Beginning in the mid-eighteenth century, there was a steady, if not large, stream of freed slaves returning to Africa, encouraged, but not entirely successfully, by the American Colonization Society (ACS). Among those who left, there were some well-documented cases of African Muslims.[12]

But the failure of enslaved African Muslims to perpetuate their faith was largely due to environmental factors, which precluded them from engaging in the kinds of activities by which other groups perpetuated their faith. These were problematic for slaves as a whole, but even more so for African Muslims. The great majority of them were male (perhaps separated from their wives when they were captured) and, by virtue of their religion, not as easily assimilated among the other slaves, whereby they could establish strong family ties and transmit their faith to successive generations. Some did marry, but it appears that most African Muslims that did, married non-Muslims, and though they may have practiced their faith, their children and their grandchildren did not.[13]

Further, their environment included the absence of circumstances under which they could proselytize among other slaves, among whom they were few in number and in competition with practitioners of many other African religions and, increasingly, Christianity. Not only was their faith foreign to the overwhelming number of traditional African slaves, but its rigor was so demanding on anyone considering adopting their faith in terms of discipline and education, that it discouraged converts. Often considering themselves superior to other slaves, and even their Christian owners, they rejected any form of syncretism that became commonplace among other religious groups. As Africanized Christianity became a force, Islam would suffer.[14]

Ultimately, their numbers depended on the arrival of newly enslaved Muslim Africans, which all but disappeared after 1808. As Silviane Diouf as pointed out, indicative of the failure of African Muslims to make any long-term impact on the religion of the slaves: "It is remarkable that among the thousands of slave testimonies recorded in the United States, there is nothing but silence concerning the Muslims: no description of their particular rituals, comments about their habits, mention of their religion or eagerness to share it."[15]

The influence of Christianity on African Americans

Regardless of the degree to which most historians believe African religion survived among slaves, most agree that Christianity became the dominant element in African American religion. Slaves reshaped the Christianity they embraced and a "black Christian consciousness" arose that has led many to conclude that: "They conquered the religion of those who had conquered them." In its new formulation African American Christianity lacked both the sense of guilt and mission central to Western Christendom, but gained a "humanism that affirmed joy in life in the face of every trial."[16]

If there was any initial opposition to their christening, as initially some believed that would call into question their continued enslavement, that disappeared by the early years of the

Figure 6.1 A slave praying on a plantation

Source: Chronicle/Alamy Stock Photo

eighteenth century as new laws made clear that slaves would not become free through their acceptance of Christianity (see Figure 6.1). Thus, many slaves were baptized either soon after their arrival or as they became the first generation born into slavery, especially in the wake of the First Great Awakening and later during the Second Great Awakening. This was critical, as a consequence of their conversion to Christianity was that they came to view their new land though the lens of evangelicalism, which in turn influenced their reformist activities in community building and even abolitionism. At first, the Anglican Church took the lead, but the most significant missionary efforts toward African Americans came at the hands of Methodists and Baptists.[17]

   Baptist and Methodist preachers, who generally lacked the formal education of Anglican ministers, were more effective in appealing to the poor, uneducated, and outcast. Similarly, slaves found in their fiery message of salvation hope for, and even the prospect of, escape from their earthly woes. The emphasis that the preachers placed on feeling as a sign of conversion found a ready response in slaves who were repressed in many ways, as did the opportunity for the social solidarity camp meetings and other revivals offered.[18]

Some owners feared teaching slaves the Bible, much as they did reading and writing, for what use they might make of such knowledge. Slaves might well find in the Bible implications of human equality, which would incite them to take steps to free themselves. Others saw religion as a means of control and even exhibited genuine concern for the spiritual welfare of their slaves. As a result, the religion of the slaves was in large part an "invisible" institution. Black churches did exist in the South before emancipation. Slaves were often allowed to worship in white churches, and masters commonly employed ministers to provide spiritual care for their slaves. But in most such "visible" forums, the message was carefully controlled. Moreover, not all masters provided such opportunities, prompting a 1723 letter from a groups of slaves in Virginia "humbly beg[ging]" the Bishop of London to intervene on their behalf. They had been baptized and raised Anglican, whereby they were commanded to keep holy the Sabbath, only to be denied the opportunity to attend church. Thus, slaves also participated in a religious life hidden from their masters in illicit meetings during which they controlled who and what would be preached.[19]

Whether presented in the "visible" or "invisible" church, the Bible provided the means by which slaves acquired a new theology. From the Bible slaves learned that God, ultimately revealed in Jesus, was the ruler of the universe and superior to all other gods and that God punished and rewarded men, black and white, for their deeds. Whites might stress those passages that encouraged slaves to accept their lot in this world, and, if they were obedient, honest and truthful, to believe that they would be rewarded in the next. Slaves adapted this and other messages and passages from the Bible to their own psychological and social needs. The Old Testament notion of God as avenger, conqueror, and liberator became an important part of their faith, as did the image of Moses as the deliverer of his people. From the New Testament the reality of Jesus as the Son of God made flesh found a deep response among blacks. The experience of oppression found immediate resonance with the view of the suffering, humiliation, death, and eventual triumph of Jesus in the resurrection. In sum, the Bible presented a pervasive theme of deliverance.[20]

One of the best examples of how slaves adapted Christianity to their peculiar needs is the sacred folk music known as the Negro spiritual. Although adopted from whites, African Americans invested spirituals with elements of their African and American experiences and made them their own. There has been considerable effort on the part of scholars to invest black spirituals with a revolutionary meaning or to claim that they represented disguised plans for escape from slavery. "The Gospel Train" and "Swing Low, Sweet Chariot," for example, are commonly cited as associated with the Underground Railroad. Clearly, such messages were incorporated. Slave spirituals, however, were also otherworldly in outlook. They expressed the awe and wonder of the slaves in regard to life and death, their emotional reactions to the complexity of their existence, and their desire to escape from the uncertainties and frustrations of this world. Simply put, slaves did not have to choose between the two; their spirituals could be worldly, spiritual, or both.[21]

The single most persistent image of the slave spirituals was that of relief from their worldly oppression and the promise of life eternal with Jesus in a world yet to come. "There is Balm and Gilead" and, once again, "Swing Low, Sweet Chariot [coming forth to carry me home]" are just two examples. Similar images were present in the religious singing of white evangelical churches during the first half of the nineteenth century. White Americans sang of triumph and salvation, given their long-standing heritage of the idea of a chosen people, but for this message to be expressed by slaves who were told endlessly that they were members of the lowliest of races is significant. As Lawrence Levine put it: "It offers an insight into the kinds of barriers the slaves had available to them against the internalization of the stereotyped images their masters held and attempted consciously and unconsciously to foist upon them."[22]

As previously noted, many slaveholders tried to control African American religion by employing white preachers, upon whose biblical interpretations and spiritual messages they could rely. A few of those preachers appear to have earned the slaves' respect, both by their preaching and their concern for the slaves' welfare. Most were greeted with indifference and a few with hostility, forcing an increasingly large number of slaves to worship in private. Since all forms of organized social effort were forbidden among the slaves, in the absence of an established priesthood the black preacher played an important role in the invisible church. The black preacher was "called" to his office and through his personal qualities achieved a position of dominance. The call came through some religious experience that indicated that God had chosen him as a spiritual leader, and as a result, he became a leader among slaves. Quite often, however, black preachers were forced to hide their calling from their masters.[23]

The African American preacher had to combine his knowledge of the sacred scriptures with an ability to speak and communicate his special knowledge to the slaves. As W.E.B. DuBois found, black slave religion depended on three particular characteristics: "the preacher, the music, and the frenzy." If you had the first two, the third followed. The preacher was an orator who could deliver a plain message that could reach the heart. Slaves looked to him because he could understand and address them, their hopes, and their misery. But he also had to be able to sing. Employing both, he could move his congregation toward an ecstatic form of worship intended to provide a purifying emotional catharsis and a moment of spiritual ecstasy by which, at least for the moment, they could escape the harshness of their reality.[24]

Where he was unknown to his master, the black preacher was free to exercise his gifts and to direct his followers as he saw fit. Where he was known, he was always subject to at least some supervision, and that supervision grew more intense over time. Each insurrection scare – Gabriel Prosser's (1800), Denmark Vesey's (1822) and Nat Turner's (1831) – connected in some way to black preaching and provoked further repression. Nat Turner was not a preacher in the formal sense of the word, but he was an exhorter, and he convinced his fellow slaves in Southampton County, Virginia, by the power of his message, that he was the anointed one of God for their deliverance. They killed fifty-seven white men, women, and children. The governor of Virginia blamed the revolt on the evil doings of black preachers, and state legislatures throughout the South passed laws forbidding free blacks to preach to slaves, to register and control black preachers, and to require whites to be present when they preached.[25]

At the same time, the period after 1831 constituted a very fruitful period for the spread of Christianity among the slaves. After 1831, Southern planters, motivated both by fear of insurrection and desire for social control, as well as a sincere concern for the salvation of slaves, heavily promoted Christianity in a spiritually starved slave community. The result was a dramatic increase in the number of conversions by the time of the Civil War.[26]

The pioneering work of black Baptist preachers was most successful in those areas of the South where the interests of the ruling whites were not so deeply rooted in the plantation system – in the cities of Virginia, for example. A few even preached to whites, but there was always some question concerning the propriety of blacks preaching to whites or even their worshipping together. Where large numbers of black communicants existed, they worshipped in separate wings of congregations and under different preachers. Presbyterians, Episcopalians, Baptists, and Methodists built separate churches for their black members, and in those churches, blacks tended to conduct their services according to their own mode of religious expression.[27]

In the North, as in the South, a number of black preachers acquired some distinction and preached to mixed congregations, but similar problems arose. Among the most famous of early African American preachers in the North was Richard Allen, both because of his preaching and because of the role he played in organizing an independent black church. Allen was born a slave in Philadelphia but was sold to a planter who took him to Delaware, where he came under the influence of Methodist preachers and converted. He aided in the conversion of his master, was allowed to conduct prayers and preach in his master's house, and was permitted to purchase his freedom when his master became convinced that slavery was wrong.[28]

In 1780, Allen became a preacher, and Methodist Bishop Asbury gave him assignments whereby he was allowed to travel with white Methodist ministers. Six years later, he was invited to preach in the St. George Methodist Episcopal Church in Philadelphia, where he observed the need of blacks for religious leadership and a benevolent voluntary association. Allen and others organized the Free African Society. He also proposed that a separate church be established for blacks, but his proposal was opposed by both whites and blacks until blacks attending St. George Church were removed from the seats around the wall and ordered to sit in the gallery.[29]

After Allen and Absalom Jones left St. George Church, they differed as to whether blacks should model their church organization after the Methodist or the Episcopal Church. Jones organized the St. Thomas African Protestant Episcopal Church and in 1804 became the first black Protestant Episcopal minister. The majority of seceding blacks followed Allen, who organized the Bethel Church for which a building was purchased and dedicated in 1794. Bishop Asbury ordained Allen a deacon. Later he became an elder and the movement spread to other cities, largely in the North. The representatives of those churches met in Philadelphia in 1816 and established the African Methodist Episcopal Church. Allen was elected bishop and a book of discipline was adopted that embodied the same articles of religion and rules as the Wesleyans.[30]

The secession of blacks from the white Methodist church in Philadelphia was followed by secessions in New York City. Peter Williams, a sexton for a number of years in the John Street Methodist Church, was distinguished for his piety and faithfulness among white communicants. However, being influenced by the general movement among African Americans to establish their own churches, he joined with other blacks in organizing the Zion Church out of which, in 1801, developed the African Methodist Episcopal Zion Church. The African Methodist Episcopal Zion Churches did not completely separate from the Methodist Church until after the Methodists' 1824 General Conference, the Zion Churches' First General Conference being held in 1828.[31]

In the North, ministers of the African Methodist Episcopal Church and the African Methodist Episcopal Zion Church became outspoken and often leaders in the abolitionist movement. In the South, where that was not possible, at least in such an open manner, African Americans, slave and free, sought asylum from "the spirit of slavery and the spirit of caste" in independent Baptists churches. By 1850, the number of black Baptists reached 150,000, and by 1870, 500,000, but it was only later that the black Baptist churches were brought together in a national convention.[32]

The Civil War and emancipation destroyed whatever stability and order had developed among African Americans under the slave regime. Nevertheless, the strength of the slaves' religion became clear. The religious intensity of the ex-slave Union troops, the freedmen's translation of their political position into religious terms and the extraordinary mushrooming of black churches told their story. Emancipation provided the opportunity for the fusion of the invisible institution of the African American church, which had taken root among the slaves, and the visible institutional church that had grown up among free blacks before the Civil War. The result was rapid growth in the size of the black church. But there was a more important result of this merger, namely the structuring or organizing of African American life to an extent that had not previously existed. Religious life became the chief means by which this organization came about.[33]

Roman Catholicism

Although hard to fathom for most today, historian Arthur M. Schlesinger, Sr., once described anti-Catholicism as "the deepest bias in the history of the American people." Schlesinger did not mean to suggest that it was the most violent of American prejudices, though violent it was at times, but that it struck a chord in the depth of the American consciousness. As Michael Schwartz has put it:

> It is woven into the fabric of our culture. For the most part unconsciously and unintentionally, as a sort of tacit assumption this prejudice has helped to shape our national character, mold our institutions, and influence the course of our history.[34]

Although by the end of the nineteenth century it would become the largest denomination in the United States, for the first two centuries of the nation's history Roman Catholicism had to do battle for freedom and dignity in a Protestant empire. As noted in the opening chapter of this book, the oldest colonial power in what is now the United States was Catholic Spain; the first permanent Spanish continental settlement was established at St Augustine, Florida, in 1565. Catholic France also planted settlements in Maine as early as 1604, eventually spreading along the St. Lawrence River Valley into the Ohio River Valley and south along the Mississippi. As a result of the treaty process, westward expansion, purchases, and war, Spanish and French Catholic lands, and the people therein, became part of the United States by the Civil War.[35]

As discussed in Chapter 2, the British settlements of North America – the civilization and culture that laid the foundation of the United States – was overwhelmingly Protestant and hostile to Roman Catholics. As the result of the cruelties of the English Reformation, alleged subversive activities such as the Gunpowder Plot, and continued international quarrels with Catholic France and Spain, opposition to Roman Catholicism was widespread and deeply imbedded throughout the colonies. The intellectual center of English America developed in Puritan Massachusetts, and the Puritans not only represented the dissenting wing of England's Reformation but also the most ardent opposition to Roman Catholicism. For Puritans, Catholicism was a corruption of the Christian message, Rome was Babylon, and the Pope was the Antichrist, images that would not be lost in the United States for centuries.[36]

The threat of Catholicism concerned more than religion. New Englanders believed that Catholics were part of a vast international conspiracy to seek world domination. They believed that Catholics owed their loyalty first and foremost to that conspiracy and its leader, the Pope. They held that the Pope used his religious influence to maintain his tyrannical grip, and because they owed their allegiance to the Pope, Catholics could not be trusted with any civil power in Protestant countries.[37]

A Massachusetts statute of 1647 identified any Catholic priest discovered on its territory as "an incendiary and disturber of the public peace and safety, and an enemy to the true Christian religion" and, if apprehended, subject to "perpetual imprisonment" or, for second offenders, possible death. Similar laws could be found in other colonies, making it at least theoretically the case that Catholics could enjoy full civil and religious rights only in Rhode Island. But in fact, in the colonial period prosecutions of Catholics were rare, largely because there were so few Catholics in the colonies.[38]

Roman Catholics did find their way to British America, especially to Maryland and Pennsylvania. The most substantial Catholic settlement was in Maryland, a proprietary colony founded by the Lords Baltimore and dedicated to religious toleration for Catholics. Toleration was provided for by law beginning in 1639 but made more specific in the 1649 Act Concerning Religion, and for a time Roman Catholics enjoyed most of the civil rights guaranteed Protestants under English law. But, as they soon became a distinct minority among Protestants, acts concerning Catholic toleration were repeatedly rescinded until England's Glorious Revolution of 1688, whereupon toleration was lost for the duration of the colonial period.[39]

Significant numbers of Roman Catholics migrated to William Penn's Holy Experiment, as well. Although not as obviously a Catholic haven as Maryland, Pennsylvania offered Catholics religious toleration. And Catholics were treated comparatively well, even if the colony did require oaths of allegiance and supremacy and a test act that denied them membership in the assembly and other public offices.[40]

By 1763, there were about 20,000 to 25,000 Roman Catholics in the thirteen colonies, or about 1 percent of the population. But as the colonies slipped toward war with England, anti-Catholic sentiment among Protestants continued, even among rebel leaders. Sam Adams, for example, insisted that there was "much more to be dreaded from the growth of Popery in America than from the Stamp Act." Harvard College had its Dudleian Lectures, the fourth in each annual series devoted to "detecting, convicting and exposing the idolatry, errors and superstitions of the Romish church." At least in New England, the belief that it was becoming "popish" contributed to the growing antipathy of Whigs toward Britain.[41]

The Quebec Act, which British colonists assumed was promulgated in response to the Boston Tea Party and further evidence of the influence of Catholicism on the British throne, was "intolerable." It inflamed prejudice by establishing the Roman Catholic religion in Canada, where most residents were, in fact, Catholic. But when the first shots of the Revolutionary War were fired, attempts to establish friendly relations with Catholic Canada, France and Spain required efforts on the part of revolutionary leaders to suppress at least outward expressions of hostility toward that faith. Canadians were never persuaded to join the colonial effort for independence, and some American Roman Catholics joined the Tory side. But most Roman Catholics in the thirteen colonies rallied to the independence movement.[42]

Maryland's Charles Carroll was among the most eloquent spokesmen for independence. Employing the pseudonym "First Citizen," Carroll challenged Tory Daniel Dulany in public debate over colonial grievances, only to be criticized by Dulany for even calling himself a citizen, having been disqualified by law from any legal participation in colonial government simply because he was not a Protestant. Citizen or not, Carroll served on Maryland's Committee of Correspondence, in its state Senate, as representative to the Continental Congresses, and as signer of the Declaration of Independence. "When I signed the Declaration of Independence," he later wrote, "I had a view not only of our independence from England but the toleration of all sects, professing the Christian religion, and communicating to them all great rights." Charles Carroll and his cousin John Carroll, a former Jesuit priest, joined the nation's first, if failed, diplomatic mission to Canada in 1776.[43]

With independence and the creation of new state constitutions, several states continued established Protestant churches, while most continued restrictions of one sort or another on Roman Catholics. Typically, state law required office-holders not to "deny the being of God or the truth of the Protestant religion." Nevertheless, conditions were more favorable for Catholics, and step by step, state by state, by 1868, such restrictions fell and religious freedom was extended to them but not without a period of heightened hostility toward Catholics.[44]

Following the signing of the peace treaty with Great Britain, steps had to be taken to organize the Roman Catholic Church in the United States. That, of course, would be a delicate matter, given Protestant Americans' antipathy both to Catholics and bishops, the latter issue dating to opposition to the establishment of an Anglican bishop in the colonies. Beginning in 1782, John Carroll began the process of organizing America's Catholics by working out a "Constitution of the Clergy," which detailed financial arrangements and rules of behavior, as well as a panel for arbitration and conciliation. But a replacement had to be found for the English vicar apostolic of the London district who had previously exercised church authority over American Catholics. Until such time, two sacraments – holy orders and confirmation – could not be conferred. In 1784, Rome named Carroll Superior of the Mission in the United States; in 1789, it made Carroll the nation's first bishop.[45]

It fell to Carroll and his successors to deal not only with increasing anti-Catholic sentiment in the face of Catholic immigration, but also the problem of reconciling a native Catholic tradition, which had grown up in a Protestant environment and adopted some Protestant ways, as well as the ethnic divisions that developed within American Catholicism. Given the Protestant tradition of congregational autonomy, which American Catholics had come to appreciate, the establishment of a traditional Roman Catholic hierarchy was problematic.

Carroll had a strong sense of the need for a national church that would largely shape its own destiny, including a comparatively autonomous body of clergy that might choose its own bishops and be presided over by the bishop of its own choosing. He envisioned a church in communion with the see of Rome, but internally autonomous, self-perpetuating, and free of any taint of foreign jurisdiction. Carroll's plan would not be realized, as the Roman Church's magisterium, traumatized by actions taken against the Church during the French Revolution, took steps toward greater centralization throughout the Catholic world. This not only caused dissent among American Catholics but also added fuel to the fire of Protestants who saw opposition from Rome to such republican ideas indicative of the retrogressive and harmful authority with which it had to deal.[46]

Nevertheless, the American Roman Catholic Church flourished in the nineteenth century, largely because of unprecedented immigration: about 250,000 in the 1830s; 700,000 in the next decade; and a million in the ten years before the Civil War. By 1860, there were nearly 2.5 million American Catholics, making them second in number only to American Methodists. By 1890, they topped 7.3 million and all other American denominations. As James Hennesey put it, in reference to this great migration: "Many shed their ancestral religion along with allegiance to European princes, but most retained it. Those who remained Catholic, and their descendants, became American Catholicism." Nativism, however, had not completely disappeared, and with the dramatic growth of Roman Catholicism in the early nineteenth century, it reappeared with unprecedented hostility.[47]

Early to mid-nineteenth-century, Catholic immigrants, largely Irish and German, found themselves tied to the industrialization and urbanization that swept the nation beginning in this period and posed a direct threat to what was seen as the traditional Protestant way of life. Indeed, Irish Catholics, fleeing a potato famine and repressive measures in their homeland, and largely destitute, became indelibly linked with that threat. Their growing involvement in urban Democratic politics and insistence on their own schools only added to feelings of hostility. As even the father of Protestant American theological liberalism, the Reverend Horace Bushnell of Hartford, Connecticut put it in 1847: "Our first danger is barbarism, Romanism next."[48]

Protestants, by far the dominant religious group in the new nation, set the early years of the republic socially and culturally, as well as religiously. Their presumption was that the republic would continue to reflect that relative homogeneity, which provided the underpinnings upon which the nation had been erected. At the same time, however, they committed themselves to the free exercise of religion and a separation of church and state embodied in the First Amendment to the US Constitution and in short order at the state level.[49]

Protestant fears of the incongruity of Roman Catholicism to American republicanism were enhanced by pronouncements from the Vatican. In response to reform movements and revolutions, which would peak in 1848 and that posed threats to Roman Catholic European establishments, the papacy issued a series of statements which signaled opposition to liberty of conscience and the separation of church and state. In 1832, Pope Gregory XVI set the tone for what was to follow in an encyclical that read, in part:

> From the polluted fountain of indifference flows that absurd and erroneous doctrine, or rather raving, in favor and in defense of 'liberty of conscience,' for which most pestilential error, the course is opened by the entire and wild liberty of opinion, which is everywhere attempting the overthrow of religious and civil institutions and which the unblemished impudence of some has held forth as an advantage of religion.[50]

But then, Roman Catholics had their own "conundrum." They faced the challenge of "reconcil[ing] their appreciation for the political freedoms that facilitated the growth of their churches in the United States with their own particularist view of Catholicism as the one true faith." As John Hughes, Archbishop of New York, made clear in his public pronouncements, he – as most Catholics – was an American citizen "not by chance but by choice." He contended that America's commitment to the free exercise of religion was the primary reason for his coming to America. "I know the value of civil and religious liberty, which our happy government secures for all." Nevertheless, Hughes and others added, Catholicism, not Protestantism, was the great hope for America. As Martin Spalding, Bishop of Louisville, explained, Protestantism's fatal deficiency was its inability, largely due to its liberality, to contend with "indifferentism and infidelity," which threatened to engulf the nation as it already had the countries of Europe. As native-born Catholic convert Orestes Brownson wrote in his 1856 essay, "The Mission of America": "As our country is the future hope of the world, so is Catholicity that hope of our country."[51]

A spate of anti-Catholic literature accompanied and added to the conflict between American Protestants and Catholics. Samuel F. B. Morse, the inventor, wrote *Foreign Conspiracy against the Liberties of the United States* (1834), in which he charged various European missionary support organizations, such as the Leopoldine Foundation, with papal support, and with using poor, ignorant immigrants as its shock troops to bring about a monarchist-papist putsch in the United States. Lurid tales of convent horrors appeared, such as Rebecca Reed's *Six Months in a Convent* (1835) and Maria Monk's *Awful Disclosures of the Hotel*

Dieu Nunnery in Montreal (1836). They told of atrocities committed behind convent walls, often running to the pornographic, with tales of priest-nun rendezvous and murdered infants (the product of those rendezvous). Investigators found no evidence to support the allegations made against the Hotel Dieu Nunnery. Nevertheless, Monk's *Awful Disclosures* became the best-selling book in America prior to publication of *Uncle Tom's Cabin* in 1852. Reed and Monk became regulars on the lecture circuit, and a storm of violence brewed.[52]

The first major violence occurred in Charlestown, near Boston, at a convent school run by sisters of the Ursuline community. Enjoying the heavy patronage of more liberal Protestants (Unitarians, for example) for the education of their children, the area's more conservative Protestants (including Congregationalists) increased their anti-Catholic rhetoric, which literally burst into flames in 1834. Rebecca Reed came to town for a public lecture on her life in the convent, where, she alleged, young women were being held against their wills. One of the Ursulines, Elizabeth Harrison, later determined to be suffering from mental depression, briefly fled the community creating a public stir. And Lyman Beecher of Cincinnati's Lane Theological Seminary delivered a series of sermons, one provocatively titled "The Devil and the Pope of Rome." Ostensibly, Beecher was in Boston to raise money for his seminary. But the author of *Plea for the West* made his case for the seminary in the context of the need to deter papal plans to take over the Mississippi River Valley. Charlestown selectmen inspected the Ursuline convent and reported that nothing was amiss, but a mob gathered, and when they could not be persuaded that they had nothing to fear, they ransacked and burned the convent to the ground. Only one rioter was ever convicted, and he was pardoned.[53]

Philadelphia burst into flames in the spring and summer of 1844 over complaints of the city's Catholics against the reading of the King James Version of the Bible in the public schools. When, on May 3, the nativist American Republican Party held a meeting in the Irish district of Kensington, an Irish mob demolished the speaker's platform and forced the "native Americans . . . to flee under a shower of missiles, accompanied by shouts, oaths, hisses, and groans." Not to be outdone, the nativists regrouped and marched on the Irish neighborhood and the war was on. In a matter of days, despite calls for calm from the governor, the mayor, and city elite, thirty homes, two churches, and an Irish volunteer fire department went up in flames. In July, rumors spread of the stock-piling of arms in one of the city's Catholic churches. When muskets were actually found in the church, having been supplied by the state arsenal for self-defense, a mob marched on the church, only to be met by a heavily armed group of Irish Catholic defenders. Before it was over, fourteen lay dead or dying. Another fifty were wounded.[54]

Bishop Kendrick of Philadelphia was criticized for his passive role in the Philadelphia riots; not so Bishop Hughes of New York. Hughes also challenged the reading of the King James Version of the Bible in New York City's public schools but was soon engaged in the larger issue of local control and public funding of schools in Catholic neighborhoods. Once again, the outcome was not what either side intended. Hughes was successful in amassing sufficient political support to block Protestant reformers from creating a public schools system as "homogenizing agencies" of "pan-Christian instruction." He failed in realizing his goal of securing religiously separate – meaning Catholic – locally controlled and publicly funded schools, and that ultimately led to the development of parochial schools, which further inflamed nativist sentiment. When nativist disturbances threatened his city, Hughes demanded a meeting with the mayor, where he demanded protection and, failing that, issued a thinly veiled threat by allusion to the fires that welcomed Napoleon to Moscow in 1812. A nativist rally was subsequently cancelled and the city, though tense for some time, did not burn. Other cities, like St. Louis, Louisville, and Detroit, were not so lucky.[55]

The nativist movement spilled over into national politics with the formation of the American Republic Party in 1843. It reorganized into the Native American Party and was soon joined by the Order of the Star Spangled Banner, devoted to excluding Roman Catholics from public office and even from the country. It spawned the Know Nothing Movement, which took political shape as the American Party and achieved its greatest success at the polls in the early 1850s. Governors, senators, congressmen, and a host of state and local officials owed their election to Know Nothing support in the northeastern, border, and southern states.[56]

In 1853, papal diplomat Archbishop Gaetano Bedini visited the United States. His arrival went peacefully enough; he even met with President Franklin Pierce. But he was soon attacked by the nativist press and when he traveled to the Midwest, trouble started. A former priest turned anti-Catholic spokesman, Alessandro Gavazzi, charged Bedini, when Papal Governor of Bologna, with being responsible for executions carried out there by Austrian military authorities. Mobs promptly labeled him the "Butcher of Bologna" and hounded his every step until he was spirited out of the country.[57]

When the Know Nothing phase of nativism died in the mid-1850s, it did so not because of any lessening of antipathy toward Catholics, but rather because American concern with Catholics was overcome by concern over slavery. Hostility toward Catholics would rise again, at the end of the nineteenth century.

The Mormons

In some respects, the Church of Jesus Christ of Latter-day Saints was distinctly American. It was born of the evangelically sowed seeds in the soil of the American frontier and reflected elements of both evangelicalism and the frontier in its character. But it also faced the same "conundrums" with which Catholics and Protestants contended, as just noted. The young nation into which the Church was born believed, simultaneously, that the success of the new republic depended on a people united in their commitment to essentially Protestant values at the same time that they were committed to the free exercise of religion as enshrined in its founding documents. Mormons posed a threat to both, in that they were seen as beyond the pale in their beliefs and called into question whether or not, for the sake of the nation, free exercise could be provided them. And much like Catholics, Mormons sought a reasonable level of acceptance even where it involved some accommodation, while drawing a line at that point where they would lose their particularism, or that which set them apart from mainstream Protestant America. The result, much like that experienced by Catholics, was considerable resistance, even at time violence, and in their case occasionally at the hands of the law.[58]

The Church of Jesus Christ of Latter-day Saints' founder, Joseph Smith, Jr., (see Figure 6.2) was born in 1805 into a struggling farm family in Vermont. In 1816, the family moved to Palmyra, in the "burned-over district" of western New York, so known because of the frequency of religious revivals in the area in the first half of the nineteenth century. The Great Revival of 1816–1817 was in progress when the Smiths arrived in Palmyra, and it was in the immediate wake of that revival that the 12-year-old Joseph first became concerned about religion. "My mind became seriously impressed with regard to the all-important concerns for the welfare of my immortal soul," he later reported, "which led me to searching the scriptures." Two years later, the Methodists organized a camp meeting nearby, and he was tempted, but for the moment resisted, making any formal commitment to them. Soon, he had little good to say about it or any other denomination.[59]

Figure 6.2 Joseph Smith, Founder of the Church of Jesus Christ of Latter-day Saints

Source: Pictorial Press Ltd/Alamy Stock Photo

Financially, the Smiths were no more successful in their new home than in their old, and Joseph took up treasure hunting and money digging. At one point, he was arrested and found guilty of being "a disorderly person and an impostor," the specific evidence used against him being that he employed a "seer stone." In 1827, however, his luck began to change, if in ways he did not anticipate. He became the author of a new bible and the founder of a new religion, that would outdistance every other sect brought into being in America. As Smith's biographer Fawn Brodie wrote: "Joseph's was no mere dissenting sect. It was a real religious creation, one intended to be to Christianity what Christianity was to Judaism: that is, a reform and a consummation."[60]

Smith reported that his first vision came to him in 1820, but that he did not fully understand it. By the time he reported it in 1832, Smith knew that the vision was one of the steps
in "the rise of the church of Christ in the eve of time" and the restoration of the Aaronic
Priesthood. "The Lord opened the heavens upon me and I saw the Lord and he spoke unto
me saying Joseph my son thy sins are forgiven thee, go thy way, walk in my statutes, and
keep my commandments." Like countless other revival subjects who had come under conviction, Joseph Smith received assurance of forgiveness from the Lord. His "soul was filled
with love," and for many days, he could "rejoice with great joy"; the Lord was with him.[61]

Smith's conversion was different from nearly all others brought about by the revivals of
the period. Smith claimed that the angel Moroni appeared to him in a vision and led him to
a cache of gold plates inscribed in "reformed Egyptian" hieroglyphics, as well as to a set of
seer stones (Urim and Thummim) with which he was able to read the plates. Although Martin Harris and Oliver Cowdery claimed to have received visions attesting to the existence
and authenticity of the plates, no one ever actually saw them. Smith translated them – he on
one side of a curtain, his wife, Cowdery and two other copyists on the other. The task was
completed in 1829, and in March 1830, the *Book of Mormon* was published.[62]

Although interspersed with exhortations on topics of doctrinal and social consequence,
the *Book of Mormon* is primarily historical in form. It is a 500-page account of the wander-
ings and experiences of America's pre-Columbian inhabitants: first, the Jaredites, who left
the Tower of Babel and crossed the Atlantic to America, only to extinguish their numbers
through continuous internecine wars; second, the evil sons of Laman (the Lamanites), who
were the American Indians; and third, the good sons of Nephi, who after many battles were
all but extinguished by the Lamanites. Only Mormon and his son Moroni were left, and
they buried their chronicles in 384 CE so that whenever God chose they could be revealed
again to their spiritual descendants, who would establish the Nephite stake in Zion before
the Last Day.[63]

Controversy surrounded the *Book of Mormon* from its first appearance. Actual authorship
of the *Book of Mormon* has been contested, as has the very existence of the golden plates,
but most scholars agree that the book and its subsequent use at the hands of Joseph Smith
captured both the spirit and needs of those in the region. Smith may, or may not, have had a
decisive religious crisis in which his agony over the multiplicity of sects led to the vision that
made him a seer and prophet. But he clearly had experienced revival preaching, and he was
familiar with the large number of doctrinal issues it raised. His father had been influenced
by Universalism, Methodism, and even skepticism. His mother was a seeker after cultic
certainties, and in 1824, Joseph himself had heard a local preacher consign his dead brother
to hell. He was also well versed in the King James Version of the Bible, a point made clear
by his having appropriated from it about 27,000 words for the *Book of Mormon*, as well as
its English style and structure.[64]

As Sydney Ahlstrom has written, the *Book of Mormon:*

> brought a satisfying answer to many needs: it undercut sectarian pluralism and emotion-
> alism with objectivity, moral legalism, a liberal answer to many old issues, a positive
> this-worldliness, and even a kind of rationalism that had grown out of Joseph's own
> disdain for frontier sermonizing.

Smith himself made his opposition to sectarian pluralism clear, when he wrote that "if God
had a church, it would not be split into factions." Such factions, he insisted, were "devoted

to destruction." The book, however, did not make Mormonism. Joseph Smith, and, after Smith's death, Brigham Young did that.[65]

Soon after publication of the *Book of Mormon* in 1830, Smith baptized six of his followers and formed a church. Within a month, forty people acknowledged Smith a seer, translator, prophet, and apostle of Jesus Christ. Church doctrine, rules of ritual, and direction as to the myriad of other organizational concerns with which churches are normally concerned were minimal at first. Joseph Smith, however, spoke for the Lord, and his revelations were non-stop. A steady flow of revelations began to define the shape and goals of Mormonism. Infant baptism was ruled out in favor of limiting receipt into the church to those old enough to be accountable for their sins before God and to repent. The Calvinist principle of irresistible grace was struck down in favor of the idea that "there is a possibility that man may fall from grace and depart from the living God." But at least for the first few years, there was little to distinguish Mormon belief from that of other Protest denominations. Richard Bushman has suggested that the articles promulgated in the first years of the church's history made no effort to distinguish the new church from other denominations. Instead, the purpose was to identify the new organization as a respectable Christian church, holding to the established principles of the gospel. "Joseph's visions were not flaunted before the world. They were simply acknowledged as part of the church's history."[66]

Smith's well-staged and publicized healings drew converts, as did his warnings about the imminent Second Coming, but they also drew an increasing number of critics. Hecklers and then mobs began to frequent Mormon gatherings, threatening bodily harm as well as creating a situation where Smith was subjected to arrest warrants for disturbing the peace. Smith began advocating a move west, and five months after the church's founding Smith announced that the New Jerusalem would be found "on the borders by the Lamanites." Mormonism's first westward trek began.[67]

In Kirtland, Ohio, the "United Order of Enoch" took form from Smith's continued revelations. A theocratic government was established, and the notion that the Latter-day Saints were soon to rule on the earth became widely accepted among them. As in New York, however, hostility arose among the group's neighbors in part fueled by fear of the potential political power of the large group of new settlers, but also by concern for reports of Smith's antirepublican civil and unorthodox spiritual ways. Converts continued to pour in and a temple was built and dedicated with festivities pervaded by pentecostal fervor. What amounted to a bank, though called the Kirtland Safety Society Anti-Banking Company, was organized, notes issued, and a large debt accumulated until the panic of 1837 burst the bubble and brought creditors to its gates. Schism, rioting, and fires followed. Smith fled to Missouri, but his woes did not end.[68]

The Mormons were chased out of Jackson County, Missouri, by an angry mob that resented their presence and feared they would incite an Indian uprising against them. Rumors abounded that the Mormons were taking their faith to the Indians and slaves, a situation made worse by Smith's promise on July 4, 1838, that he would wreak vengeance on his oppressors and that he would be a "second Mohammed." Violence escalated. Missouri Governor Lilburn Boggs called out the militia, vowing to run Smith out of the state. Smith was arrested, and he and his followers left Missouri for Illinois, where they founded the town of Nauvoo.[69]

It was election time 1840, and with Whigs and Democrats vying for support in the newly settled territory both parties sought the 15,000 Mormon votes. Nauvoo was promptly given a charter that made it almost an autonomous theocratic political unit, and Nauvoo became the fastest growing city in Illinois. By 1842, it boasted a population of about 10,000 people.

Evangelistic efforts were extended even to the poor of England, who began emigrating by the thousands, and Smith organized a military force known as the Nauvoo Legion. Smith was declared King of the Kingdom of God, and he gathered to him ever-increasing civil and spiritual powers. He continued to receive revelations, including, between 1841 and 1843, the concept of plural marriage, polygyny, to be more specific.[70]

In 1844, Joseph Smith announced his candidacy for the presidency of the United States. Some argue that his decision to run for office was motivated by his desire to publicize his grievances against the federal government after he had tried unsuccessfully to enlist the aid of federal officials to secure compensation for losses suffered during the Mormon expulsion from Missouri. Others insist that he was encouraged by a strong sense of millennialism, by his belief that the US government was on the verge of collapse to be replaced by the just rule of the King of Kings. A few have concluded that Smith believed that his election would dissolve all distinctions between sacred and secular and make them one.[71]

Regardless of his motives, Smith's candidacy provoked dissidence, apostasy, fear, and violence. Non-Mormons accused him of conspiring to establish a theocratic empire. Ex-Mormons published lurid tales of polygyny corruption and lawlessness, and dissidents set up a rival newspaper called the *Nauvoo Expositor*. Smith responded with crushing authority, and the Illinois militia threatened to intervene. Joseph and his older brother Hyram Smith surrendered to authorities, whereupon they were moved to a Carthage, Illinois, jail. While awaiting trial, a mob broke into the jail and lynched both of them.[72]

Although challenged in his bid for leadership of the church by Sidney Rigdon and Joseph's younger brother William Smith, and faced with a separationist movement led by James Strang, Brigham Young was recognized as Smith's successor. Young, born to a devout Vermont Methodist family, moved to western New York as a young man. Like Smith, he was influenced by the religious enthusiasm of the burned-over district, but he became a Methodist exhorter. In 1830, Young came into contact with Mormonism when Samuel Smith, one of Joseph's younger brothers, arrived in the town where Young was living to preach Mormonism and to sell copies of the *Book of Mormon*. It took two years, but in 1832, Young cast his lot with the new church. He travelled to Kirtland, Ohio, where he met Joseph Smith, and in 1835, Smith appointed Young to the newly created Council of Twelve.[73]

In the midst of the controversy surrounding Joseph Smith, the Illinois state legislature revoked the Nauvoo charter. Upon his assuming power over the church, a warrant was issued for Young's arrest, and although Young was able to persuade those who came to arrest him to at least temporarily allow him his freedom, he had little choice but to leave. On February 15, 1846, Young departed Nauvoo, beginning the harrowing Mormon trek across America to the Great Salt Lake basin. They arrived in July 1847. A constitutional convention was held in 1849, and the autonomous state of Deseret took shape. Within a decade, ninety communities were formed and the future of Mormonism seemed assured, at least for the moment.[74]

In 1850, Utah became a United States territory. Young tried to have Utah admitted to the union as a state, bypassing territorial status and thereby strengthening control by the Mormon majority. He was made territorial governor, but old quarrels were renewed, including word of the continued practice of polygyny among the Mormons. Rather than avoid the issue, Young and other leaders of the church sought to defend the practice. First, they defended it on hereditary grounds as an essential practice for procreation. Polygyny would facilitate the peopling of this world by producing numerous posterity through a righteous chosen (Mormon) lineage. Second, they pointed to the Old Testament precedents of Abraham, Isaac, and Jacob. And third, they argued that it was consistent with man's nature, meaning that his basic sexual drive was polygamous and should be allowed legitimate outlet. Women, by nature, were monogamous.[75]

Mormon attempts to defend polygyny did not persuade many to their cause, and the conflict between the Mormons and federal troops in the region escalated. When the Mormons were blamed for the Indian killings of eight members of a US Army Topographical Survey team, known as the Gunnison Massacre, federal troops were assigned to the area against Young's wishes. In 1857, when President James Buchanan replaced Young with a non-Mormon as territorial governor, Young decided that the Mormons must stand their ground and what became known as the Utah, or Mormon, War began.[76]

Although the war was officially declared ended in 1858, a cold war of sorts continued between the Mormons and the US government for the rest of the century. In 1879, the US Supreme Court ruled against polygamy by upholding the constitutionality of an 1862 Act of Congress against bigamy, noting that religious freedom did not involve the right to subvert an institution upon which "society may be said to be built." The Edmunds Act of 1882 brought stringent political pressures to bear on the Mormons, to which was added a federal act of 1884 applying economic penalties. Finally, in 1890, the church revised its teaching on polygyny, thus bringing peace to the area and opening the way to statehood, which was granted in 1896.[77]

Over the course of the next century, the Church of Jesus Christ of Latter-day Saints gained broad, if not total, acceptance and attracted numbers sufficient to make it one of the largest religious bodies in the United States, with adherents worldwide. The phrase "broad, if not total, acceptance" seems appropriate, given the lingering questions concerning Republican presidential candidate Mitt Romney's Mormon faith in the 2012 campaign. To a considerable extent, this can be attributed to still widespread ignorance of the Mormon faith. But it might also be attributable to continued Mormon insistence on their particularism or, as Mormon leader Joseph Young put it in 1855, and as it had been repeated many times by church leaders ever since, on their being a "peculiar people."[78]

The question that usually arises from these considerations is: Are Mormons Christians? Given the widespread assumption that the United States is a Christian nation, this question takes on greater importance than its being merely an academic inquiry. Some evangelicals bristle at the very idea that Mormons could be considered Christians. Many Mormons might agree that they have Christian origins but that, with a new prophet and scripture, they are distinctly different. While still others see it as the latest, major division of Christianity. The matter cannot be resolved here, although it is worth concluding with what several Mormon writers have argued as of late, which serves not only to help us identify the church but also to remind us of its mission: They see "the Protestant Reformation as a prerequisite for the restoration of true Christianity through Joseph Smith."[79]

Summary

Jon Butler has described antebellum America as a "spiritual hothouse," both for the expansion of already established denominations and for the creation of new ones. Sydney Ahlstrom called it a "sectarian heyday" and Nathan Hatch "a sea of sectarian rivalries." As Christianity – Protestant Christianity, to be more specific – advanced, however, so too did new and sometimes ugly demands for government guarantees of Protestant hegemony. In the case of African Americans, control was intended to preserve the slave economy and racial social hierarchy. In the case of Roman Catholics and Mormons, nativists responded to what they saw as a threat to their divinely ordained Protestant empire. Resistance emerged from strong, unresolved tensions accompanying America's advancing religious complexity, Protestant institutional prowess, and persistent desires for simplification and individual freedom. The players would change, but the nation's even greater future religious complexity would continue.[80]

Review questions

1   What were some of the common elements among the various traditional African religions?
2   What characteristics of African Muslims set them apart from their fellow slaves who practiced traditional African religions?
3   How would you defend the statement that African Americans reshaped and embraced Christianity, giving rise to a "black Christian consciousness"?
4   Historians have argued that the arrival of a large number of Roman Catholics in the nineteenth century gave rise to the first major test of "Protestant America." What accounted for that test and how did it play out?
5   In some respects, the Church of Jesus Christ of Latter-day Saints was distinctly American. Yet it was met by hostility on the part of many Americans. Why was that the case?

Notes

1   Catherine L. Albanese, *America: Religions and Religion*, 4th edn. (Belmont, CA: Thomas Wadsworth, 2007), 134; Peter W. Williams, *America's Religions: From Their Origins to the Twenty-First Century*, 3rd edn. (Urbana: University of Illinois Press, 2008), 225–6. See also: Albert J. Raboteau, *Slave Religion: The "Invisible Institution" in the Antebellum South* (New York: Oxford University Press, 1978); Benjamin C. Ray, *African Religion: Symbol, Ritual and Community* (Englewood Cliffs, NJ: Prentice Hal, 1976).
2   Albanese, *America*, 134–5; Williams, *America's Religions*, 25–2, 29.
3   Williams, *America's Religions*, 29.
4   Williams, *America's Religions*, 25–9; Albanese, *America*, 135; William Bascom, *Sixteen Cowries: Yoruba Divination from Africa to the New World* (Bloomington: Indiana University Press, 1997).
5   Albanese, *America*, 136.
6   Albanese, *America*, 137–8; Williams, *America's Religions*, 27, 30. See also: Yvonne P. Chireau, *Black Magic: Religion and the African American Conjuring Tradition* (Berkeley: University of California Press, 2003); Theophus H. Smith, *Conjuring Culture: Biblical Formations of Black America* (New York: Oxford University Press, 1994).
7   Michael A. Gomez, *Black Crescent: The Experience and Legacy of African Muslims in the Americas* (New York: Cambridge University Press, 2005), 143, 150, 166; Philip D. Curtin, *The Atlantic Slave Trade: A Census* (Madison: University of Wisconsin Press, 1969), 334–5; James A. Rawley, *The Transatlantic Slave Trade: A History* (New York: Norton, 1981), 114–15; Daniel C. Littlefield, *Rice and Slaves: Ethnicity and the Slave Trade in Colonial South Carolina* (Baton Rouge: Louisiana State University, 1981), 31–2; For a more complete discussion of why the study of enslaved African Muslims was late in being explored, see: Sylviane A. Diouf, *Servants of Allah: African Muslims Enslaved in the Americas* (New York: New York University Press, 1998), 2, 198–205; Edward E. Curtis, IV, *Muslims in America: A Short History* (New York: Oxford University Press, 2009), xi–xii.
8   Allan D. Austin, *African Muslims in Antebellum America* (New York: Garland, 1984), 515; Gomez, *Black Crescent*, 179; Diouf, *Servants of Allah*, 126–8. See: Ronald Judy, *(Dis)forming the American Canon* (Minneapolis: University of Minnesota Press, 1993).
9   Sylviane Diouf suggests that one reason for the dearth of African-born Muslim slave narratives was the lack of interest in them by abolitionists. She also notes that, in the case of Muslim slave narratives, as opposed to other slave accounts, neither editors nor the assistance of abolitionists in commissioning, revising, and publishing their accounts were necessary. Diouf, *Servants of Allah*,

2, 107–23, 140–4, and ch. 2; Omar Ibn Said, "Autobiography of Omar Ibn Said," *American Historical Review*, 30 (1925): 793–4; Richard Madden, *A Twelve Months' Residence in the West Indies* (Philadelphia, PA: Carey, Lea & Blanchard, 1835), 126, 129; "Documents," *Journal of Negro History*, 21 (1936): 55; Austin, *African Muslims in Antebellum America*, 69, 466, 662; Theodore Dwight, "Condition and Character of Negroes in Africa," in *The People of Africa: A Series of Papers on Their Character, Condition, and Future*, ed. Henry Schieffelin (New York: A. D. F. Randolph, 1871), 48; Lamin Sanneh, *The Crown and the Turban: Muslims in West African Pluralism* (Boulder, CO: Westview Press, 1997), 148.

10 Michael Gomez has written that a factor that may have encouraged the African Muslim sense of superiority among other African slaves and even Christians was the increasingly intolerant society they were leaving behind, which was marked by jihads against non-Muslims and the establishment of Muslim theocracies in West Africa. Diouf, *Servants of Allah*, 94, ch. 2; Gomez, *Black Crescent*, 143, 156, 171, 179. Muslims were not opposed to slavery; in fact, they participated in it. But they placed restrictions on those who could be enslaved, namely non-Muslim war captives and the progeny of slaves. Race was not a factor. Theophilus Conneau, *A Slaver's Log Book or Twenty Years' Residence in Africa* (Englewood Cliffs, NJ: Prentice Hall, 1976), 69; Paul Lovejoy, "Background in Rebellion: The Origins of Muslim Slaves in Bahia," *Slavery and Abolition*, 15 (1994): 164; Philip Curtin, "Ayuba Suleiman Diallo of Bondu," in *Africa Remembered: Narratives by West Africans from the Era of the Slave Trade*, ed. Philip Curtin (Madison: University of Wisconsin Press, 1967), 40; Curtis, *Muslims in America*, 1–5, 11–22; Austin, *African Muslims in Antebellum America*, 309–408, 445–524; ibn Said, "Autobiography of Omar ibn Said, Slave in North Carolina, 1831," *American Historical Review*, 30 (1925), 787.

11 Gomez, *Black Crescent*, 173–6; Diouf, *Servants of Allah*, 99, 102–3; Paul Barringer, *The Natural Bent* (Chapel Hill: The University of North Carolina, 1949), 12. For information on the involvement of African Muslims in slave revolts in Latin America and the Caribbean, especially in the Haitian Revolution, see: Diouf, *Black Crescent*, chs. 3–5.

12 Diouf, *Servants of Allah*, 166–9, ch. 6; Francis Moore, *Travels into the Inland Parts of Africa* (London: E. Cave, 1738), 204–5; Curtis, *Muslims in America*, 1–4, 6–11. See: Terry Alford, *Prince among Slaves: The True Story of an African Prince Sold into Slavery in the American South* (New York: Oxford University Press, 1977), especially 120: When his owner realized he was from a high-status West African family, he nicknamed him Prince. Austin, *African Muslims in Antebellum America*, 121–264.

13 Michael Gomez has found in the stories of the grandchildren and subsequent generations of the African-born Muslims considerable pride and admiration for their originating family members, including their Islamic heritage even though they no longer embraced Islam. Gomez, *Black Crescent*, 153, 161, 172.

14 Gomez, *Black Crescent*, 160.

15 Diouf, *Servants of Allah*, 179–82; Gomez, *Black Crescent*, 143, 160. For a slave's observation on the absence of Muslim practitioners, see: Charles Bell (enslaved in Maryland, South Carolina, and Georgia), *Fifty Years in Chains* (New York: Dover Publications, 1837; rpt. 1970), 165. Ball observed that he knew several Africans who "must have been . . . Mohammedans," but at that time, he "never heard of the religion of Mohamed." On Muslim resistance to syncretism, see Lamin, *The Crown and the Turban*, 20.

16 Eugene D. Genovese, *Roll, Jordan, Roll: The World the Slaves Made* (New York: Vintage Books, 1976), 211–2; Albert J. Raboteau, "The Black Experience in American Evangelicalism: The Meaning of Slavery," in *African-American Religion: Interpretive Essays in History and Culture*, ed. Timothy E. Fulop and Albert J. Raboteau (New York: Routledge, 1997), 89–106; Timothy L. Smith, "Slavery and Theology: The Emergence of Black Christian Consciousness in Nineteenth-Century America," in *Critical Issues in American Religious History*, ed. Robert R. Mathisen (Waco, TX: Baylor University Press, 2006), 297–303.

17 Genovese, *Roll, Jordan, Roll*, 183, 185; Edward Franklin Frazier, *Negro Church in America* (New York: Schocken Books, 1969), 6–7; Donald G. Mathews, *Slavery and Methodism* (Princeton, NJ: Princeton University Press, 1965), 293–9; Raboteau, "Black Experience in American Evangelicalism," 92–3; Rita Roberts, *Evangelicalism and the Politics of Reform in Northern Black Thought, 1776–1863* (Baton Rouge: Louisiana State University Press, 2010), Introduction.

18 Frazier, *Negro Church in America*, 9. See also: Catherine C. Cleveland, *The Great Revival in the West 1797–1805* (Chicago: University of Chicago Press, 1916); Elizabeth K. Nottingham, *Methodism and the Frontier Indiana Proving Ground* (New York: Columbia University Press, 1941).

19 Susan M. Fickling, *Slave Conversion in South Carolina: 1830–1860* (Columbia: University of South Carolina, 1924), 18; Genovese, *Roll, Jordan, Roll*, 189; William Sumner Jenkins, *Pro-Slavery Thought in the Old South* (Gloucester, MA: Peter Smith, 1935;1960), 13, 17; Clement Eaton, *Growth of Southern Civilization, 1790–1860* (New York: Harper and Row, 1961), 87; Albert J. Raboteau, "Slave Religion: The 'Invisible Institution' in the Antebellum South," in *Critical Issues in American Religious History*, ed. Robert R. Mathisen (Waco, TX: Baylor University Press, 2006), 297–303; Thomas N. Ingersoll, "Releese Us Out of This Cruell Bondage: An Appeal from Virginia in 1723," *William and Mary Quarterly*, 3rd sers, 51 (October 1994): 776–82.

20 Charles Eric Lincoln and Lawrence H. Mamiya, *Black Church in the African American Experience* (Durham, NC: Duke University Press, 1990), 3–4; Genovese, *Roll, Jordan, Roll*, 252–3.

21 Lawrence W. Levine, "Slave Songs and Slave Consciousness: An Exploration in Neglected Sources," in *African-American Religion: Interpretive Essays in History and Culture*, ed. Timothy E. Fulop and Albert J. Raboteau (New York: Routledge, 1997), 60–2; Miles M. Fisher, *Negro Slave Songs in the United States* (Ithaca, NY: Cornell University Press, 1983); Frazier, *Negro Church in America*, 12–3; Howard Thurman, *The Negro Spiritual Speaks of Life and Death* (Richmond, IN: Friends United, 1947; rpt. 1975), 17, 27–8, 38, 51; Vincent Harding, "Religion and Resistance among Antebellum Slaves," in Fulop and Raboteau, *African-American Religion: Interpretive Essays in History and Culture*, ed. Timothy E. Fulop and Albert J. Raboteau (New York: Routledge, 1997), 109–11.

22 Levine, "Slave Songs and Slave Consciousness," 69.

23 Genovese, *Roll, Jordan, Roll*, 202–9; Lincoln and Mamiya, *Black Church in the African American Experience*, 24.

24 Genovese, *Roll, Jordan, Roll*, 258; Frazier, *Negro Church in America*, 18; Lincoln and Mamiya, *Black Church in the African American Experience*, 5–6.

25 Genovese, *Roll, Jordan, Roll*, 257, 259; Harding, "Religion and Resistance among Antebellum Slaves," 117–18; Herbert Aptheker, *Nat Turner's Slave Rebellion* (New York: Humanities Press, 1966).

26 Raboteau, *Slave Religion*, 155–62; Genovese, *Roll, Jordan, Roll*, 187–8.

27 Leroy Fitts, *A History of Black Baptists* (Nashville, TN: Broadman, 1985); Frazier, *Negro Church in America*, 25–6; Genovese, *Roll, Jordan, Roll*, 235, 240.

28 Will B. Gravely, "The Rise of African Churches in America (1786–1822): Reexamining the Contexts," in Fulop and Raboteau, *African-American Religion: Interpretive Essays in History and Culture*, ed. Timothy E. Fulop and Albert J. Raboteau (New York: Routledge, 1997), 136–7; Richard Allen, *The Life, Experience and Gospel Labors of Rt. Rev. Richard Allen*, ed. George A. Singleton (New York: Abingdon Press, 1960), 12; Charles H. Wesley, *Richard Allen, Apostle of Freedom* (Washington, DC: Associated Publishers, 1935), 15–7.

29 Wesley, *Richard Allen*, 52–3; Lincoln and Mamiya, *Black Church in the African American Experience*, 50–1.

30 Allen licensed a woman, Jarena Lee, a member of Bethel AME Church, to preach and facilitated her work as a traveling preacher. Carter G. Woodson, *The History of the Negro Church* (Washington, DC: Associated Publishers, 1972), 75–7; Lincoln and Mamiya, *Black Church in the African American Experience*, 51–2; Daniel A. Payne, *History of the African Methodist Episcopal Church* (New York: Arno Press, 1891; rpt. 1969).

31 Lincoln and Mamiya, *Black Church in the African American Experience*, 56–7; Frazier, *Negro Church in America*, 28. See also: William J. Walls, *The African Methodist Episcopal Zion Church: Reality of the Black Church* (Charlotte, NC: AME Zion Publishing House, 1974); Howard D. Gregg, *History of the African Methodist Episcopal Church* (Nashville, TN: AMEC Publishing House, 1980).

32 Lincoln and Mamiya, *Black Church in the African American Experience*, 25; Frazier, *Negro Church in America*, 28; see also: Gerald Sorin, *Abolitionism: A New Perspective* (New York: Praeger Published, 1971).

33 Frazier, *Negro Church in America*, 29–30; Lincoln and Mamiya, *Black Church in the African American Experience*, 7; Raboteau, *Slave Religion*.

34 Michael Schwartz, *The Persistent Prejudice: Anti-Catholicism in America* (Huntington, IN: Our Sunday Visitor, 1984), 13–4.
35 James Hennesey, *American Catholics: A History of the Roman Catholic Community in the United States* (New York: Oxford University Press, 1981), chaps. 1–3.
36 Hennesey, *American Catholics*, 36–7; Ray Allen Billington, *The Protestant Crusade, 1800–1860* (New York: Macmillan Company, 1938), 1–4.
37 Francis D. Cogliano, *No King, No Popery: Anti-Catholicism in Revolutionary New England* (Westport, CT: Greenwood Press, 1995), 14.
38 Hennesey, *American Catholics*, 37; Billington, *Protestant Crusade*, 7–9.
39 Hennesey, *American Catholics*, 37–42; Billington, *Protestant Crusade*, 5–7.
40 Hennesey, *American Catholics*, 49.
41 Hennesey, *American Catholics*, 55–6; Charles H. Metzger, *Catholics and the American Revolution: A Study in Religious Climate* (Chicago: Loyola University Press, 1962), 14; Cogliano, *No King, No Popery*, 8–9, 35.
42 Cogliano, *No King, No Popery*, 51; James H. Hutson, ed., *A Decent Respect for the Opinions of Mankind, Congressional State Papers 1774–1776* (Washington, DC: Library of Congress, 1975), 29; Hennesey, *American Catholics*, 59.
43 Daniel Dulany, *Maryland and the Empire, 1773: The Antilon-First Citizen Letters*, ed. Peter S. Onuf (Baltimore, MD: Johns Hopkins University Press, 1974), 121–2; Edmund C. Burnett, ed., *Letters of Members of the Continental Congress*, 8 vols. (Washington, DC: Carnegie Institution, 1921–1931), 1: 354; Martin I. J. Griffin, *Catholics and the American Revolution*, 2 vols. (Ridley Park, PA: Published by the Author, 1907–1911), 1: 352; Hennesey, *American Catholics*, 64–5.
44 John E. Semonche, *Religion and Constitutional Government in the United States* (Carrboro, NC: Signal Books, 1985), 22–3.
45 Hennesey, *American Catholics*, 69–70.
46 Hennesey, *American Catholics*, 85, 89.
47 Hennesey, *American Catholics*, 102; For a discussion of the controversy surrounding the counting of American Catholics, see: Finke and Stark, *Churching of America*, 110–5.
48 Hennesey, *American Catholics*, 118–19.
49 Jon Gjerde, *Catholicism and the Shaping of Nineteenth-Century America*, ed. S. Deborah Kang (New York: Cambridge University Press, 2012), ix.
50 Gjerde, *Catholicism and the Shaping of Nineteenth-Century America*, 54–5.
51 Gjerde, *Catholicism and the Shaping of Nineteenth-Century America*, ix–x, 64–5, 79–90.
52 Billington, *Protestant Crusade*, 90–2, 99–108, 122–5; James T. Fisher, *Communion of Immigrants: A History of Catholics in America* (New York: Oxford University Press, 2002), 45. Coincidently, the author of *Uncle Tom's Cabin*, Harriet Beecher Stowe, was the daughter of Lyman Beecher.
53 Billington, *Protestant Crusade*, 68–76; Hennesey, *American Catholics*, 122; Jon Gjerde, *Catholicism and the Shaping of Nineteenth-Century America*, ed. S. Deborah Kang (New York: Cambridge University Press, 2012), 96–8.
54 Billington, *Protestant Crusade*, 220–34; Michael Feldberg, *The Philadelphia Riots of 1844: A Study of Ethnic Conflict* (Westport, CT: Greenwood Press, 1975).
55 Richard Shaw, *Dagger John: The Unquiet Life and Times of Archbishop John Hughes of New York* (New York: Paulist Press, 1977), 197.
56 Billington, *Protestant Crusade*, 200–11.
57 James F. Connelly, *The Visit of Archbishop Gaetano Bedini to the United States, June 1853–February 1854* (Rome: Universita Gregoriana, 1960).
58 J. Spencer Fluhman, *"A Peculiar People": Anti-Mormonism and the Making of Religion in Nineteenth-Century America* (Chapel Hill: The University of North Carolina Press, 2012), 9–10
59 Richard L. Bushman, *Joseph Smith and the Beginnings of Mormonism* (Urbana: University of Illinois Press, 1984), 52–3; Marvin S. Hill, *Quest for Refuge: The Mormon Flight from American Pluralism* (Salt Lake City, UT: Signature Books, 1989), 9, 12, 28.
60 Sydney E. Ahlstrom, *A Religious History of the American People* (New Haven, CT: Yale University Press, 1972), 502; Fawn M. Brodie, *No Man Knows My History: The Life of Joseph Smith* (New York: Alfred A. Knopf, 1979), viii.
61 Bushman, *Joseph Smith*, 56–7.
62 Bushman, *Joseph Smith*, 61–4, 87–102; Ahlstrom, *Religious History of the American People*, 502.

63 Bushman, *Joseph Smith*, 115–19; Ahlstrom, *Religious History of the American People*, 502–3.
64 Bushman, *Joseph Smith*, 115–40; Ahlstrom, *Religious History of the American People*, 503–4.
65 Ahlstrom, *Religious History of the American People*, 504; Hill, *Quest for Refuge*, xi, xiv.
66 Bushman, *Joseph Smith*, 157.
67 Bushman, *Joseph Smith*, 149–68; Ahlstrom, *Religious History of the American People*, 503–5.
68 Hill, *Quest for Refuge*, xix, 55–98; Kenneth H. Winn, *Exiles in a Land of Liberty: Mormons in America, 1830–1846* (Chapel Hill: University of North Carolina Press, 1989), 63–84; Newell G. Bringhurst, *Brigham Young and the Expanding American Frontier* (Boston: Little, Brown and Company, 1986), 32–5.
69 Bringhurst, *Brigham Young*, 36–41; Winn, *Exiles in a Land of Liberty*, 85–105.
70 Bringhurst, *Brigham Young*, 44–9, 51–4; Leonard J. Arrington, *Brigham Young: American Moses* (New York: Alfred A. Knopf, 1985), 79–97; Ahlstrom, *Religious History of the American People*, 506.
71 Bringhurst, *Brigham Young*, 60; Hill, *Quest for Refuge*, 138.
72 Winn, *Exiles in a Land of Liberty*, 182, 212–14; Arrington, *Brigham Young*, 103; Bringhurst, *Brigham Young*, 62; Ahlstrom, *Religious History of the American People*, 506.
73 Bringhurst, *Brigham Young*, 1–29, 64–8; Arrington, *Brigham Young*, 19–49.
74 Arrington, *Brigham Young*, 128–9; Bringhurst, *Brigham Young*, 82–3; Ahlstrom, *Religious History of the American People*, 507.
75 Bringhurst, *Brigham Young*, 111.
76 Arrington, *Brigham Young*, 250–68; Bringhurst, *Brigham Young*, 112–18, 136–9. See also: Will Bagley, *Blood of the Prophets: Brigham Young and the Massacre at Mountain Meadows* (Norman: University of Oklahoma Press, 2002).
77 Ahlstrom, *Religious History of the American People*, 507.
78 Fluhman, *"A Peculiar People,"* 1.
79 Fluhman, *"A Peculiar People,"* 2.
80 Jon Butler, *Awash in a Sea of Faith: Christianizing the American People* (Cambridge, MA: Harvard University Press, 1990), 225, 284; Ahlstrom, *Religious History of the American People*, 472; Hatch, *Democratization of American Christianity*, 62.

Recommended for further reading

Arrington, Leonard J. and Davis Bitton. *The Mormon Experience: A History of the Latter-Day Saints*, 2nd edn. Urbana: University of Illinois Press, 1992.
Billington, Ray Allen. *The Protestant Crusade, 1800–1860*. New York: Macmillan Publishing Company, 1938.
Diouf, Sylviane A. *Servants of Allah: African Muslims Enslaved in the Americas*. New York: New York University Press, 1998.
Fluhman, James Spencer. *"A Peculiar People": Anti-Mormonism and the Making of Religion in Nineteenth-Century America*. Chapel Hill: The University of North Carolina Press, 2012.
Genovese, Eugene D. *Roll Jordan, Roll: The World the Slaves Made*. New York: Vintage Books, 1976.
Gjerde, Jon. *Catholicism and the Shaping of Nineteenth-Century America*, ed. S. Deborah Kang. New York: Cambridge University Press, 2012.
Gomez, Michael A. *Black Crescent: The Experience and Legacy of African Muslims in the Americas*. New York: Cambridge University Press, 2005.
McGreevy, John T. *Catholicism and American Freedom: A History*. New York: W. W. Norton, 2003.
Moore, Robert Laurence. *Religious Outsiders and the Making of Americans*. New York: Oxford University Press, 1986.
Winn, Kenneth H. *Exiles in a Land of Liberty: Mormons in America, 1830–1846*. Chapel Hill: University of North Carolina Press, 1989.

Chapter 7

Civil war and the churches

Origins of the antislavery movement

By the end of the seventeenth century, African slavery became an accepted way of life in the South, and almost simultaneously, the first protests against the South's peculiar institution were heard. The earliest known petition against slavery was published in Pennsylvania in 1688 by Francis Daniel Pastorius. In 1700, Judge Samuel Sewall of Boston published his *Selling of Joseph*, and soon after, the Quakers began adding their condemning testimony, most notably in John Woolman's *Considerations on the Keeping of Negroes* (1754).[1]

In the aftermath of the American Revolution, the acceptance of Enlightenment concepts regarding natural rights and human liberty led some denominations to incorporate condemnations of slaveholding in their disciplines. In 1775, the Quakers organized the country's first antislavery society, and in 1776, Anthony Benezet led the Society of Friends in expelling its slaveholding members. John Wesley persuaded the Christmas Conference of 1784, from which American Methodism dates its formal origins, to institute measures that would exclude slave owners or dealers from membership. As slavery continued to grow and become the source of more heated debate, however, the Methodist proscription was relaxed, as it was among the other leading denominations. In 1816, some church leaders helped organize the American Colonization Society, whose mission was to encourage manumission by sending former slaves out of the country, especially to its African outpost, Liberia.[2]

If accommodation was the rule for over two centuries, the 1830s proved to be a turning point. The story of William Lloyd Garrison, the principal leader of the Abolitionist Movement, is representative. In 1829, while running a small Baptist temperance journal, Garrison was converted to the antislavery cause by Benjamin Lundy, a New Jersey Quaker.[3] Garrison helped Lundy publish his *Genius of Universal Emancipation* but, as a result, was jailed for libel. When he was released, Garrison went to Boston to found *The Public Liberator and Journal of the Times*, in the inaugural issue of which appeared the following pledge:

> I will be harsh as truth, and as uncompromising as justice. On this subject [of slavery] I do not wish to think, or speak, or write with moderation. . . . I am in earnest – I will not equivocate – I will not excuse – I will not retreat a single inch – AND I WILL BE HEARD.[4]

No longer a gradualist – urging emancipation sometime "between now and never" – Garrison, like an increasing number of abolitionists, demanded abolition immediately. "Immediate emancipation" became the new battle cry, but even Garrison did not insist that slavery cease right away. Rather, he demanded that people decide immediately to renounce slavery, thereby setting the process of emancipation in motion.[5] In 1846, abolitionist Presbyterian minister Albert Barnes spelled out what such a commitment on the part of the nation's churches would mean:

> Let the time come when, in all the mighty denominations of Christians, it can be announced that the evil [slavery] is ceased with them forever; and let the voice of each denomination be lifted up in kind, but firm and solemn testimony against the system . . . and the work is done. There is no public sentiment in this land that would resist the power of such testimony.[6]

As Lyman Beecher said of Garrison, his zeal was commendable but misguided. His absolutism, his lack of charity, his incapacity – or unwillingness – to understand the hesitancy of others, and his branding of the United States Constitution a diabolical compact alienated many initially sympathetic Northerners. It provoked heightened Southern opposition to emancipation as well. States in the upper South, including Virginia, debated emancipation until 1830, but the Nat Turner Revolt of 1831 and the growing din of Northern abolitionism of the early 1830s ended that. In 1832, Garrison organized the New England Antislavery Society on a platform of immediatism. In 1833, with the help of the wealthy merchant Arthur Tappan, he established the American Antislavery Society (AAS), and by 1838, the AAS claimed a membership of 250,000.[7]

Adding fervor to the abolitionist movement were the idealism generated by, and expressed publicly by, clerical and lay leaders of the American Revolution and the religious heat of the Second Great Awakening. The Declaration of Independence served as a symbolic benchmark dividing the ages of monarchic despotism from a new era of political liberty and self-determination, and American reformers pictured their own moral revolutions as the fulfillment of their destiny as God's chosen people. Suggestive of this, David Walker, the militant free black abolitionist, concluded his manifesto, *Appeal to the Colored Citizens of the World*, by quoting the Declaration of Independence and exclaiming: "See your Declaration, Americans!!!"[8]

That same spirit of reform was advanced by the Second Great Awakening and, in particular, the revival activity of Charles Finney in the Old Northwest. In contrast to the First Great Awakening, the participants of which generally remained silent on more worldly matters, conversion and Christian commitment to social relevant causes, like antislavery, was an earmark of the Second Awakening. The revivalists believed in a new, more immediate relation between man and God and man and his fellow-creatures – one that emphasized perfectibility rather than inability, activity rather than passivity, benevolence rather than piety.[9]

The Second Great Awakening encouraged abolitionists and most antebellum crusaders to see reform as something akin to an act of repentance. Evangelists instilled in their audiences a sense of personal responsibility for slavery and an obligation to act against it, as sin. In their bleak images of the slaveholder, the slaver, and the South, evangelical abolitionists constructed a model of what happened when any people did not conquer their worst cravings. They characterized slaveholders as lazy, irreligious, and disrespectful of family, and the slaveholding South as a place where tyranny and disorder prevailed. Moral dissolution turned the South into a cursed land. Such condemnation slighted social, political, and economic factors, and it could be narrow and self-righteous, but it had a passion and moral firmness badly needed when men and women agitated unpopular issues in a society where the instinct to compromise was second nature. Immediate emancipation jolted people out of their complacency and infused antislavery with a fervor it did not have before 1830.[10]

In 1834, Theodore Dwight Weld, one of Finney's converts and for a time one of Finney's "holy band" of assistant revivalists, was also converted to abolitionism, and he brought the antislavery gospel to Lane Theological Seminary in Cincinnati. The seminary students' nearly unanimous indictment of gradualism in the debates that resulted, not only produced a number of leading abolitionists, but also provoked administrators to adopt disciplinary measures, which in turn led one vocal group of dissidents to migrate to Oberlin, Ohio. Oberlin, and Oberlin College, under the leadership of Asa Mahon and Charles Finney, and with the financial assistance of Arthur and Lewis Tappan of New York – both of whom had also felt Finney's influence – became a center of both abolitionism and revivalism.[11]

Other influential figures joined forces with the new movement. In 1835, James G Birney, a former slaveholder, then colonizationist, was converted to abolitionism by Theodore Dwight Weld. Birney began his work in Kentucky, but when threatened by mob action, he moved to Cincinnati, Ohio, where he began publishing a crusading journal. The murder of Elijah Lovejoy in Alton, Illinois, in 1837 while defending his printing press electrified the North and led even more to conclude that slavery and freedom were incompatible. Among those brought into the movement at that point was Edward Beecher, President of Illinois College. Beecher not only condemned the Alton riots but also issued a series of articles on "organic sin," which gave evangelical abolitionism some of its major ethical and theological insights.[12]

The antislavery axis of Tappan, Garrison, Weld, Lovejoy, and Birney was forged, transforming what had been a minor, ineffective protest movement into a nationally organized crusade. The American Antislavery Society printed and distributed thousands of pieces of abolitionist literature, even in the South, and in 1837, it began to encourage and coordinate the circulation of antislavery petitions directed at Congress. In 1839, the American Antislavery Society broke in two over Garrison's insistence on involving women leaders and on non-political moral suasion, but any negative impact on the movement as a whole was brief. Antislavery was soon thoroughly politicized, leading to the creation of the Liberty and Free Soil Parties. As long as antislavery remained a third party issue, it could not carry the day. But as Ronald Walters has concluded: "In a highly political nation, electioneering and losing can serve as a valuable form of propaganda." With the rise of the Republican Party in the 1850s, they would lose no more.[13]

As noted earlier, rallying in support of slavery in the South was due to the Nat Turner revolt of 1831 and the inflammatory, vituperative language of the Abolitionist Movement. The South, which had not until that point spoken with one voice on its peculiar institution, rapidly closed ranks. Abolitionist hopes for an awakening of Southern slaveholders' consciences were dashed, and an elaborate scriptural argument that soothed Christian consciences on slavery was fused with a new Southern nationalism. By the 1850s, treatises by Thomas Dew, John C. Calhoun, Edmund Ruffin, Henry Hughes, William Grayson, George Fitzhugh, and others provided elaborate sociological defenses of African slavery, often by comparing it to the "wage slavery" of the North. Southern clergy added appeals to slaveholders to live up to the ideals expounded in those treatises and to treat their slaves humanely.[14]

Proslavery literature involved an effort to construct a coherent Southern social philosophy. In defending what they referred to as the cornerstone of their social order, Southerners presented a world-view that included social legitimization and their self-conscious definition of themselves. Non-evangelical Southerners responded to antislavery polemics with anger and indignation. Southern evangelicals responded differently. They found it necessary to challenge the abolitionist's premise that slavery was a sin before God.[15]

Southern evangelicals argued that scripture sanctioned slavery in passages like Genesis 14:14, Leviticus 25:44–55, and I Corinthians 11:21–4. They pointed to the Old Testament story of Ham. In summary form, they explained that Noah had three sons, Ham, Shem, and Japeth, from whom the earth was populated. One day when Noah lay in a drunken stupor, Ham, the father of Canaan, saw his nakedness. He told Shem and Japeth, who covered their father without looking at him. Upon waking, Noah realized what had happened and cursed Ham. "Cursed be Canaan; a servant of servants shall he be unto his brethren." Noah blessed Shem, adding that Canaan would be his servant, and prophesied that God would "enlarge Japeth," who would dwell in the tents of Shem and be served by Canaan as well (Genesis 9:20–9). Southerners understood Ham to be black, Japeth white, and Shem Indian – all prototypes of the races of America, thus offering one resolution to a tension in white Southern Christian thought: how blacks could be fellow-human beings and yet deserve to be slaves.[16]

Turning to the New Testament, Southern evangelicals pointed out that Christ and his apostles, though living where it existed and was recognized by Roman law, did not denounce slavery. Indeed, they received into the church slaves and slaveholders alike and called upon slaves to be obedient to their masters, and masters to act with humanity toward their slaves. Why should things be any different in the Christian South? The South was largely successful in its exegetical defense of slavery through direct appeal to Scripture, forcing Northern clergy to find other grounds for their claim of slavery's sinfulness. Their appeal to a Higher Law to condemn slavery constituted not an appeal to the Bible but to an individual conscience that stood above not only the Constitution but also the revealed word of God.[17]

Southern Christian missions to the slaves burgeoned during the 1840s and 1850s. Such missions, Southern evangelicals insisted, provided "a most merciful deliverance" from the "savage idolatry" of unredeemed Africa to a Christian land where they became "the most contented and happy people on earth." In sum, as Carwardine has concluded, Southern evangelicals "accepted slavery not because it was a positive good, but because it was consistent with Scripture and involved fewer evils than would result from emancipation."[18]

It should be noted that, although quite effective, the enormous pressures for conformity were never entirely successful in eliminating Southern opposition to slavery. There were clergy who dissented from the Southern proslavery position, and they paid a dear price for that dissent. Given their low profile, their exact numbers cannot be determined, but they were a distinct minority. Most were located in the upper South, as was true of dissent in the general population. Even there, however, making their sentiments known, or having them discovered, often led to severe punishment (frequently at the hands of mobs), imprisonment, and even death.[19]

Antislavery and the churches

Church history was intrinsic to both Northern and Southern anti- and proslavery developments. The many voluntary associations for evangelism and moral reform became inseparable from the humanitarian crusades that marked the first half of the nineteenth century, including the antislavery movement. The churches were slow in joining the antislavery cause, but as the movement gained momentum, the countless auxiliary organizations of mainstream Protestantism became radiating centers of concern and agitation. The national antislavery societies, now faction-ridden, were superseded by ecclesiastical organizations in which an antislavery Social Gospel was forging ahead, winning new leaders, trampling on compromisers, and bringing schism or conflict when the occasion demanded.[20]

Among the dozens, perhaps hundreds, of antislavery leaders and abolitionists, whites outnumbered blacks and, understandably, northerners were more numerous than Southerners, largely because white northerners were better positioned to publicly oppose the South's "peculiar institution." Nevertheless, the role that blacks and even Southerners played in the antislavery movement was important, even critical. Among the leading white male abolitionists were William Lloyd Garrison, Theodore Weld, David Walker, and Elijah Lovejoy. The list of prominent white women included Lydia Maria Child, Lucretia Mott, and Harriet Beecher Stowe, as well as the Grimke sisters, Angelina and Sarah, who defied their Southern slaveholding heritage. Women were often, but not always, married to abolitionists. They tended to come from the more liberal denominations, such as the Quakers and Unitarians, and as Manisha Sinha has persuasively argued, their grassroots organizing did much to assure the political impact of the antislavery movement. (It also laid the groundwork for the women's rights movement.) Nevertheless, as noted, black abolitionists, male and female, were critical and included the likes of Frederick Douglass, Sojourner Truth, Harriet Tubman, and numerous black ministers who often served several small parishes or took to the itinerant circuit where they stoked the fires of antislavery sentiment.[21]

Participation in antislavery activities created a black clerical elite. They tended to belong to traditionally white churches. They interacted with white abolitionists and were generally freer and better situated to be visibly active. Among their ranks were Congregationalists Amos Beman and Charles Ray, Episcopalians Alexander Crummell and Peter Williams, Presbyterians Samuel Cornish and Theodore Wright, and others. A much larger group of ministers served in middle-class or historically black churches (for example, the African Methodist Episcopal [AME] Church), while most worked in small congregations and on itinerant circuits. We know very little about the second two groups. Their actions were less public and their sermons seldom found their way into print.[22]

Most black ministers opposed slavery through the counseling of their church members in self-respect and a "higher manhood" and by providing aid to fugitives, often at stations on the Underground Railroad. Some offered ideological support and even antislavery activism, but most offered constant support for moral reform. Their theology, like that of most of their white abolitionist ministerial colleagues, was nineteenth-century evangelical Protestant, but it was more heavily weighted in the direction of a human god and liberating Christology. Nevertheless, as the Civil War approached, black ministers lived in an increasingly dangerous world. As one AME minister put it: "Every colored man is an abolitionist, and slaveholders know it."[23]

The South witnessed the anomaly of its equally fervent religiosity and equally strident moralism marked by a diametrically opposed view of slavery, which can be accounted for only with reference to their different cultural conditions and ethics. As Sydney Ahlstrom has put it: "The South channeled the social impact of evangelicalism and its perfectionist demands against the weaker provinces of Satan's kingdom." In other words, it was used to keep the work of the evangelical united front aimed at the tasks it had pursued before 1830.[24]

Slavery was not entirely ignored. Richard Furman's biblical argument was adopted by the South Carolina Baptist Association in 1822 and by 1841, when John England, the Roman Catholic bishop of Charleston, published his defense of slavery, this line of thought had sunk deep into the Southern consciousness. Theologians and laity alike learned to recite the standard biblical texts on African inferiority, patriarchal and Mosaic acceptance of servitude, and Saint Paul's counsels of obedience to masters. Evangelization of the slaves was pursued with increased vigor, at the same time that the emotionalism of revivalism contributed to extremist views on slavery in the South, as it had in the North. As the nation reached mid-century, evangelicals both in the North and South became increasingly more polarized and less willing to compromise.[25]

Churches rent asunder

William Lloyd Garrison never anticipated that abolitionism would cause any conflict within American churches. He and others in the antislavery movement were church leaders "tenacious of their theological views, [and] full of veneration for the organized church and ministry," confident that both would rally to their cause. They never dreamed that their opposition to the nation's "distinctive, all-conquering sin" would breed such opposition and divide American denominations so badly. Those clergy who had not yet spoken out on slavery were simply preoccupied with subjects nearer home or ignorant of the true nature of the institution.[26]

Even the ranks of the Quakers, who were the first to oppose slavery in large numbers, were divided – not on the issue of slavery, of which they were rid, but on abolition. Benjamin Lundy, James and Lucretia Mott, and others actively engaged in abolition, but theirs were individual efforts, and many of their co-religionists refused to join them. Moreover, antislavery was a factor in the struggle between 1827 and 1829 that led to separations within Quaker meetings. Elias Hicks, whose principles precipitated those separations, authored the antislavery pamphlet *Observations on the Slavery of the Africans and Their Descendants* (1810), in which he urged Friends to boycott rice, cotton, and sugar, as long as they were products of slave labor. Hicks's primary concerns were doctrinal, however, and the Hicksites were not necessarily antislavery.[27]

The Presbyterian Church did not explicitly divide on the issue of slavery until after secession. Nevertheless, Old School men had grown suspicious of the new kind of revivalism that swept the nation after 1800. Many were suspicious of its growing emphasis on conversion and religious experience, and disturbed by the apparent corresponding laxity with regard to doctrine and the sacraments. They were also skeptical of the results of an alliance New England Presbyterians had entered into with Congregationalists – the Plan of Union – whereby the two worked toward interdenominational harmony and the championing of evangelical Christianity on the region's sparsely settled frontier. By the 1830s, however, Old School Southern Presbyterians began to sense a growing antislavery spirit in the New School. That spirit, though not explicitly articulated, underscored the accusations of heresy and complicity exchanged at the Presbyterian Assembly of 1837, and that led to the two groups' separation. Antislavery memorials presented to the General Assembly of 1837 were tabled without discussion, and four synods representing the "New School" were expelled, even though they were supported by some 60,000 Presbyterians, all in the North.[28]

In 1818, the General Assembly of the undivided Presbyterian Church had unanimously adopted a manifesto that declared the institution of slavery "utterly inconsistent with the law of God." It also voted, however, that "hasty emancipation" was an even "greater curse." This compromise continued to mark the official position of both the New and Old Schools after 1837. Both continued to have minorities that represented anti- and proslavery positions, and leaders of both factions feared further divisions.[29]

Within the New School, however, more and more members made their antislavery sentiments known. The Reverend Albert Barnes of New Jersey published the influential *Inquiry into the Scriptural View of Slavery* (1846). In 1846 and 1849, a few churches even left the New School to form an antislavery union, but it was short-lived. Finally, in 1850, the New School General Assembly repudiated the view that slavery was a divinely sanctioned institution. In 1853, it took steps to implement that position and tension increased until, in 1857, the small number of remaining proslavery presbyteries withdrew to form their own assembly. The Old School Church was more successful in suppressing any official discussion of the slavery issue until 1861, when the newly constituted Presbyterian Church of the Confederate States of America declared: "We have no right, as a church, to enjoin [slavery] as a duty, or to condemn it as a sin."[30]

The Methodist Church was just as poorly equipped to deal with the slavery controversy. It was organized in a strict and inflexible way, so that disagreements over matters of consequence had to be formally resolved at a national level. Thus, when it sought to extend its membership into the South, Methodists were forced to modify John Wesley's original regulations on slavery. By 1843, there were 1,200 Methodist ministers and preachers owning about 1,500 slaves, and 25,000 members with about 208,000 slaves. If the church was going to maintain its unity, it would have to maintain a strict neutrality and silence on the slavery question. By 1836, neither was any longer possible.[31]

At first, the Methodists followed the Presbyterians' example. At their General Conference of 1836, Methodists formally conceded the evils of slavery, but they condemned as well, in very forceful terms, "modern abolitionism." This measure managed to get the church through its annual meeting in one piece, but it only incited the increasing number of Methodist abolitionists led by the Vermont circuit preacher Orange Scott. Scott, influenced by William Lloyd Garrison and the *Liberator*, turned the Methodist organ, *Zion's Herald*, to antislavery, while his "Appeal to the Methodist Episcopal Church," printed in 1838 in the *Wesleyan Anti-Slavery Review*, made the struggle within the church for a change in its stern antiabolitionist policy inevitable.[32]

By the General Conference of 1844, a sizable number of Methodists was prepared to call for separation. The debate was precipitated by an outcry over the slaveholding of Bishop James Andrew of Georgia. When a motion to force Andrew to "desist from the exercise of his functions" as long as he owned slaves passed – voted along sectional lines – all was lost. Neither side was willing to compromise and the two sides agreed to "an amicable plan of separation," in which the two groups pledged to remain in fellowship with each other.[33]

On May 1, 1845, the Methodist Episcopal Church, South, was born at a convention in Louisville, Kentucky. Since the South had been able to stave off any attempt to condemn slavery in the undivided church, no changes in the new church's constitution were necessary. In the North, however, the process of reorganization did not go as smoothly. Northern Methodists condemned the Compromise of 1850, but they did not formally commit themselves to the Abolitionist Movement. Instead, foreshadowing the response of Lincoln and Unionists to Southern secession, when word of the separation of Southern Methodist congregations reached the membership in the North, several leaders, including abolitionists, issued charges of unconstitutionality. At the 1848 General Conference, the South's delegate was rebuffed and the Plan of Separation declared null and void. The Northern Methodist Church did not redress its actions of 1848 by sending a delegate southward until 1872; by then the issue of slavery had been settled, but not separation. Northern and Southern Methodists had gone their own way.[34]

Finally, there were the Baptists. In theory, the Baptists were better prepared for the challenge of slavery than either the Presbyterians or Methodists, in that their polity was primarily congregational; Baptist national organization was seen as a "cooperative agency" of its various churches. Founded in 1814 to support missionaries to foreign countries, the General Convention met triennially after 1832 in conjunction with the new Home Missionary Society. During the volatile 1830s, the Convention managed to avoid the issue of slavery. In 1840, antislavery Baptists organized the National Baptist Anti-Slavery Convention and tried to force the issue among their brethren. In the same year, however, the Foreign Missions Board formally declared its neutrality, and in 1843, it was supported in this by the General Convention.[35]

The Anti-Slavery Convention continued to meet and to agitate, and by 1844, abolitionism gained in both numbers and stridency among Baptists in the North. Antislavery talk began to be heard in state conventions, and soon both mission boards were faced with decisions deliberately thrust upon them by the South in an attempt to head off any actions by the North. In October 1844, the Home Board declined to appoint as a missionary the nominee of the General Baptist Convention, James Reeves, because he was a slaveholder. It insisted, however, that it would continue to embrace slaveholding members and contributions.[36]

Two months later the Foreign Board took a similar position when petitioned to state its policy by the Alabama Baptist Convention. The Southern response was predictable. They called for a meeting of their similarly aggrieved brethren to take a united stand against what they saw at the aggression of their Northern brethren. Delegates from nine states met on May 8, 1845, in Augusta, Georgia, and gave birth to the Southern Baptist Convention. Its first regular triennial session was held in 1846. The Southern Baptist Convention issued no formal statement on slavery. Northern Baptists avoided further division by retaining their congregational format, but their American Baptist Missionary Union excluded proslavery members from its ranks.[37]

Churches that escaped schism

As previously noted, the Civil War was a theological crisis. Although most Americans agreed with one another that the Bible was authoritative, there was widespread disagreement about what the Bible taught about slavery. As a result, none of the several American churches of the antebellum period could escape the impact of the slavery debate. Some, however, were able to escape the full brunt of its divisiveness. Some of those churches were able to survive schism because they did not have significant membership in both the North and South. Congregationalists and Unitarians, for example, not only made their antislavery position public but also made major contributions to the antislavery movement. Their members, however, were almost entirely from the North and increasingly antislavery.[38]

Other churches – the Lutheran, Episcopal, and Roman Catholic churches, for example – remained undivided until secession. Despite their having comparatively large constituencies in the North and South and contributing vigorous polemicists to both sides of the controversy, they were able to avoid any showdown on the matter. Lutheran synods and Episcopal and Roman Catholic dioceses tended to be organized on a territorial basis, thereby limiting the meeting of controversial issues at the national level. The Lutheran General Synod, for example, which did take a strong antislavery stand, had little more than advisory or coordinating functions, thereby leaving each territorial synod to deal with the issue much as it chose.[39]

The general conventions of the Episcopal Church did provide the opportunity for controversy, but the church was able to avoid schism by remaining extraordinarily passive. Historians remain divided in explaining this, but they agree that Episcopalians were generally conservative and satisfied with the *status quo*. In the end, separate dioceses could and did adapt themselves to local conditions with no interference from above.[40]

The Roman Catholic Church was unique among all the previously mentioned American denominations in that it was international, and the official position of the church in the antebellum period – issued from the Vatican – was that slavery as a principle of social organization was not in itself sinful. In 1838, Pope Gregory XVI did reiterate the church's condemnation of the slave trade, but not slavery itself. As Archbishop of Baltimore, thereby occupying the most influential post in the American hierarchy, Bishop Francis Kenrick continually sought to interpret the church's teachings on slavery. He regretted that there were so many slaves whose liberty and education were so restricted, but he otherwise equivocated, thereby placing himself much in the same company with Episcopal leaders who favored the *status quo*.[41]

Much the same can be said of the pastoral letters of the assembled American Catholic bishops, which studiously avoided any reference to the national dilemma. The single exception was a letter of 1840 in which the bishops made an ambiguous, indirect allusion to the nation's political parties having avoided the issue of slavery. Historians have interpreted that letter as an admission that the hierarchy was divided, and divided it remained. Even when the war came and churches existed in the Union and Confederacy, the church at large maintained its position on slavery, while bishops North and South continued to keep in contact with each other "so far as circumstances would allow."[42]

One last interesting example of compromise comes from none other than the African Methodist Episcopal Church. When a majority report on slavery, denying membership to those who held slaves, was presented to the 1856 AME general convention, it was labeled radical and hotly debated. Obviously, there were few slaveholders, if any, in their ranks, but they feared that adoption of the proposed measure would result in closings of its Southern congregations and encourage the intimidation of its itinerants in Border States. The convention passed a milder compromise report.[43]

Some have argued that the split in the churches was the chief cause of the final rupture of the Union. To be sure, churchmen played leading roles in the moral revolution that swept the North and South in opposite directions between 1830 and 1860. Churchmen converted the antislavery movement into a massive juggernaut and dedicated the South to preserving a biblically supported social order. To both causes they transmitted the overcharged intensity of revivalism, carrying it even to the troops when war finally came. "We are charged with having brought about the present contest," declared northern Methodist Granville Moody in 1861. "'I believe it is true that we did bring it about, and I glory in it, for it is a wreath of glory around our brow." Ministers on both sides of the Mason-Dixon Line shared Moody's sentiment.[44]

The churches amid civil war

"When the cannons roared in Charleston Harbor . . . two divinely authorized crusades were set in motion, each of them absolutizing a given social and political order. The pulpits resounded with a vehemence and absence of restraint never equaled in American history." So wrote Sydney Ahlstrom in his assessment of the churches' role in the American Civil War. Once disunion was a reality politically, so too it became an ecclesiastical reality. Even those churches that had not formally divided, professed their patriotism in unquestionable terms.

Northern clergy who believed slavery was an institutional evil, but were reluctant to resort to war for its destruction, now saw no alternative. Southern clergy who accepted slavery as a necessary evil, and opposed secession in its defense, no longer had any choice.[45]

At its meeting in 1862, the General Synod of the Lutheran Church, now without its Southern members, appointed a special committee to apprise President Abraham Lincoln of its wholehearted support, characterizing the "rebellion" as most wicked, unjustifiable, unnatural, inhuman, oppressive and "destructive in its results to the highest interests of morality and religion." Southern Presbyterians, who had with equal vigor insisted on neutrality on the issue of slavery, also shifted their position. In the same year, they expressed their deep conviction "that this struggle is not alone for civil rights and property and home, but also for religion, for the church, for the gospel, for existence itself."[46]

Not only did the churches attest to their respective governments and armies through sermon and prayer, but also they actively participated in the war effort by bringing a Christian ministry to the soldiers and by organizing non-combatant support among their constituencies. A remarkably large number of chaplains volunteered, and they carried on their ministries with astounding success, actually precipitating revivals among the rank and file. Estimates of conversions vary between 100,000 and 200,000, but regardless of the exact number many agreed with J. William Jones, a chaplain in Lee's Army of Northern Virginia, that:

> any history of that army which omits an account of the wonderful influence of religion upon it – which fails to tell how the courage, discipline, and morale of the whole was influenced by the humble piety and evangelical zeal of many of its officers and men – would be incomplete and unsatisfactory.

As Ahlstrom found: "A fervently pious nation was at war, and amid the carnage and slaughter, amid the heroism and weariness, men on both sides hungered for inspiration and peace with God." Dedicated ministers on both sides responded, and on both sides "the soldier's sense of duty was deepened, his morale improved, his loyalty intensified." Perhaps the war itself was lengthened, as well, and its carnage made worse.[47]

More complicated are the various ways in which the churches interpreted the Civil War. Historians have argued that the crisis significantly modified Americans' theological understanding of history. Such interpretations did not surface, however, until the war was at an end and more patriotic stances were neither no longer needed nor viable. In some ways postwar assessments reflected earlier positions; in other cases they were quite different. Ministers on both sides, however, asked themselves why they had fought and why so many of their number had died.[48]

At the war's end, in both the North and South, there were feelings of relief, dejection and smoldering rage. In the South, Father Abram Ryan, Confederate chaplain, gave voice to what many surely continued to believe when he wrote that the South would "keep watch over the Stars and Bars until the morning of the Resurrection." Their hearts would remain with the Lost Cause even after they had been defeated on the battlefield.[49]

Similarly, Southern Presbyterian theologian Robert Lewis Dabney, who had served as adjutant under Stonewall Jackson, continued to insist that the war had been caused deliberately by abolitionists who "with calculated malice" goaded the South to violence in order to revolutionize the government and "gratify their spite." "I do not forgive," he declared. "What! Forgive those people, who have invaded our country, burned our cities, destroyed our homes, slain our young men, and spread desolation and ruin over our land! No, I do not forgive them." He continued to yearn for a "retributive Providence" that would demolish the North and abolish the Union.[50]

Henry Ward Beecher took a page from Lincoln's Second Inaugural Address and counseled compassion for the South, but he, like most in the North, mourned the war dead and the loss of his leader, nearly deified by an assassin's bullet. His indictment of the South was no less direct and only slightly more temperate than Dabney's condemnation of the North:

> I charge the whole guilt of this war upon the ambitious, educated, plotting political lead-
> ers of the South. . . . A day will come when God will reveal judgment and arraign these
> mighty miscreants . . . and every maimed and wounded sufferer, and every bereaved
> heart in all the wide regions of this land, will rise up and come before the Lord to lay
> upon these chief culprits of modern history their awful witness. . . . And then these
> guiltiest and most remorseless traitors, these high and cultured men with might and
> wisdom . . . shall be whirled aloft and plunged downward forever and ever in an endless
> retribution.[51]

Some Northern clergy made note of the wrath God had already unleashed on the South, as promised in her battle hymn by Julia Ward Howe, and saw the resultant desolation as deserved. Theodore Munger, a pastor-theologian in New Haven, Connecticut, was representative of this group when he explained in his essay on "Providence and the War," two decades after Appomattox, the divine logic by which the South had been punished for its sins, with the North as the "sacrificing instrument." Not only had a deathblow been dealt to a diabolical slave state so that America could realize its destiny, but also justice had been done in a most devastating manner, appropriate to the nature and severity of the crime or sin.[52]

Yet another group of theologians was less confident of God's intentions in the war. Some Southern evangelicals found the answer to their questions about defeat in the individual vices and sins of their own people, rather than in the shape and fabric of their empire. Otherwise, they could only make reference to God's will. God, wrote a Georgia Baptist editor in 1866, "has done what He thought best." He may have "laid His hand heavily upon us; certainly we are deeply smitten, but in the midst of it all, we rely on His goodness, and would not, if we could, interfere with the workings of His providence."[53]

A Virginia editor could not believe that God had designed the Civil War to overthrow slavery, an institution which God himself "ordained, established and sanctioned" forever. He could not have intended that an "inferior race might be released from a nominal bondage and endowed with a freedom which, to them, is but another name for licentiousness, and which must end in complete extermination." He concluded: "It was Satan that ruled the hour of emancipation." For this editor and others in the South the war settled the problem of power, not of morality.[54]

Northern views of historical events could be ambiguous as well, and less than certain of their own or their region's moral purity, but at the same time strike a jeremiad-like position intended to restore the postmillennial faith of the early decades of the century. Agents of both the North and South, they occasionally charged, shared complicity in the institution of slavery to which God was so opposed that He plunged the nation into war. These clergy searched for a way of seeing the entire tragedy – its triumphs and defeats, on both sides – as meaningful to the nation as a whole. Though perhaps no less certain of the nation's destiny, they saw the need to bring all Americans, not just Southerners, to penitence, reformation, and reconciliation with God as His chosen people.[55]

Horace Bushnell of Massachusetts was a spokesman for this position, as was Philip Schaff of Pennsylvania. So too was Abraham Lincoln, perhaps no less a student of the Bible in his own way. Bushnell and Schaff held the special view that suffering was the instrument by which the nation would be purged of the sins that had brought about the conflict and experience a new birth. Both used the symbol "baptism by blood." According to Schaff: "This very baptism of blood entitles us also to hope for a glorious regeneration." By references to the Crucifixion and vicarious sacrifice, Bushnell sought to explain the suffering and sacrifice of the war as an act of expiation of corporate sin, thereby opening the way for the atonement of the nation.[56]

Bushnell said that the great sin for which the nation was suffering was the failure in the founding of the nation to recognize that God must be the author of a true and lasting community. He believed that the war would result in a new national consciousness which would rest on a deeper foundation than the illusion of a man-made compact. So too Schaff saw the possibility of a new and redeemed sense of nationhood rising out of the death and carnage. What he added was a more pronounced sense that the war had ultimately readied America for its great role in the cause of human freedom, thereby identifying the war as an event of world-historical significance.[57] And then there was Lincoln's Second Inaugural Addresses.

Lincoln's "Sermon on the Mount"

Try as they might to associate the martyred president with any particular Christian denomination, the task proved futile. Although shot on Good Friday, April 14, and mourned in churches across the land on Easter Sunday, April 16, the savior of the nation, who shed his blood as an atonement for the sins of the nation, belonged to no church.

Lincoln grew up in an austere predestinarian separatist Baptist, Kentucky family, where the Bible was not only the primary, but likely the only, book available to him – long passages of which, he committed to memory. After he left home, however, Lincoln also read the works of Tom Paine, Voltaire, and other deists and skeptics, his response to which has led some to describe Lincoln for most of his adult life alternately as "inhabit[ing] a twilight of belief and doubt somewhere between evangelical Protestantism and Enlightenment skepticism," or more specifically as an atheist, agnostic, deist fatalist, spiritualist, or Christian. Lincoln referred to himself as "a seeking spirit," and when asked why he never joined a church responded:

> When any church will inscribe over its altar as its sole qualification for membership the Savior's condensed statement of the substance of both the law and gospel, thou shalt love the Lord thy God with all thy heart, and with all thy soul, and with all thy mind, and thy neighbor as thyself – that Church will I join with all my heart and soul.

That never happened.[58]

Perhaps a more fruitful avenue to investigate may be how Lincoln's evolving religious beliefs "laid a foundation for his political thinking" and for his understanding of meaning of the Civil War, the best articulation of which came in his Second Inaugural Address, delivered on March 4, 1865 (see Figure 7.1). As Ronald White, the leading authority on Lincoln's Second Inaugural has put it, with the end of the bloody, four year struggle finally in sight, "most people came to the inaugural event expecting that the bugle sounds of marching soldiers would be accompanied by the trumpet sounds of an inaugural address. . . . The inaugural seemed the moment for vindication, for the Union and for the president." Instead, what Lincoln gave them was a "benediction."[59]

Figure 7.1 Lincoln's Second Inaugural Address

Source: Everett Collection Historical/Alamy Stock Photo

What White found in his study was convincing evidence that, regardless of his religious beliefs as a younger man, in his presidential years Lincoln came to embrace "a faith that would sustain him in times of stress and grief," and that "the bulk of his reflection about the meaning of God and faith evolved in the context of the political questions and issues of the Civil War." Underscoring his newfound faith was his newfound belief that the purposes of the Almighty are perfect, even though we mortals may fail to understand them, and perhaps most difficult for many to understand them, and perhaps even today, that God intended "some great good to follow this mighty convulsion" – the Civil War. But just what was that good?[60]

In his final and supreme statement on the war, his Second Inaugural Address, Lincoln expounded on the significance of the war for an "almost chosen people." He held to the proposition that nations and men are instruments of Almighty God, a proposition at which Lincoln arrived nearly three years earlier following the Union's crushing defeat at the Second Battle of Bull Run, when the President was struggling "to understand the meaning of God's activity in the Maelstrom of war."[61] In a private reflection found among Lincoln's papers only after his death, and named by his private secretary John Hay "Meditation on the Divine Will," Lincoln wrote:

The will of God prevails. In great contests each party claims to act in accordance with the will of God. Both may be, and one must be, wrong. God can not [sic] be for, and against the same thing at the same time. In the present war it is quite possible that God's purpose is something different from the purpose of either party – and yet the human instrumentalities, working just as they do, are of the best adaptation to effect His purpose. I am almost ready to say this is probably true – that God wills this contest, and wills that it shall not end yet. By his mere quiet power, on the minds of the now contestants, He could have either saved or destroyed the Union without a human contest. Yet the contest began. And having begun He could give the final victory to either side any day. Yet the contest proceeds.[62]

The contest did proceed for another three years and Lincoln, perhaps because he was not quite ready to make his thoughts public, kept them to himself until his Second Inaugural Address.

In what remains the second shortest inaugural address in United States history (Washington's Second, delivered on March 5, 1793, was even shorter) – some 701 words, 25 sentences, and 4 paragraphs long – Lincoln, who made no references to God in his First Inaugural, mentioned God 14 times, quoted or paraphrased the Bible 4 times, and made mention of prayer 3 times. Whether Lincoln used the many religious references in his Second Inaugural for political reasons or because his beliefs had evolved over the course of the past four years, Lincoln chose his references carefully. By way of example, White has titled the address Lincoln's "Sermon on the Mount" because of one particular choice of words from the New Testament and the message it conveyed for the entire address: "Judge not, that ye be not judged," Matthew 7:1. White has explained that, in these words, taken from Jesus's "Sermon on the Mount," Jesus "advocates an ethic rooted in humility and compassion . . . grace and mercy." So too would Lincoln.[63]

Given the brevity of his address, Lincoln wasted no time in turning directly to that matter over which the war had been fought. "Both parties deprecated war; but one of them would make war rather than let the nation survive; and the other would accept war rather than let it perish." "Both read the same Bible," Lincoln continued, "and pray to the same God; and each invokes His aid against the other. . . . [But] the prayers of both could not be answered"; and indeed even the North's had not been answered fully.[64]

By employing the words, "The Almighty has His own purposes," White has argued, "Lincoln brought the idea of God to the rhetorical center of his Second Inaugural Address."[65] But Lincoln went on to explain: "If we shall suppose that American slavery is one of those offenses which, in the providence of God," had to be, it had "continued through its appointed time," and God now willed that it be removed. Toward that end, God had given both the North and South this terrible war, as the woe due to those by whom the offense came. "Fondly do we hope – fervently do we pray," he continued, "that this mighty scourge of war may speedily pass away. Yet, if God wills that it continue . . . so still it must be said the judgments of the Lord are true and righteous altogether."

It was in the last paragraph of his Second Inaugural that Lincoln, unexpectedly to many, drove home the point of his address. In brief, speaking as the war was drawing to an end, when many might have expected words of celebration, Lincoln called to his audience's attention "a perilous evil in their midst" – the evil of slavery that had been at the heart of the American body politic from the nation's very founding. Lincoln was about to enter into a type of sermon with which the reader is already familiar – the Jeremiad.[66]

Although it may not sound it at the start, the purpose of these sermons was neither to merely chastise people, nor to discourage them from believing in God's having chosen them to carry out his will. Rather, it was a means by which God's chosen people could be reminded of their "backsliding" and encouraged to renew their covenant with God and regain his love and protection. The jeremiad thus combined criticism and reaffirmation with the purpose of encouraging reform.[67]

Lincoln's Second Inaugural resembled a jeremiad because it combined criticism and reaffirmation. Because of the evil of slavery, the nation deserved God's indignation and wrath. Further, the evil of slavery, though most obvious in the South, could not be laid at the feet of the South alone, as the North, too, was complicit in its creation and perpetuation, long after it had eliminated what became the South's "peculiar institution." The war, Lincoln suggested, was "divine retribution aimed at both sides," but it was also a means of purging the nation of its sins. At the moment when victory celebrations were in order, as most no doubt perceived it, Lincoln put forth the argument that "the war was divine retribution aimed at both sides."[68]

It is important to note that Lincoln believed that God had blessed America, or, as he put it in his second Annual Message to Congress on December 1, 1862, America was "the last, best hope of earth." But even then he warned: "The fiery trial through which we pass, will light us down, in honor or dishonor, to the latest generation. . . . In giving freedom to the slave, we assure freedom to the free – honorable alike in what we give, and what we preserve. We shall nobly save, or meanly lose, the last best hope of earth." Lincoln shared what we have seen in earlier chapters was a belief in the special destiny of America. "Where he distinguished himself," White has argued, "was in his willingness to confront its ambiguities. Brooding over the honor and dishonor in his nation's actions, he was unwilling to reduce political rhetoric to national self-congratulation."[69]

Thus Lincoln concluded his inaugural by confirming his belief in the Union, one nation under God with a moral purpose, which had undergone a great and tragic test of its central proposition, but could be born again by way of charity toward the vanquished:

> With malice toward none; with charity for all; with firmness in the right, as God gives us to see the right, let us strive on to finish the work we are in; to bind up the nation's wounds; to care for him who shall have borne the battle, and for his widow, and his orphan – to do all which may achieve and cherish a just, and a lasting peace, among ourselves, and with all nations.[70]

It would take decades for most Americans to see their way to Lincoln's call for charity.

Reconstruction and the churches

For most Southerners reconstruction meant one thing: to put back the pieces so far as possible to the way they were in 1860. When the old social and economic structure fell, the South began erecting a new structure, a biracial social and economic order, on the foundation of its old philosophy. The South's new philosophy was in part a yearning for a simpler, lost civilization, but it also bolstered Southern resistance to federal control of the region under radical Republican reconstruction and, ultimately, the New South that resulted.[71]

Few Southern whites advocated re-enslavement, but most continued to envision blacks as slave-like inferiors. They remained determined to keep blacks entrenched as a subordinate laboring class. They clutched dearly to every remaining shred of racial control and added some new methods. They resurrected virtually all of the old rationales for enslaving blacks. As one historian put it: "Though many of the more obscure and theoretical aspects of the proslavery argument became moot points after 186S, death of slavery failed to destroy the institution's intellectual foundation." The Lost Cause became the central religious myth of the time. As Phillip Paludan has put it, the Lost Cause:

> anointed not just a status quo but also a status pre-quo – a world of the past that the future celebrated. Little reform was possible when the most Christian of acts was to try to live up to the standards of a slave society in the name and memory of the pure white soldiers who had died. The white southerner's conviction was that his regional values and cultural symbols were holy.[72]

Northerners, by and large, believed that God had vindicated their cause, and they presumed God would stand with them in support of repressive policies against the defeated South. To justify the killing, in often strident, self-righteous terms, they clamored for change, for the rebuilding of the South in such manner as the ideals for which they believed the war had been fought would not be lost. "The Devil is in the people of the South," one preacher proclaimed, and he needed to be exorcised. The result was an unprecedented time of testing of resolve that had mixed results. In time Republican reconstruction would give way to political reality, or compromise, and after 1877, which marked the end of Southern occupation, the "solid South" would rise again. The South would embark on its own course, remaining profoundly separate in its own mind and memory and in its own distinctive religious history.[73]

Northern churches provided the major institutional context in which the antislavery impulse could thrive during the Civil War, and they provided a place for its survival during Reconstruction, even when much of the rest of the nation lost interest. During Reconstruction, Union armies made substantial inroads on Confederate territory, and the Northern Protestant churches were a mainstay of the Radical program. They regarded themselves as the custodians of the moral factor in the entire sectional crisis, and with the coming of peace they remained the chief popular support for the political leaders who wished to prevent any compromise. This involved them inescapably in the Republican strategies, which were designed to prevent or delay the rise of the politically potent South. Yet the needs of the freedman and a grim determination to reform the South best explain why the churches made Reconstruction an extension of the antislavery crusade and why they won such powerful support.[74]

Exalted principles were more easily formulated than implemented. Republicans learned that social structures, tradition, and the legacy of slavery could not be transformed by governmental fiat. Yet recovery and even advances were made. The Bureau of Refugees, Freedmen, and Abandoned Lands, established in 1865, never did fulfill the freedman's hope for a place on lands abandoned during the war, but it did ease his transition from bondage to freedom. The cause of civil rights, then and later, was advanced by the Civil Rights Act of 1866, as it was by the Thirteenth Amendment (1865), which abolished slavery; the Fourteenth Amendment (1868), which incorporated the principles of the Civil Rights Act and forbade the abridgement of any citizen's privileges or immunities; and the Fifteenth Amendment (1870), which guaranteed to all citizens the right to vote.[75]

Though not all men acted with pure motives, it is unfair and misleading to deny the reality of most Radical Republican leaders' moral fervor and humanitarian idealism. The efforts of Northern churchmen in this regard can be seen in the hundreds of relief associations they organized throughout the South, even while the war continued to be fought. To coordinate this work the United States Commission for the Relief of the National Freedman was formed in 1863 followed by the American Freedman's Union Commission (AFUC), organized in 1866 to embrace a still larger range of such societies. After 1869, Congress took increasing control of Reconstruction and freedman's aid, and the activities of the AFUC declined. Nevertheless, several denominational societies continued to act independently. The Northern Presbyterians organized their freedmen's commission in 1864, the Methodists their much more vigorous Freedman's Aid Society in 1866. By far the most effective of these church-oriented agencies, however, was the American Missionary Association, founded in 1846 by the merger of several small societies of Congregational origin who shared a missionary commitment to non-white peoples and a strong antislavery bent. By the end of the war, it had 128 missionaries and teachers at work in the South.[76]

Church efforts in the South were not limited to humanitarian efforts. They also pursued ecclesiastical changes with similarly mixed results. The three large denominations that had divided over slavery projected plans for displacing the Southern branches of their denominations. Because the Southern schismatics had proclaimed slavery as God's will, they were now considered disqualified from church membership. As one church organ put it: "The apostate church is buried beneath a flood of divine wrath; its hideous dogmas shine on its brow like flaming fiends; the whole world stands aghast at its wickedness and ruin. The northern church beholds its mission."[77]

The mission, however, was not easily achieved. Although some large churches did at one time or another use the opportunities provided by military occupation to occupy Southern churches, their efforts at converting the membership to their ways ultimately failed. Presbyterians, Methodists, and Baptists remained divided. The only successful reunion efforts among the larger churches were carried out by the Episcopal and Roman Catholic churches. In those churches, as we have seen, a diocesan polity and a record of ambivalent moderation on the central issues allowed for reunion.[78]

When Southern Episcopalians organized the Protestant Episcopal Church, Confederate States of America, in 1861, they did so with no changes of doctrine, polity or liturgy. The Northern church merely noted the absence of Southern representatives at the 1862 meeting of its General Convention. Three years later unity was restored with a minimum of bitterness. The Roman Catholic Church could not formally divide, inasmuch as the Holy See was outside and above the conflict. When hostilities ceased, the hierarchy resumed its normal functioning, and in the Plenary Council of 1866 all of the country's dioceses were represented. Neither the Episcopal nor the Catholic Church sought to press reconstructionist policies on their Southern dioceses.[79]

The chief new ecclesiastical development of the era of Reconstruction was neither reconquest nor reunion of the alienated regions, but rather the rise of independent black churches from their Baptist and Methodist origins. These churches played a significant role during Reconstruction when the Federal army, the Freedman's Bureau, and the Union Leagues utilized them to strengthen Radical Republican power. But after 1877 they, too, became a part of the "Southern solution" (segregation, subservience and tenantry), not to emerge as a radical social force again until the 1950s. Nevertheless, these churches grew apace during the late nineteenth century and gradually developed a distinctive religious ethos, which traditional denominational allegiances could neither submerge nor alter. Through a long and bitter century, they became the chief bearers of the African American heritage.[80]

Summary

Abolition was no mere political slogan. Economic and political motives were important, but separated from moral considerations, they lost much of their impact. The union of politics and morality was not forged until the 1830s, but once forged, it became a force that would not, perhaps could not, be stopped, or even curtailed until the issue of slavery was resolved. An important step in that direction would be forcing national institutions – not just local or regional institutions – to repudiate slavery. In some cases, as we have seen, for churches as well as other institutions, and ultimately the nation itself, such pressure would result in disunion.[81]

The Civil War was the turning point in the emergence of the new nation. It meant the establishment of a unified national life and the beginning of the American emergence with growing power in the community of nations. Such unity would take time. The wounds of war needed to be healed and sectional tensions eased, and nowhere was that more apparent than in the nation's major churches.

In 1865, the Reverend C. B. Boynton, chaplain of the House of Representatives, described to members of Congress gathered for a Thanksgiving service his expectations for the future:

> The American nation occupies a position never held by any people before. It stands the representative and champion of a true Christian democracy in church and state. . . . We stand on the threshold of this new era the mightiest Christian nation on earth . . . mighty through the teaching of war . . . with a national life strong enough to control a continent, and which will brook no dictation from a foreign power.[82]

Review questions

1   In what ways did the churches in the North and South contribute to the outbreak of the Civil War?
2   How did the coming of the Civil War impact American churches?
3   What churches managed to escape the most dire consequences of the Civil War and how?
4   What role did the churches in the North and South play in Reconstruction?
5   What impact did Reconstruction have on American churches?

Notes

1   Sydney E. Ahlstrom, *A Religious History of the American People* (New Haven, CT: Yale University Press, 1972), 649–50.
2   Ahlstrom, *Religious History of the American People*, 650; John R. McKivigan, *The War against Proslavery Religion: Abolitionism and the Northern Churches 1830–1865* (Ithaca, NY: Cornell University Press, 1984), 25; Ronald G. Walters, *American Reformers, 1815–1860* (New York: Hill and Wang, 1978), 78; Richard J. Carwardine, *Evangelicals and Politics in Antebellum America* (New Haven, CT: Yale University Press, 1993), 141.
3   Gerald Sorin, *Abolitionism: A New Perspective* (New York: Praeger Publishers, 1972), 49.
4   William E. Cain, ed., *William Lloyd Garrison and the Fight against Slavery: Selections from the Liberator* (Boston: Bedford Books, 1995), 72.
5   Walters, *American Reformers*, 79.
6   McKivigan, *War against Proslavery Religion*, 7, 40–3.

7 Mckivigan, *War against Proslavery Religion*, 13; Carwardine, *Evangelicals and Politics in Antebellum America*, 140; Walters, *American Reformers*, 80; Russel B. Nye, *William Lloyd Garrison and the Humanitarian Reformers* (Boston: Little, Brown and Company, 1955).

8 David Brion Davis, *Slavery and Human Progress* (New York: Oxford University Press, 1984), 150–1.

9 Sorin, *Abolitionism*, 44–5; Davis, *Slavery and Human Progress*, 136; Gilbert H. Barnes, *The Anti-Slavery impulse, 1830–1844* (New York: Harcourt, Brace and World, 1933; rpt. 1964), 3–16; McKivigan, *War against Proslavery Religion*, 19; George M. Fredrickson, "The Coming of the Lord: The Northern Protestant Clergy and the Civil War Crisis," in *Religion and the American Civil War*, ed. Randall M. Miller, Harry S. Stout and Charles Reagan Wilson (New York: Oxford University Press, 1998), 115.

10 McKivigan, *War against Proslavery Religion*, 19, 21; Nye, *William Lloyd Garrison*, 79, 83; Sorin, *Abolitionism*, 45; Eugene D. Genovese, "Religion in the Collapse of the American Union," in *Religion and the American Civil War*, ed. Randall M. Miller, Harry S. Stout and Charles Reagan Wilson (New York: Oxford University Press, 1998), 76.

11 Ahlstrom, *Religious History of the American People*, 6; Sorin, *Abolitionism*, 49–50.

12 Ahlstrom, *Religious History of the American People*, 650–2.

13 Walters, *American Reformers*, 80; McKivigan, *War against Proslavery Religion*, 6–73; Walters, *American Reformers*, 89–90.

14 Drew Gilpin Faust, ed., *The Ideology of Slavery: Proslavery Thought in the Antebellum South, 1830–1860* (Baton Rouge: Louisiana University Press, 1981), 3; McKivigan, *The War against Proslavery Religion*, 22; Carwardine, *Evangelicals and Politics in Antebellum America*, 153–4; Phillip Shaw Paludan, "Religion and the American Civil War," in *Religion and the American Civil War*, ed. Randall M. Miller, Harry S. Stout and Charles Reagan Wilson (New York: Oxford University Press, 1998), 23.

15 Faust, *Ideology of Slavery*, 1–2; Mark A. Noll, "The Bible and Slavery," in *Religion and the American Civil War*, ed. Randall M. Miller, Harry S. Stout and Charles Reagan Wilson (New York: Oxford University Press, 1998), 43.

16 Kenneth S. Greenberg, *Honor and Slavery* (Princeton, NJ: Princeton University Press, 1996), 110–1; McKivigan, *War against Proslavery Religion*, 30; Thomas Virgil Peterson, *Ham and Japeth: The Mythic World of Whites in the Antebellum South* (Metuchen, NJ: Scarecrow Press, 1978); Noll, "Bible and Slavery," 43–4.

17 Carwardine, *Evangelicals and Politics in Antebellum America*, 155; Noll, "Bible and Slavery," 49; Genovese, "Religion in the Collapse of the American Union," 74, 77–83.

18 Carwardine, *Evangelicals and Politics in Antebellum America*, 156–8; Bertram Wyatt-Brown, "Church, Honor, and Secession," in *Religion and the American Civil War*, ed. Randall M. Miller, Harry S. Stout and Charles Reagan Wilson (New York: Oxford University Press, 1998), 91.

19 See: David D. Chesebrough, *Clergy Dissent in the Old South, 1830–1865* (Carbondale: Southern Illinois University Press, 1996); Georgia Lee Tatum, *Disloyalty in the Confederacy* (Chapel Hill: University of North Carolina Press, 1934); Carl N. Degler, *The Other South: Southern Dissenters in the Nineteenth Century* (New York: Harper and Row, 1974).

20 Ahlstrom, *Religious History of the American People*, 657.

21 Carol V. R. George, "Widening the Circle: The Black Church and the Abolitionist Crusade, 1830–1860," in *African-American Religion: Interpretive Essays in History and Culture*, ed. Timothy E. Fulop and Albert J. Raboteau (New York: Routledge, 1997), 157–8; Manisha Sinha, *The Slave's Cause: A History of Abolition* (New Haven, CT: Yale University Press, 2016), 278–98.

22 Jane H. Pease and William H. Pease, *They Who Would Be Free* (New York: Atheneum, 1974), 186–93; George, "Widening the Circle," 159–60.

23 Sorin, *Abolitionism*, 101–2; George, "Widening the Circle," 164–5, 167–9. See also: Benjamin Quarles, *Black Abolitionists* (New York: Oxford University Press, 1969).

24 Ahlstrom, *Religious History of the American People*, 659.

25 Ahlstrom, *Religious History of the American People*, 659.

26 Davis, *Slavery and Human Progress*, 143–4; McKivigan, *The War against Proslavery Religion*, 13.

27 Louis Filler, *The Crusade against Slavery: Friends, Foes, and Reforms 1820–1860* (Algonac, MI: Reference Publications, 1986), 154. See also: Bliss Forbush, *Elias Hicks, Quaker Liberal* (New York: Columbia University Press, 1956).

28 Filler, *Crusade against Slavery*, 158; McKivigan, *War against Proslavery Religion*, 45–6; Carwardine, *Evangelicals and Politics in Antebellum America*, 166.
29 Ahlstrom, *Religious History of the American People*, 648.
30 Filler, *Crusade against Slavery*, 158–9; Carwardine, *Evangelicals and Politics in Antebellum America*, 167–9.
31 Ahlstrom, *Religious History of the American People*, 661.
32 McKivigan, *War against Proslavery Religion*, 46; Filler, *Crusade against Slavery*, 156.
33 Ahlstrom, *Religious History of the American People*, 161–2; Carwardine, *Evangelicals and Politics in Antebellum America*, 159–60; McKivigan, *War against Proslavery Religion*, 46–7.
34 Carwardine, *Evangelicals and Politics in Antebellum America*, 162; Filler, *Crusade against Slavery*, 157; McKivigan, *War against Proslavery Religion*, 90–1.
35 Ahlstrom, *Religious History of the American People*, 665; Carwardine, *Evangelicals and Politics in Antebellum America*, 169; Filler, *Crusade against Slavery*, 157; McKivigan, *War against Proslavery Religion*, 48.
36 Carwardine, *Evangelicals and Politics in Antebellum America*, 169.
37 Ahlstrom, *Religious History of the American People*, 664–5; Filler, *Crusade against Slavery*, 157–8; McKivigan, *War against Proslavery Religion*, 87–90. For more on the break-up of the Methodist, Presbyterian, and Baptist Churches, see: Clarence C. Goen, *Broken Churches: Denominational Schisms and the American Civil War* (Macon, GA: Mercer University Press, 1985).
38 Mark A. Noll, *The Civil War as a Theological Crisis* (Chapel Hill: University of North Carolina Press, 2006), Introduction; Sydney Ahlstrom, *Religious History of the American People*, 666; Filler, *Crusade against Slavery*, 159; McKivigan, *War against Proslavery Religion*, 48–9.
39 Ahlstrom, *Religious History of the American People*, 667; Ahlstrom, *Religious History of the American People*, 667.
40 Ahlstrom, *Religious History of the American People*, 667.
41 James Hennesey, *American Catholics: A History of the Roman Catholic Community in the United States* (New York: Oxford University Press, 1981), 145–6.
42 Ahlstrom, *Religious History of the American People*, 667–8; Randall M. Miller, "Catholic Religion, Irish Ethnicity, and the Civil War," in Miller, Stout and Wilson, *Religion and the American Civil War*, ed. Randall M. Miller, Harry S. Stout and Charles Reagan Wilson (New York: Oxford University Press, 1998), 263.
43 George, "Widening the Circle," 165.
44 William W. Sweet, *The Story of Religion in America* (New York: Harper, 1950); Ahlstrom, *Religious History of the American People*, 673.
45 Ahlstrom, *Religious History of the American People*, 672; Sorin, *Abolitionism*, 149; McKivigan, *War against Proslavery Religion*, 183; Paludan, "Religion and the American Civil War," 28. For more on specific religious groups not detailed in this section (e.g. Mormons) and more on the role of religion in the everyday life of Americans struggling to understand the meaning of the Civil War, see: George C. Rable, *God's Almost Chosen People: A Religious History of the American Civil War* (Chapel Hill: University of North Carolina Press, 2010).
46 Henry E. Jacobs, *A History of the Evangelical Lutheran Church in the United States* (New York: Christian Literature Company, 1893), 452; Thomas C. Johnson, *A History of the Southern Presbyterian Church* (New York: Christian Literature Company, 1894), 427.
47 Paludan, "Religion and the American Civil War," 24; Ahlstrom, *Religious History of the American People*, 677. See also: Steve E. Woodworth, *While God Is Marching On: The Religious World of Civil War Soldiers* (Lawrence: University Press of Kansas, 2001); Drew Gilpin Faust, "Christian Soldiers: The Meaning of Revivalism in the Confederate Army," *Journal of Southern History*, 53 (1987): 63–90.
48 Daniel D. Williams, "Tradition and Experience in American Theology," in *The Shaping of American Religion*, ed. James Ward Smith and Albert Leland Jamison (Princeton, NJ: Princeton University Press, 1961), 488.
49 Ahlstrom, *Religious History of the American People*, 682–3.
50 Ahlstrom, *Religious History of the American People*, 684.
51 Ahlstrom, *Religious History of the American People*, 684.
52 Ahlstrom, *Religious History of the American People*, 684.
53 Martin E. Marty, *Righteous Empire: The Protestant Experience in America* (New York: Dial Press, 1970), 135.

54 Marty, *Righteous Empire*, 135.

55 Paludan, "Religion and the American Civil War," 23. See also: James H. Moorhead, *American Apocalypse: Yankee Protestants and the Civil War* (New Haven, CT: Yale University Press, 1978).

56 Williams, "Tradition and Experience in American Theology," 489–90; McKivigan, *War against Proslavery Religion*, 115.

57 Williams, "Tradition and Experience in American Theology," 490; Ahlstrom, *Religious History of the American People*, 686.

58 Edwin Gaustad and Leigh Schmidt, *The Religious History of America: The Heart of the American Story from Colonial Times to Today*, rev edn. (San Francisco, CA: Harper, 2002), 109, 199; Ronald C. White, Jr. "Lincoln's Sermon on the Mount: The Second Inaugural," in *Religion and the American Civil War*, ed. Randall M. Miller, Harry S. Stout and Charles Reagan Wilson (New York: Oxford University Press, 1998), 217; Ronald C. White, Jr., *Lincoln's Greatest Speech: The Second Inaugural* (New York: Simon & Schuster, 2002), 128. For more on Lincoln's religion, see: William J. Wolf, *The Almost Chosen People: A study of the Religion of Abraham Lincoln* (Garden City, NY: Doubleday, 1959); Elton Trueblood, *Abraham Lincoln: Theologian of American Anguish* (New York: Harper & Row, 1973); Glen E. Thurow, *Abraham Lincoln and America's Public Religion* (Albany, NY: State University of New York Press, 1976).

59 White, "Lincoln's Sermon on the Mount," 211.

60 White, "Lincoln's Sermon on the Mount," 208, 219.

61 Ronald C. White, Jr., *Lincoln's Greatest Speech: The Second Inaugural* (New York: Simon & Schuster, 2002), 131.

62 White, *Lincoln's Greatest Speech*, 122–3.

63 White, "Lincoln's Sermon on the Mount," 211–2; White, *Lincoln's Greatest Speech*, 119.

64 White, Lincoln's Sermon on the Mount," 208.

65 White, *Lincoln's Greatest Speech*, 123.

66 Sacvan Bercovitch, *The American Jeremiad* (Madison: University of Wisconsin Press, 1978).

67 White, *Lincoln's Greatest Speech*, 152–3.

68 White, *Lincoln's Greatest Speech*, 157.

69 White, *Lincoln's Greatest Speech*, 159.

70 Edwin Scott Gaustad, *A Religious History of America* (New York: Harper and Row, 1966), 196–7. See Also: Wolf, *The Almost Chosen People*; White, "Lincoln's Sermon on the Mount," 208–25.

71 John David Smith, *An Old Creed for the New South: Proslavery Ideology and Historiography, 1865–1918* (Westport, CT: Greenwood Press, 1985), 7.

72 Smith, *Old Creed for the New South*, 7, 17–99; Paludan, "Religion and the American Civil War," 33.

73 Marty, *Righteous Empire*, 135–6; Paludan, "Religion and the American Civil War," 30.

74 Ahlstrom, *Religious History of the American People*, 691–2.

75 Ahlstrom, *Religious History of the American People*, 692–3.

76 Marty, *Righteous Empire*, 137–8; McKivigan, *War against Proslavery Religion*, 196–9.

77 Marty, *Righteous Empire*, 136; Ahlstrom, *Religious History of the American People*, 695–6; McKivigan, *War against Proslavery Religion*, 198–9.

78 Marty, *Righteous Empire*, 136–7.

79 Ahlstrom, *Religious History of the American People*, 696.

80 Ahlstrom, *Religious History of the American People*, 697.

81 Filler, *Crusade against Slavery*, 135; McKivigan, *War against Proslavery Religion*, 7. See also: Clarence C. Goen, *Broken Churches, Broken Nation: Denominational Schisms and the American Civil War* (Macon, GA: Mercer University Press, 1985).

82 Fredrickson, "Coming of the Lord," 124.

Recommended for further reading

Boles, John B., ed. *Masters and Slaves in the House of the Lord: Race and Religion in the American South, 1740–1870.* Lexington: University of Kentucky Press, 1988.

Carwardine, Richard J. *Evangelicals and Politics in Antebellum America.* New Haven, CT: Yale University Press, 1993.

Cole, Charles D., Jr. *The Social Ideas of the Northern Evangelists, 1826–1860*. New York: Columbia University Press, 1954.

Filler, Louis. *The Crusade against Slavery: Friend, Foes, and Reforms 1820–1860*. New York: Harper and Brothers, 1960.

Genovese, Eugene D. *A Consuming Fire: The Fall of the Confederacy in the Mind of the White Christian South*. Athens: University of Georgia Press, 1998.

Goen, Clarence C. *Broken Churches, Broken Nation: Denominational Schisms and the American Civil War*. Macon, GA: Mercer University Press, 1985.

McKivigan, John R. *The War against Proslavery Religion: Abolitionism and the Northern Churches, 1830–1865*. Ithaca, NY: Cornell University Press, 1984.

Noll, Mark A. *The Civil War as a Theological Crisis*. Chapel Hill: University of North Carolina Press, 2006.

Rable, George C. *God's Almost Chosen People: A Religious History of the American Civil War*. Chapel Hill: University of North Carolina Press, 2010.

White, Ronald C., Jr. *Lincoln's Greatest Speech: The Second Inaugural*. New York: Simon & Schuster, 2002.

Index

Note: Page numbers in *italics* indicate figures.

Aaronic Priesthood 122
abolitionist movement: African American
  ministers in 114, 135; African Americans
  in 135; and Baptists 137–8; and churches
  134–9; and Congregationalism 138; and
  Episcopalians 138–9; and idealism 132;
  leading figures in 133, 135; and Lutherans
  138; and Methodists 137; origins of 131; and
  Presbyterians 136–7; and Quakers 131, 136;
  and reform 132; and Roman Catholics 138;
  and Unitarianism 138; women in 133, 135
Abu Bakr Said (Abu Bakr al Siddiq) 109
Abzug, Robert 101
Act Concerning Religion 1649 116
Act of Toleration *see* Toleration Act 1689
Adams, John 46, 68–9, 82
Adams, Sam 116
African Americans: and baptism 111; and
  Christianity 35, 110–15; diverse religions
  of 107; enslavement of 107–13, 131;
  evangelization of 136; and invisible religious
  life 112–13; and missionaries 111, 134;
  as preachers 113–14; and religious life
  115; singing 113; slave narratives of 109;
  spirituals of 112; and white preachers 112–13
African Methodist Episcopal Church 114, 139
African Methodist Episcopal Zion Church 114
African Muslims: autobiographies of 109;
  decline in 110; enslavement of 108–10;
  literacy of 109–10; and practice of faith 109;
  and production of religious materials 109;
  and syncretism 110
African religions 108; afterlife in 107; animism
  in 108; divination in 108; and Muslims
  108–10; oral tradition of 107–8; pantheism in
  108; polytheism of 108; and spirit world 108;
  tricksters in 108
Afro-Caribbeans 108
afterlife: in African religions 107; in Native
  American religions 4, 8, 21

Age of Reason (Paine) 55
Ahlstrom, Sydney 70–1, 122, 125, 135, 139–40
Alabama Baptist Convention 138
Albanese, Catherine 23, 41
Allen, Richard 114
Amana Society 94
America: Christianization of 40, 64, 68–70;
  demographics 77; English colonization of
  27–8; and idealism 132; and millennialism
  48–9, 53–4; and national destiny 37, 92, 145;
  and the New England mind 36; and political
  liberty 132; public religion in 52–3; religious
  diversity in 40; religious freedom in 64–8;
  religious non-practice in 36; and religious
  revivals 36–40
American Antislavery Society (AAS) 132–3
American Baptist Missionary Union 138
American Bible Society 93
American Board of Commissioners for Foreign
  Missions 93
American Colonization Society (ACS) 110, 131
American Freedman's Union Commission
  (AFUC) 147
American Missionary Association 147
American Party 120
American Republic Party 119–20
American Revolution: abstention from 49; and
  Anglicanism 50–1; Baptist support for 47–8;
  and Christianity 51–2; and disestablishment
  58; evangelical support for 48–9; loyalism
  49–50; and millennialism 91; ministerial
  support for 46–7; opposition to 49–50; and
  religion 45–60; and religious discrimination
  50; Roman Catholic support for 47–8; as a
  unifying force 45
American Sunday School Union 93
American Tract Society 93
American Unitarian Association 70, 89
Amish 34
Andrew, James 137